Pocahontas

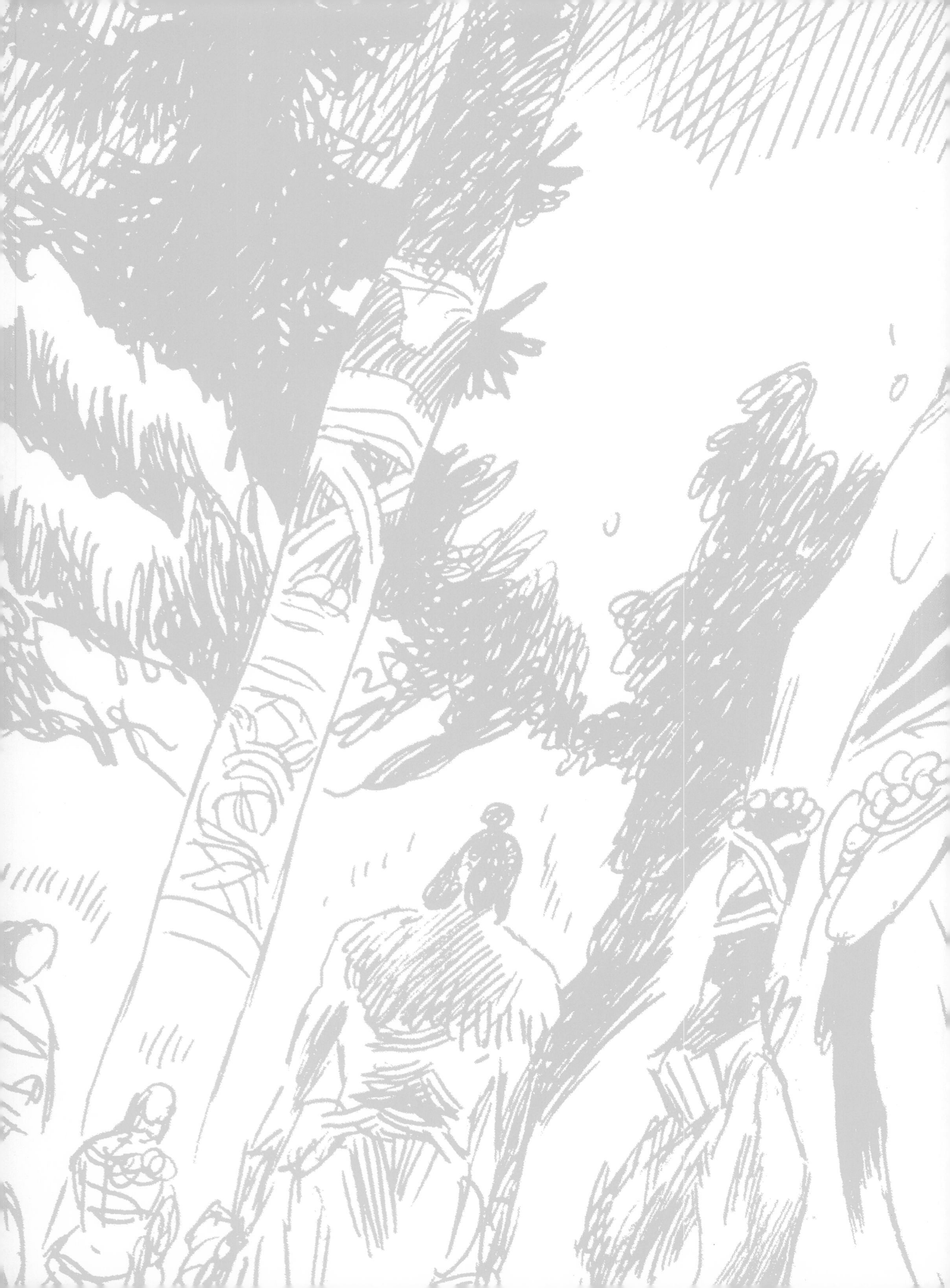

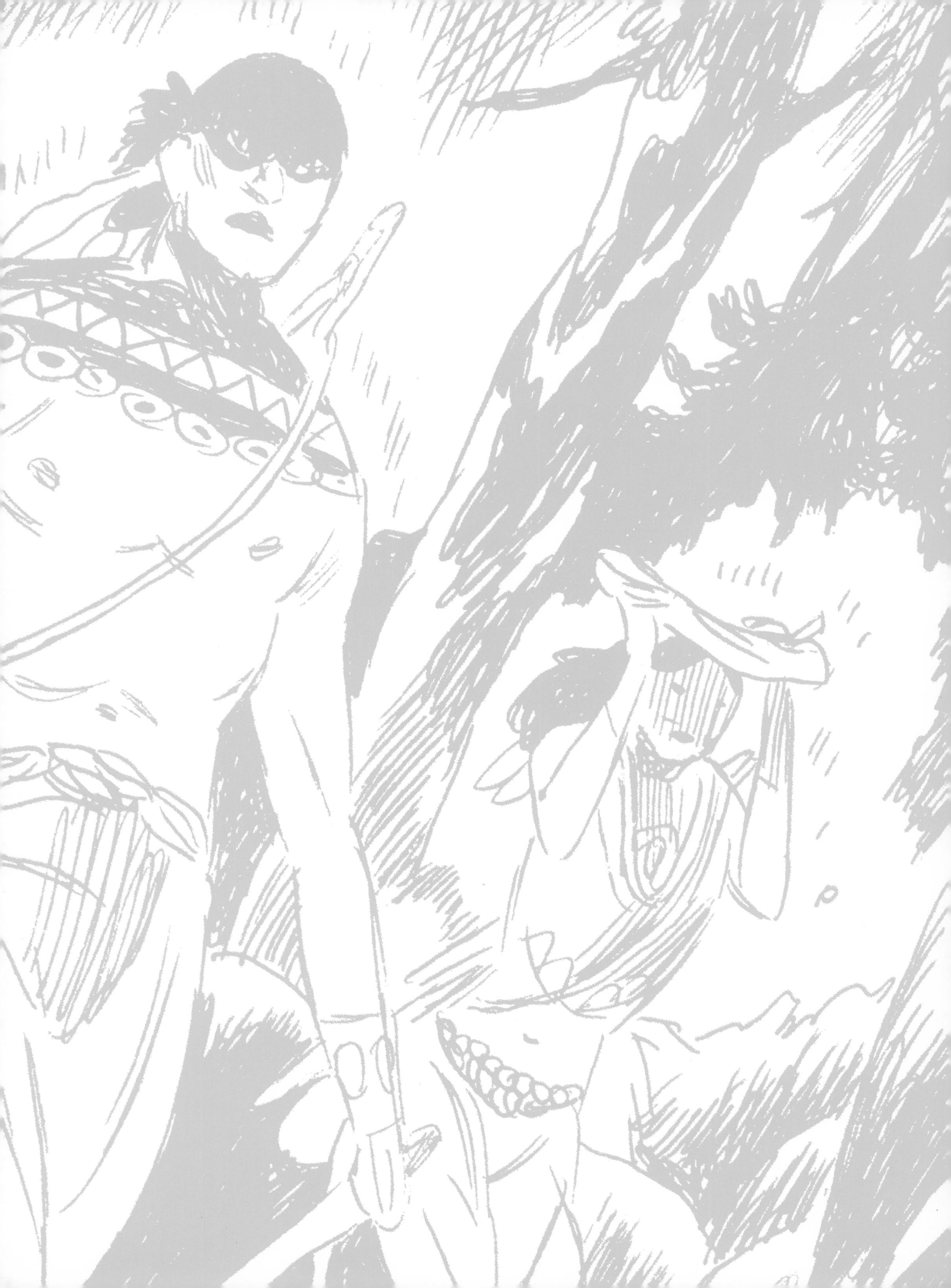

LOÏC LOCATELLI-KOURNWSKY

Pocahontas

Princess of the New World

TRANSLATED BY SANDRA SMITH

PEGASUS BOOKS
NEW YORK LONDON

POCAHONTAS

Pegasus Books Ltd.
148 W 37th Street, 13th Floor
New York, NY 10018

First Pegasus Books hardcover edition September 2016

ISBN: 978-1-68177-217-2

10 9 8 7 6 5 4 3 2 1

Printed in China
Distributed by W. W. Norton & Company, Inc.

Pocahontas

Matoaka

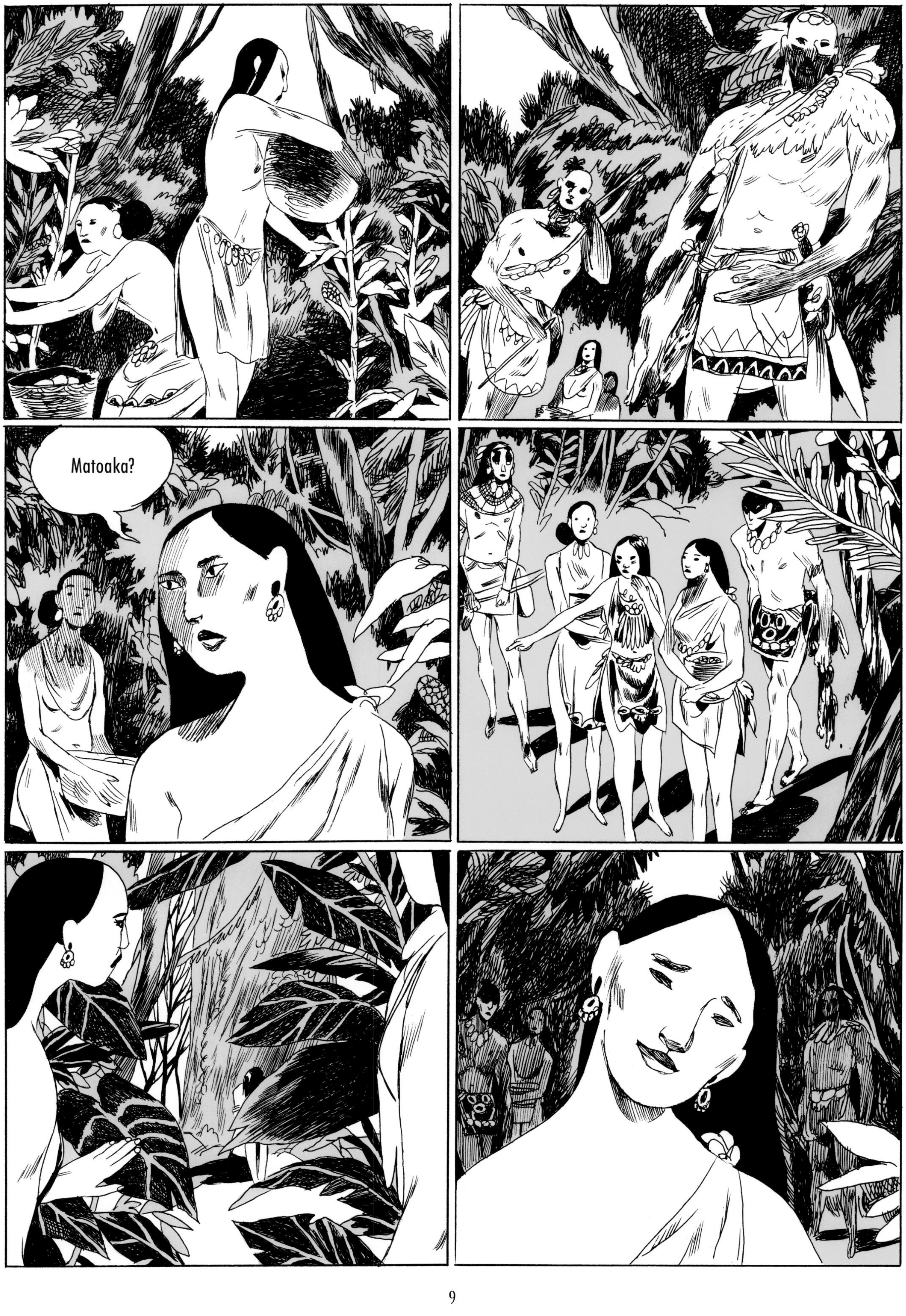
Matoaka?

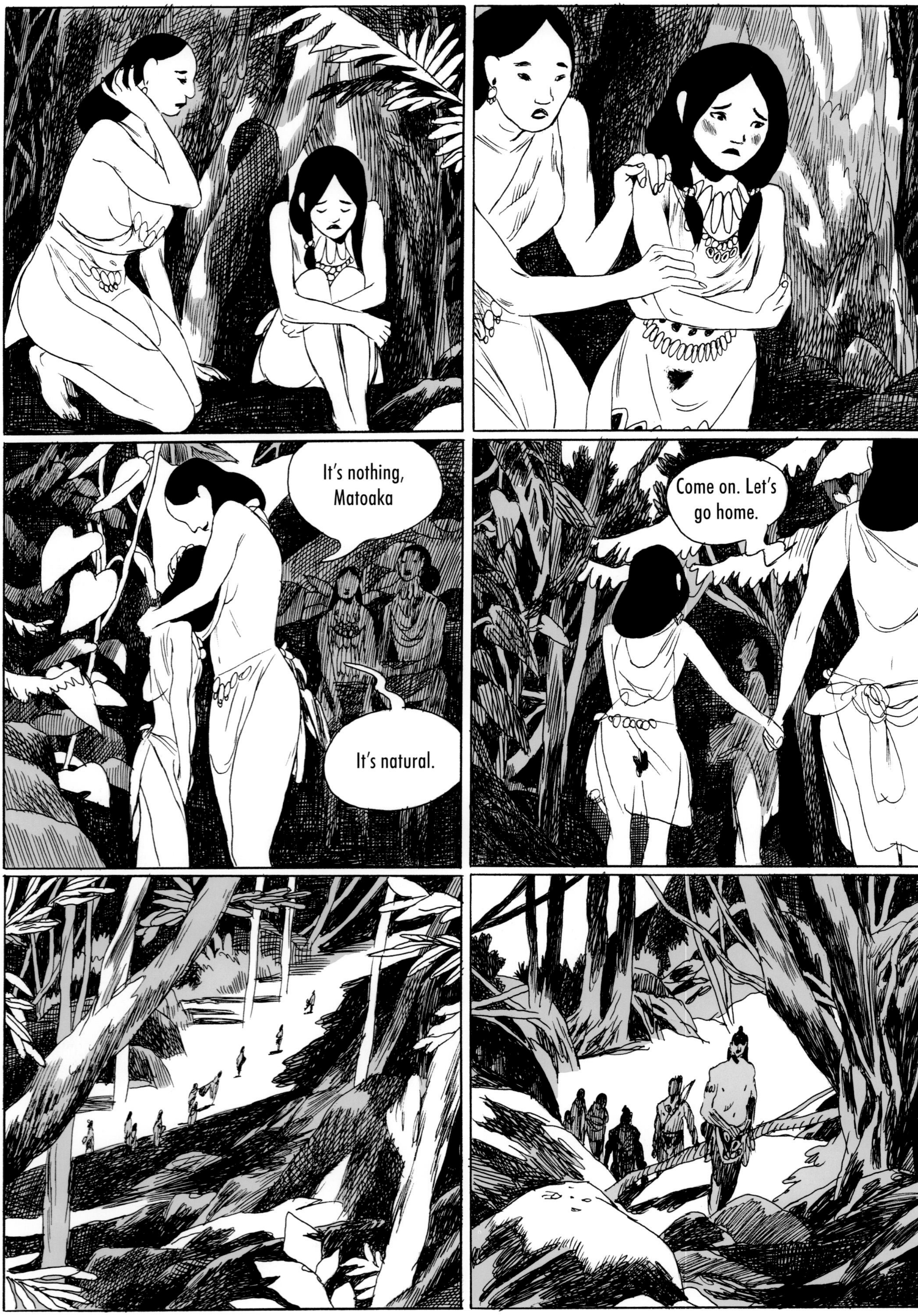
It's nothing, Matoaka
It's natural.
Come on. Let's go home.

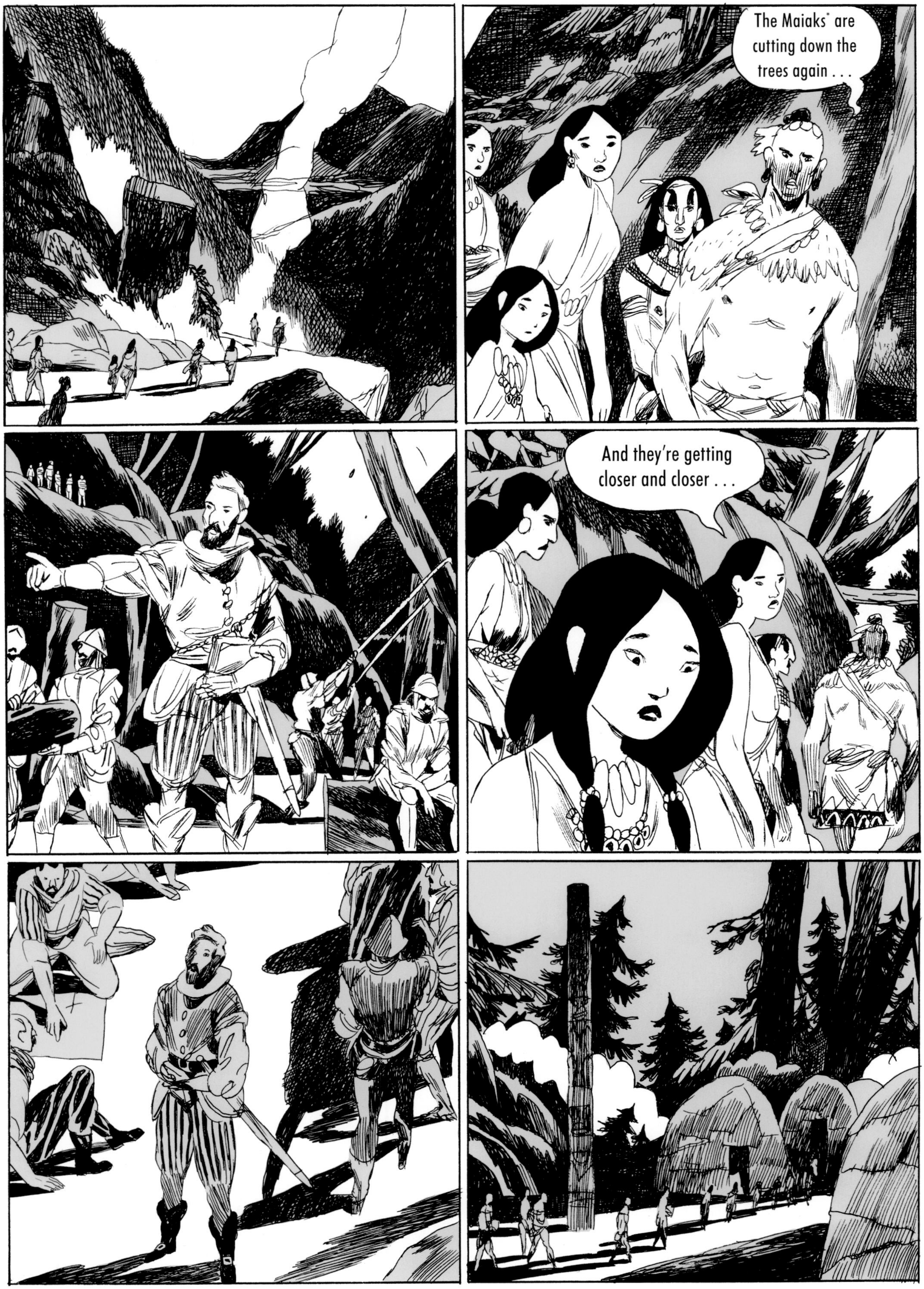
The Maiaks* are cutting down the trees again . . .
And they're getting closer and closer . . .

* Algonquin word for "foreigners"

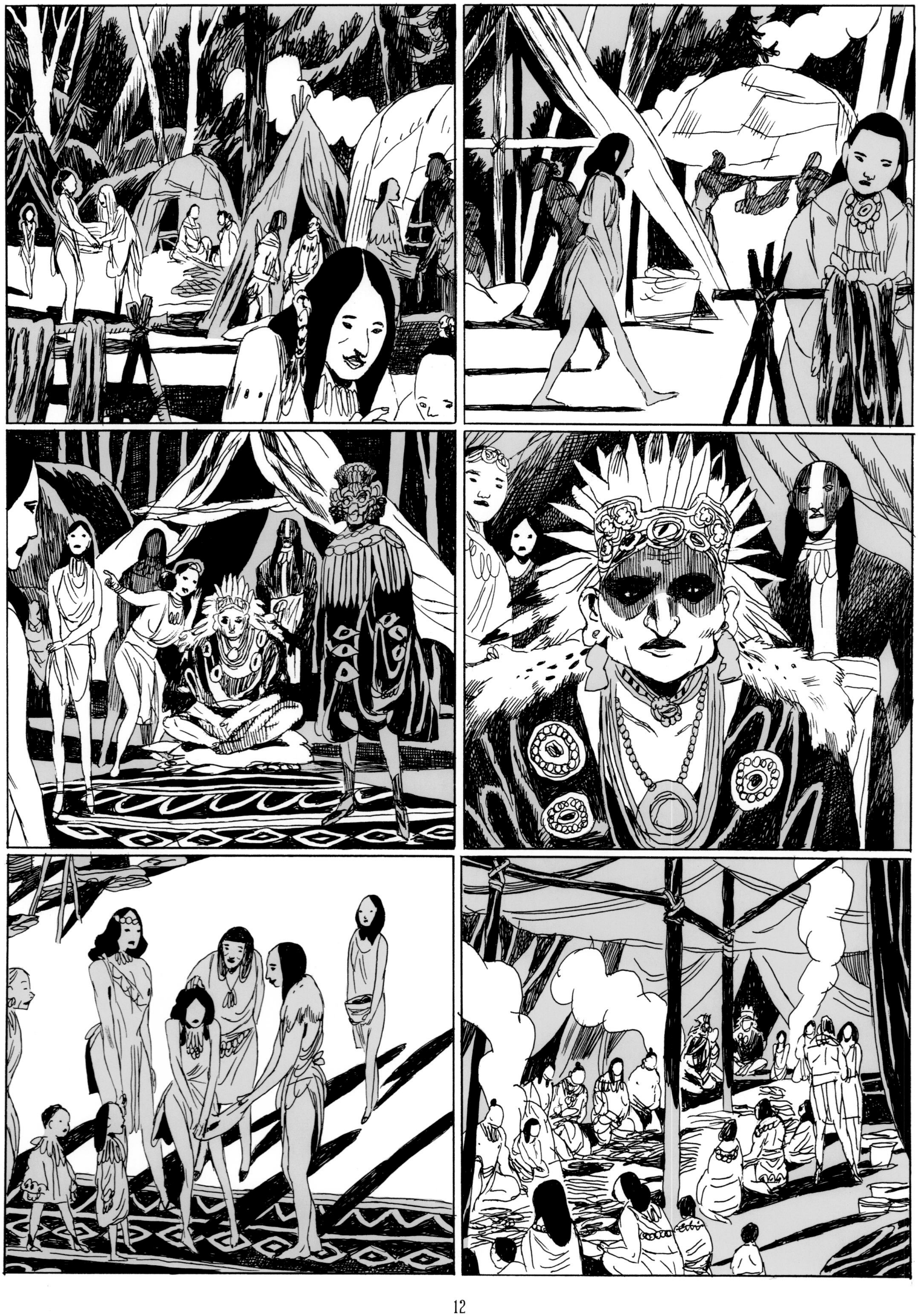

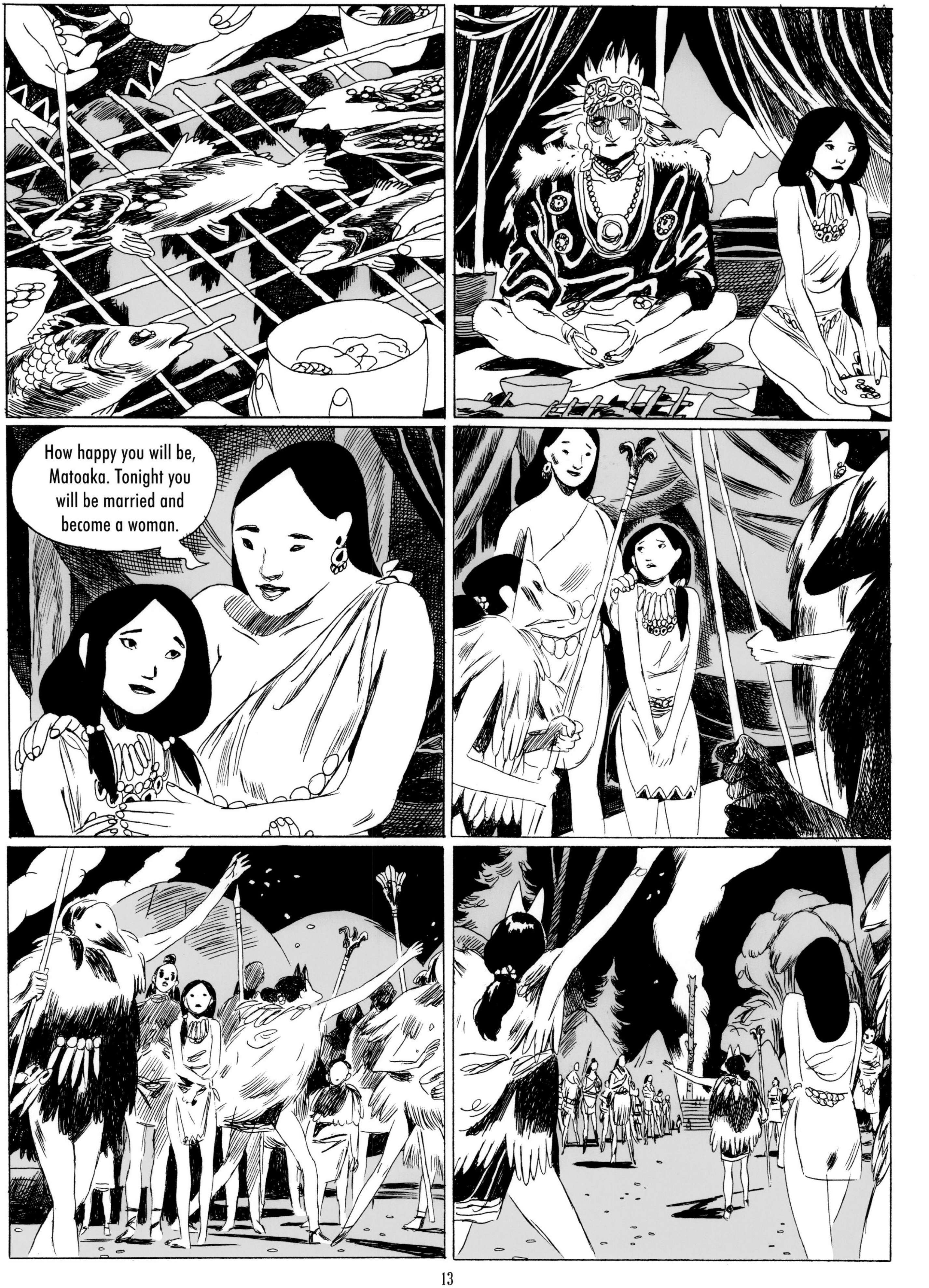
How happy you will be, Matoaka. Tonight you will be married and become a woman.

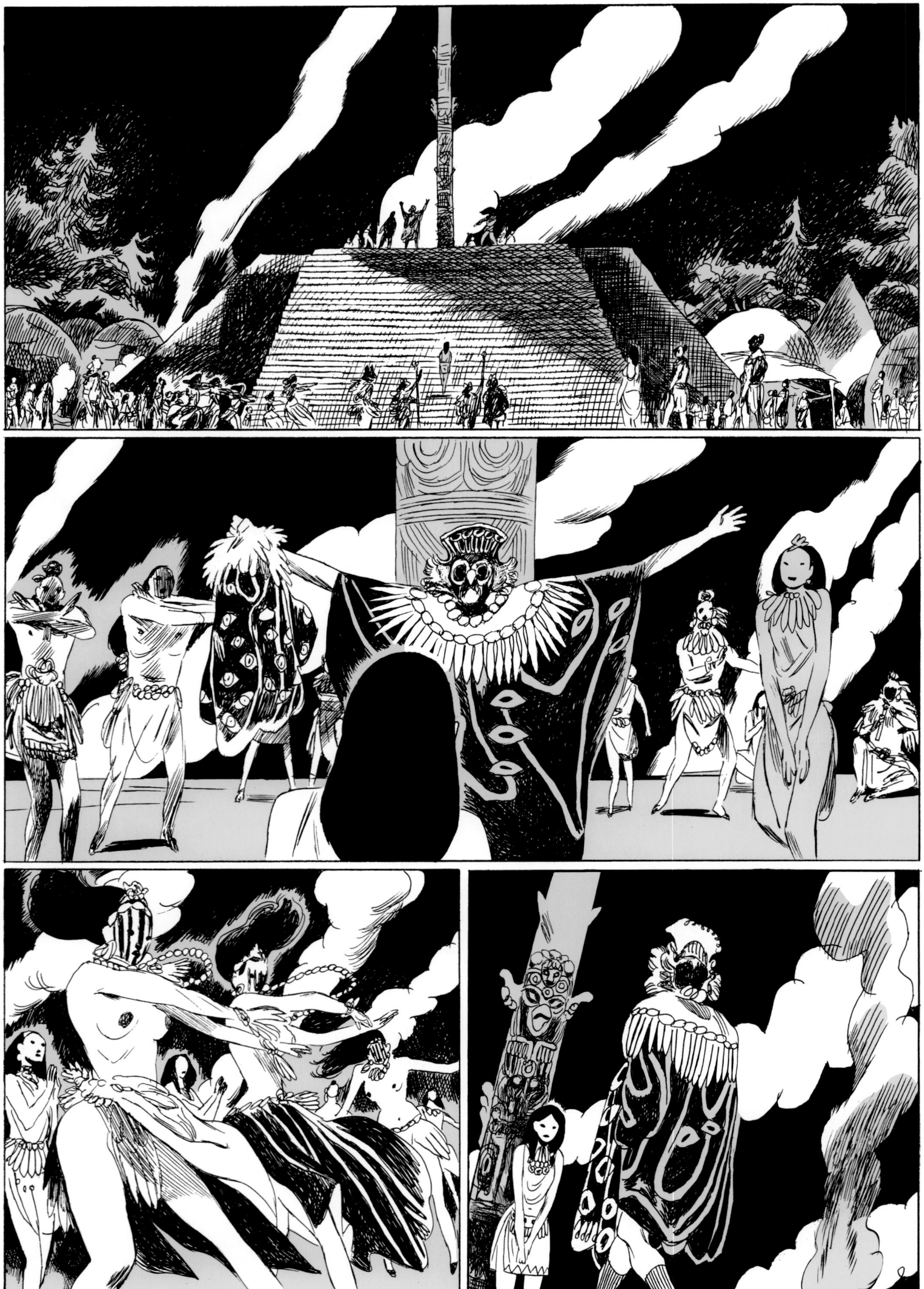

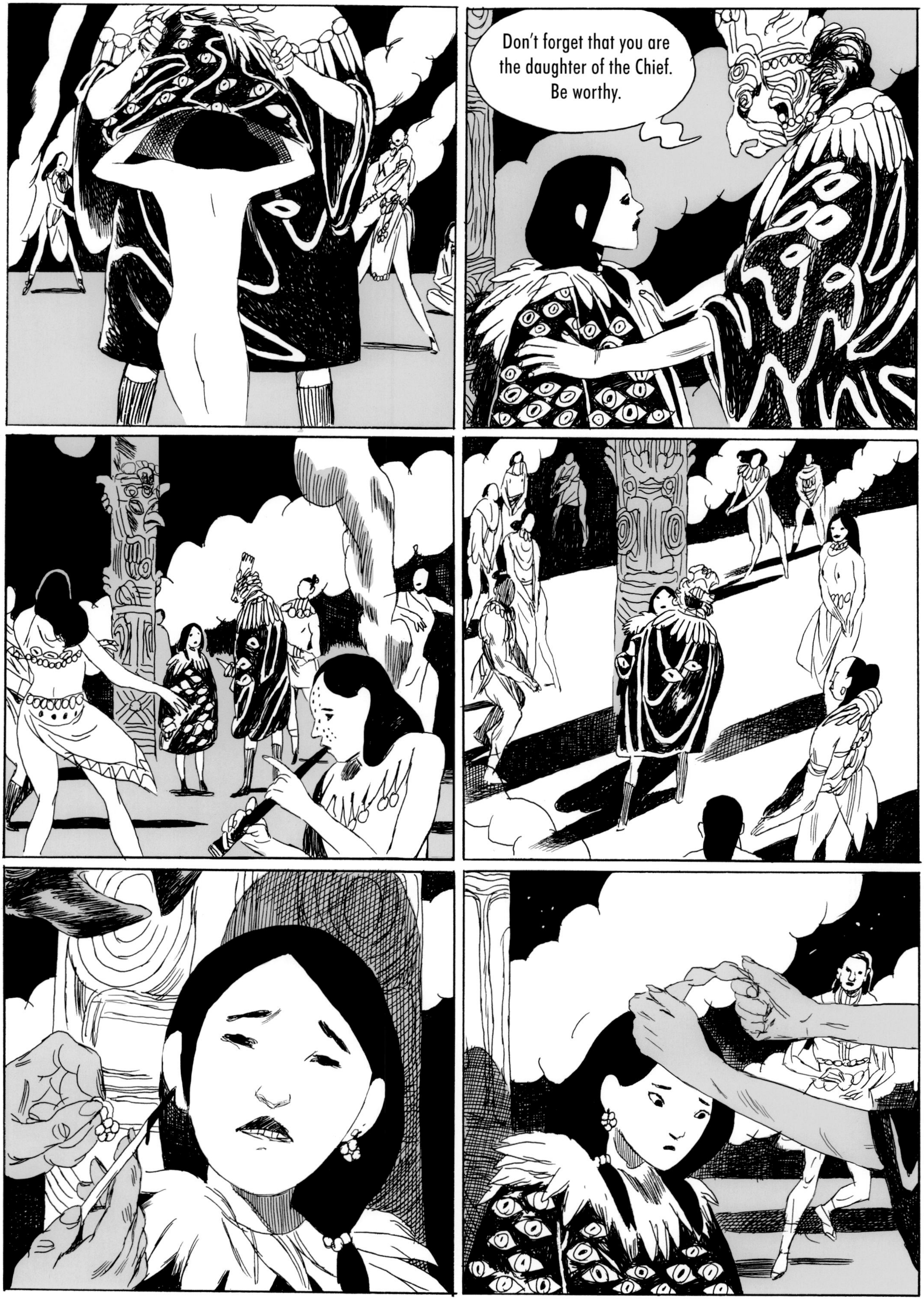
Don't forget that you are the daughter of the Chief. Be worthy.

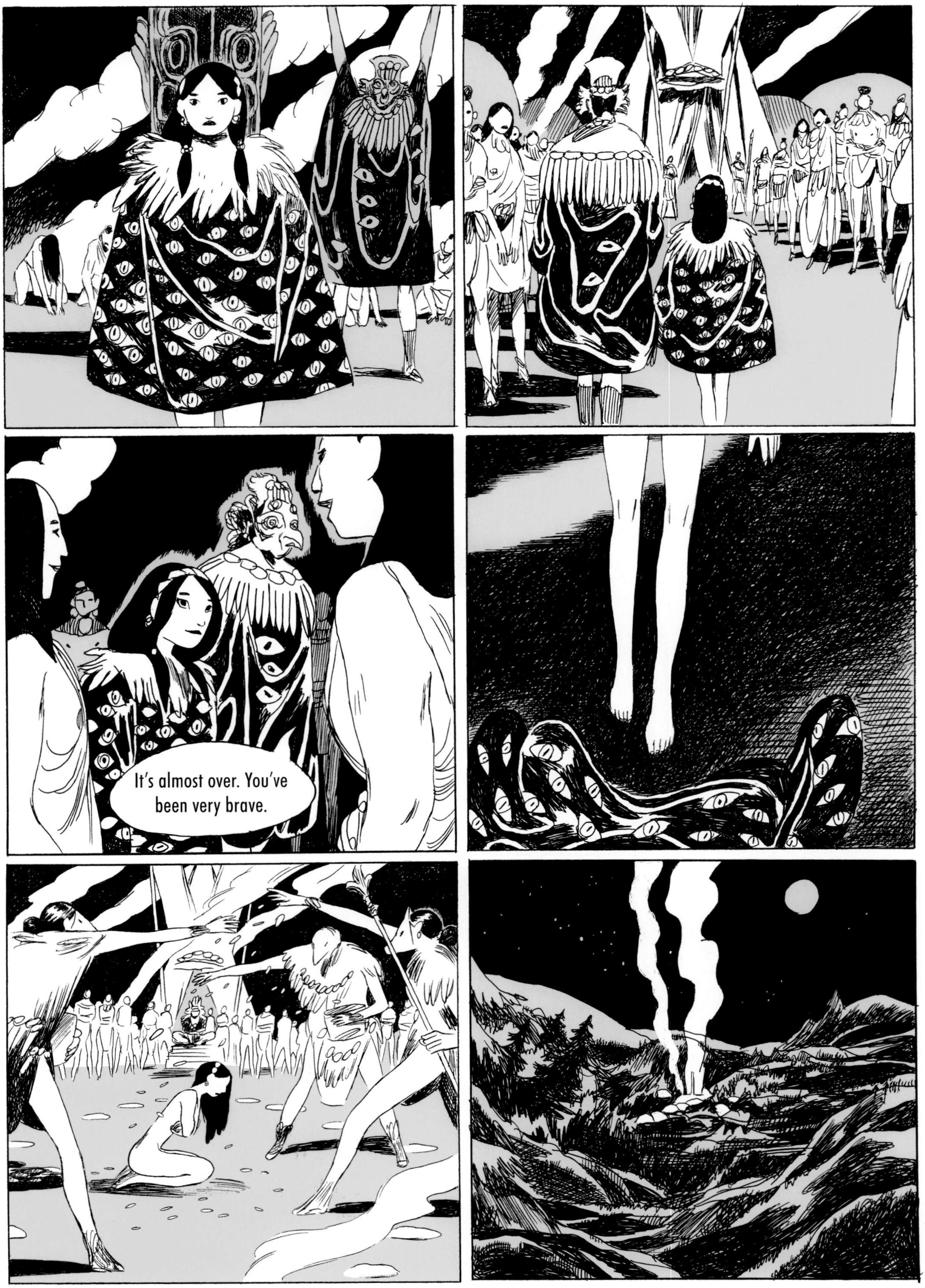
It's almost over. You've been very brave.

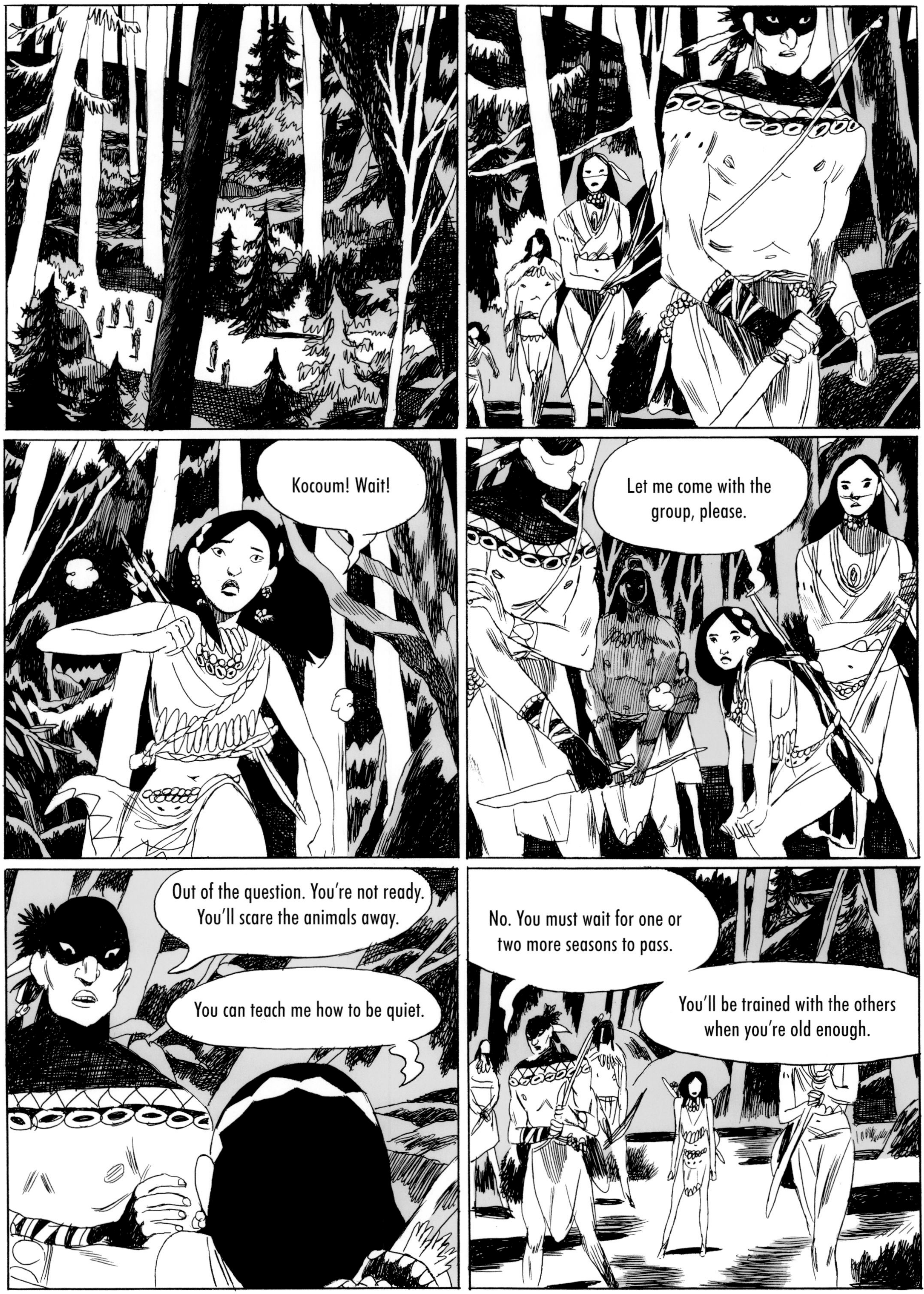
Kocoum! Wait!
Let me come with the group, please.
Out of the question. You're not ready. You'll scare the animals away.
You can teach me how to be quiet.
No. You must wait for one or two more seasons to pass.
You'll be trained with the others when you're old enough.

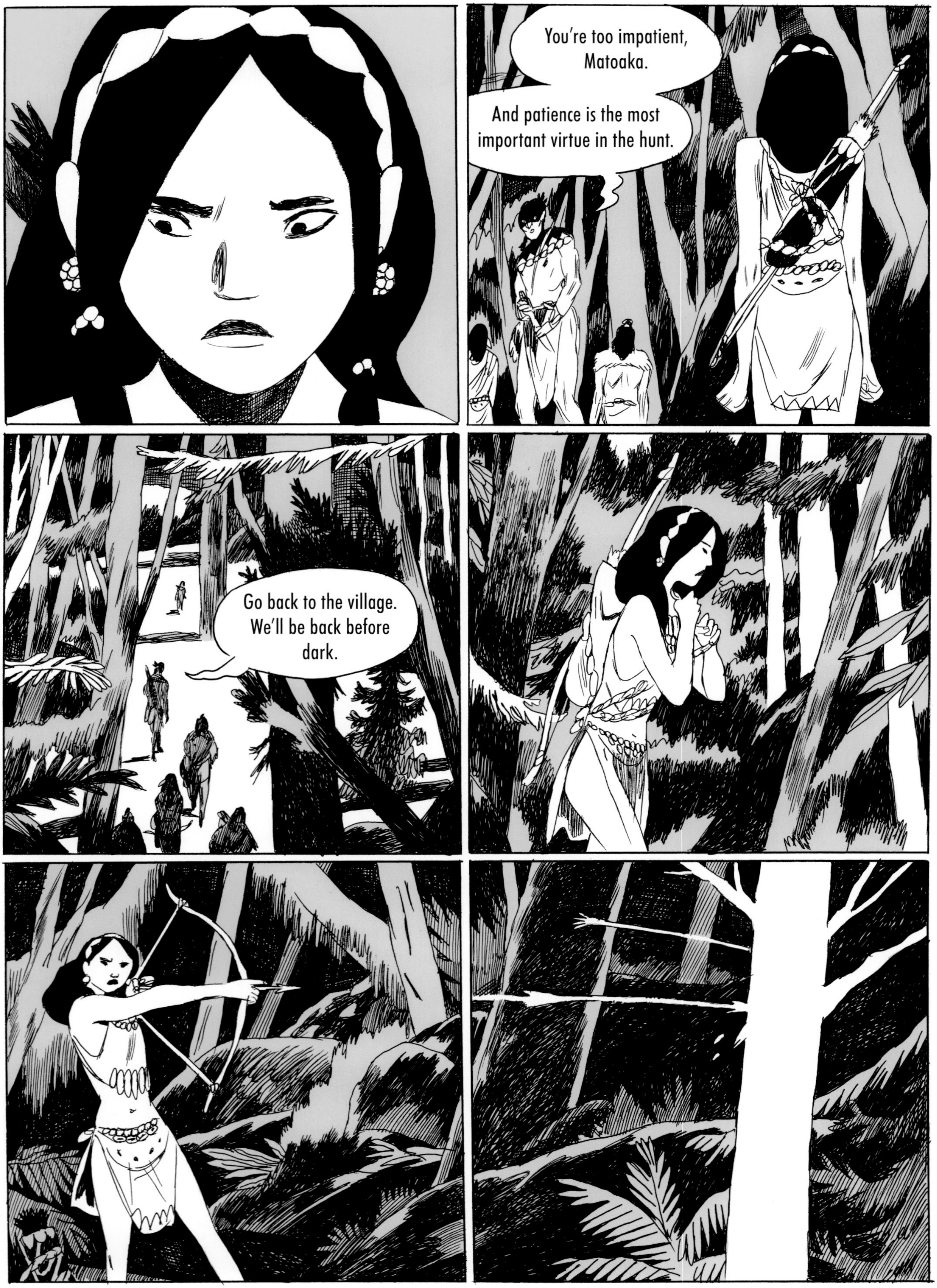
You're too impatient, Matoaka.
And patience is the most important virtue in the hunt.
Go back to the village. We'll be back before dark.

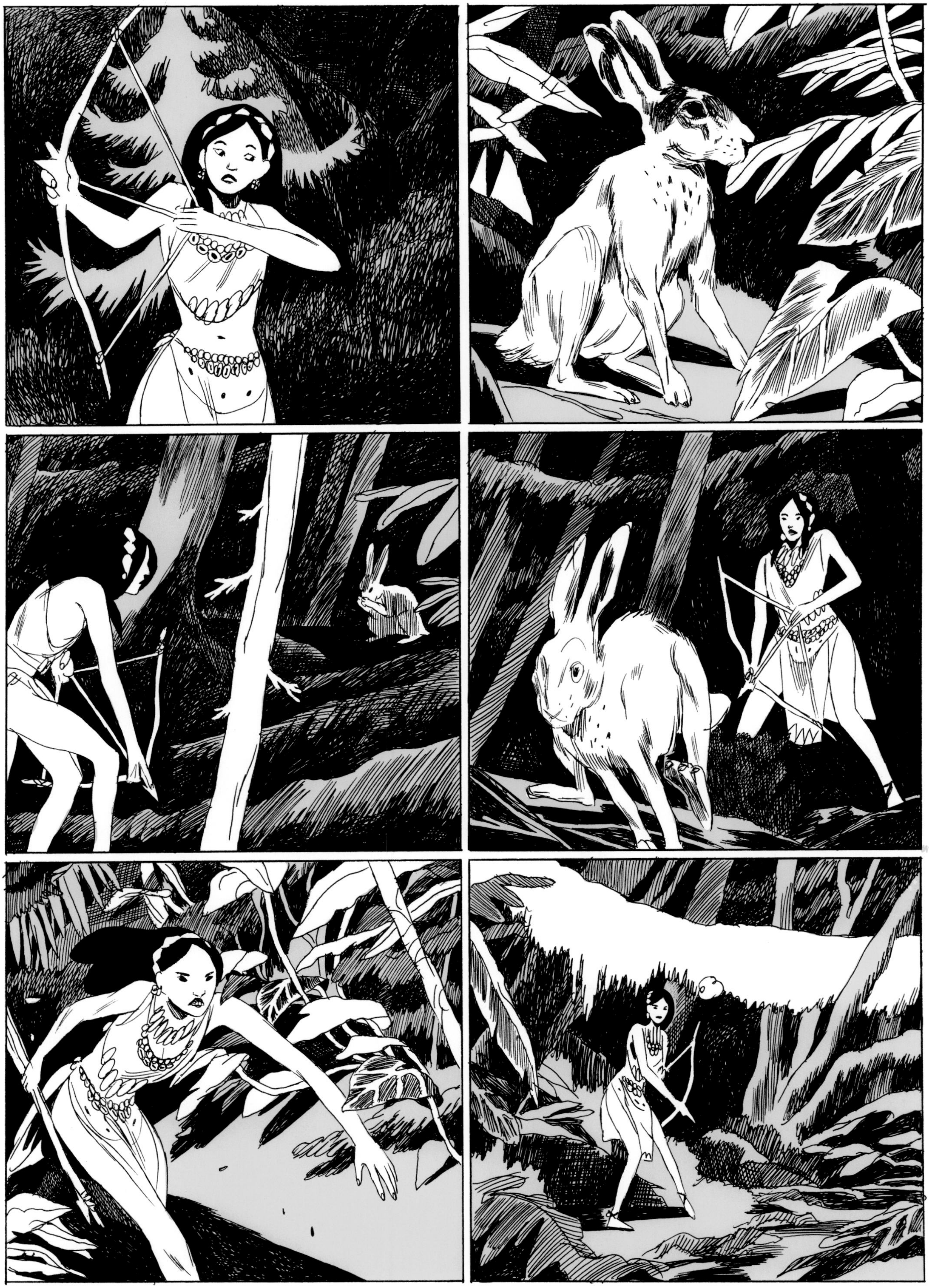

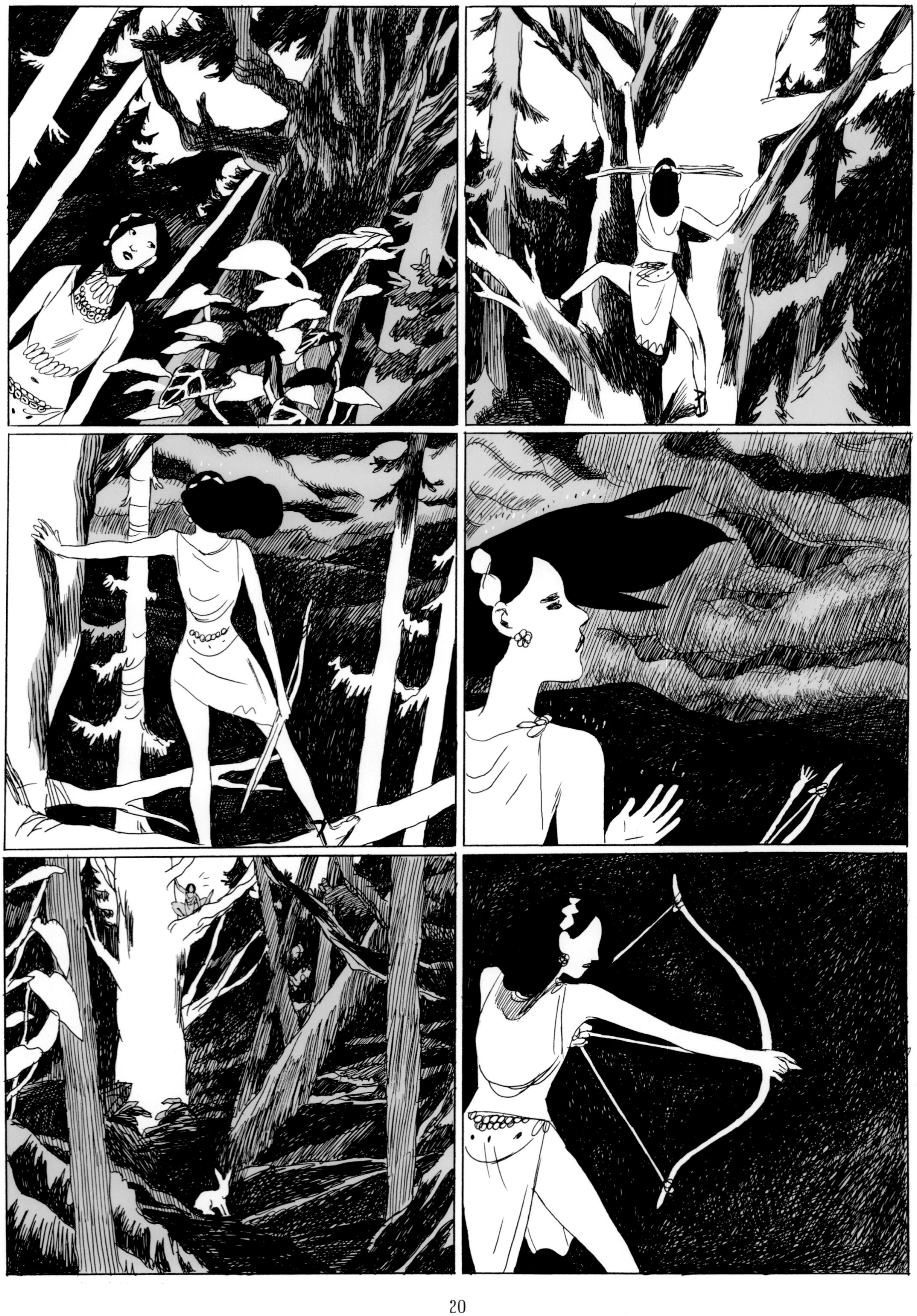

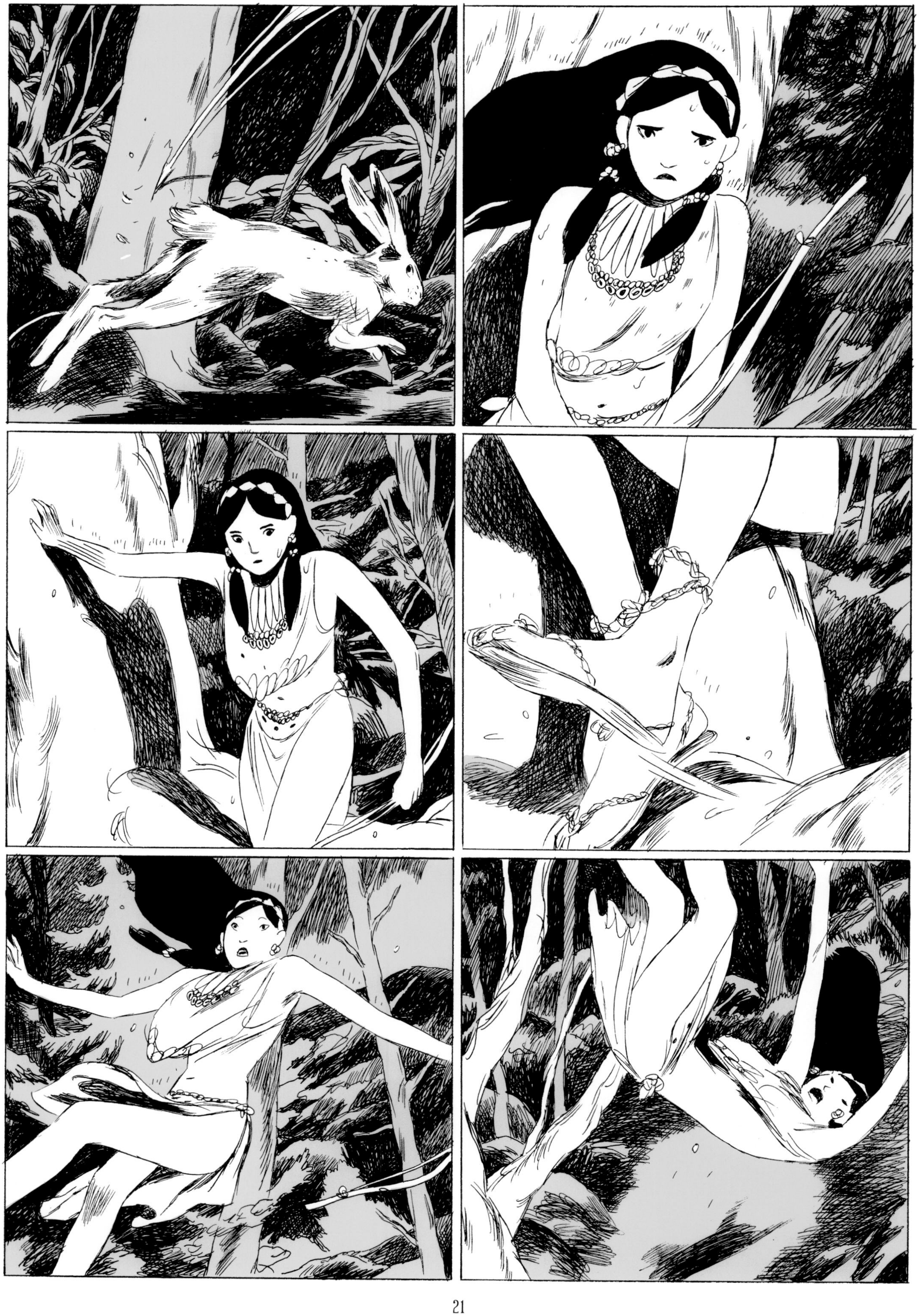

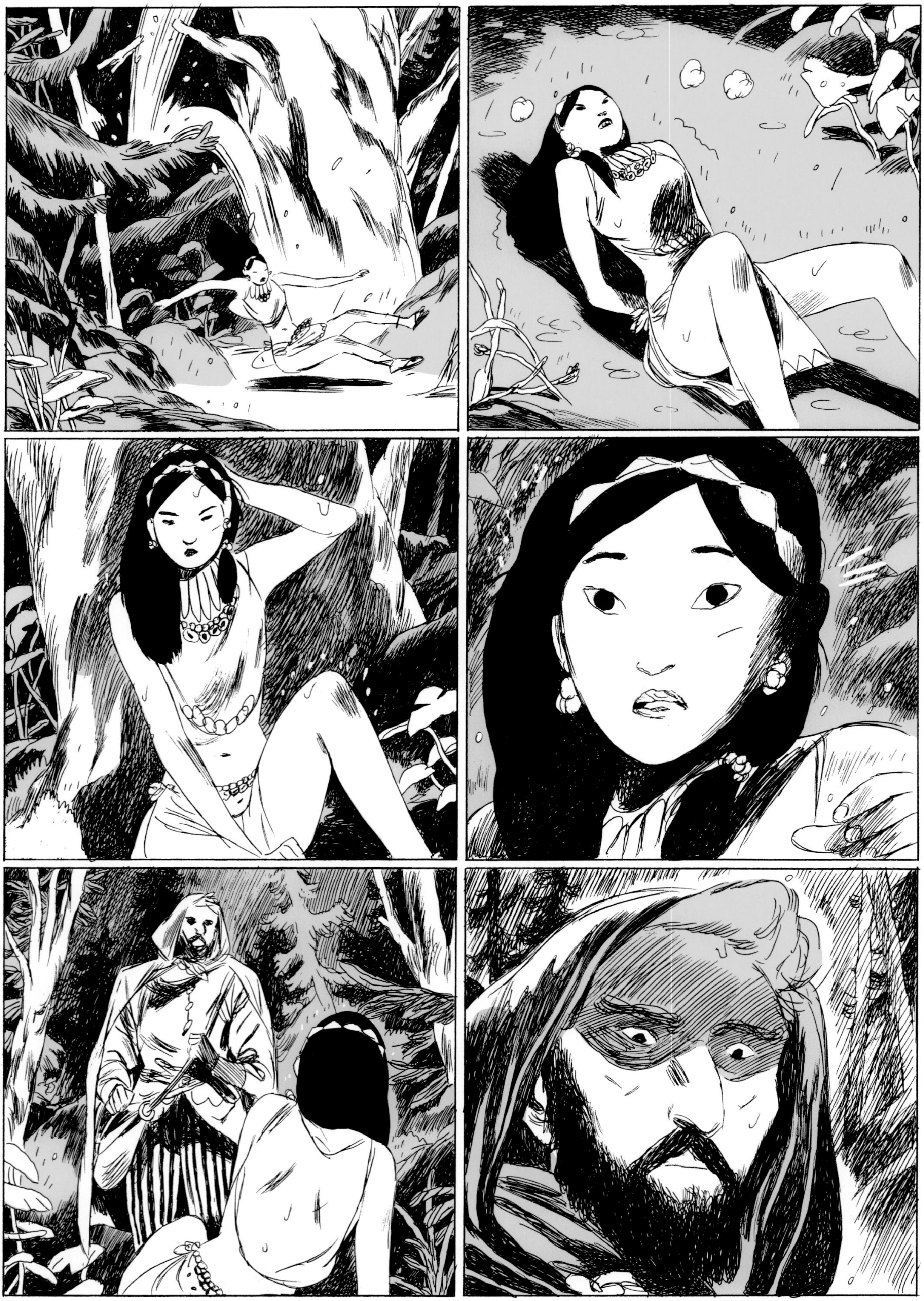

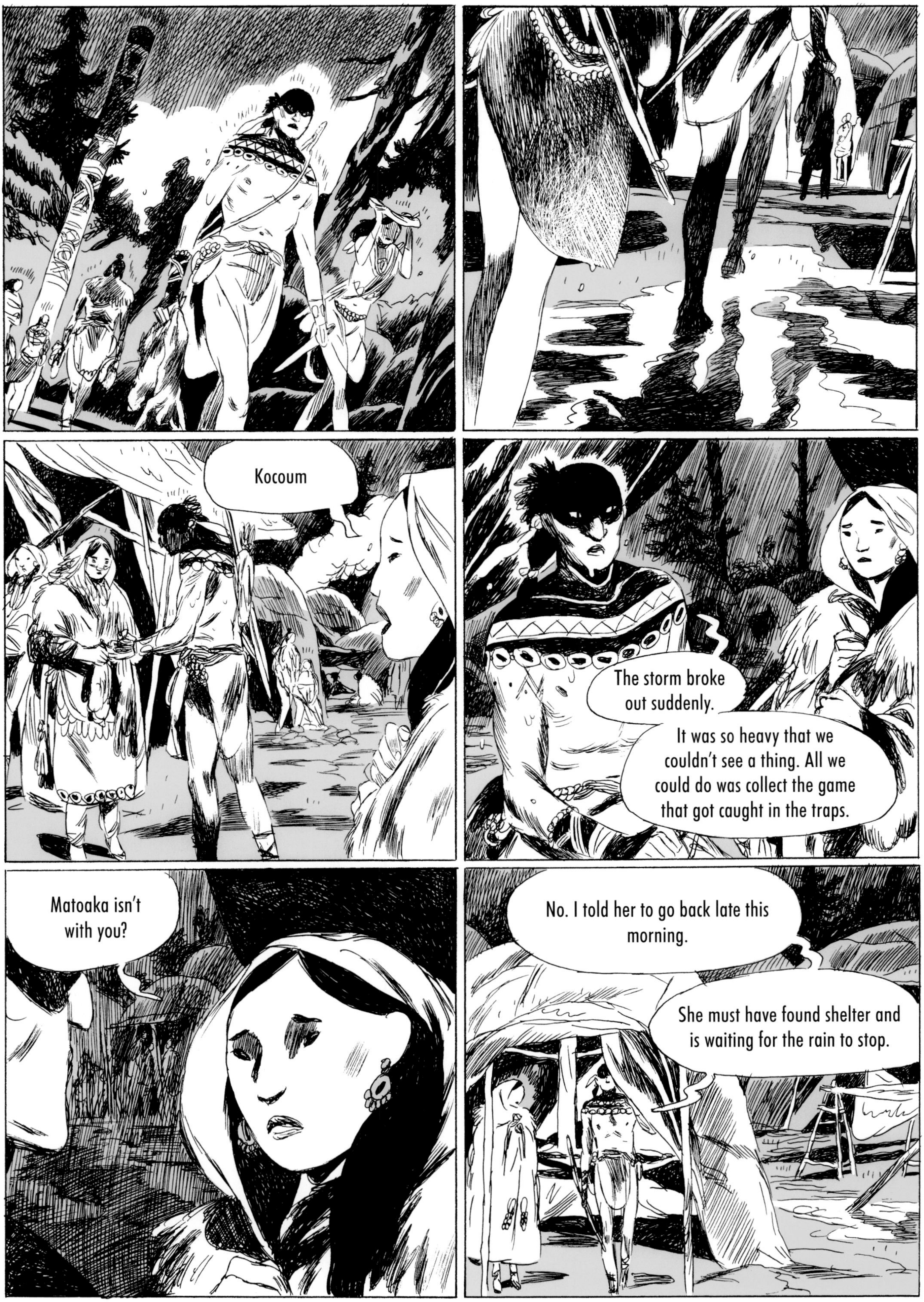

Kocoum
The storm broke out suddenly.
It was so heavy that we couldn't see a thing. All we could do was collect the game that got caught in the traps.
Matoaka isn't with you?
No. I told her to go back late this morning.
She must have found shelter and is waiting for the rain to stop.

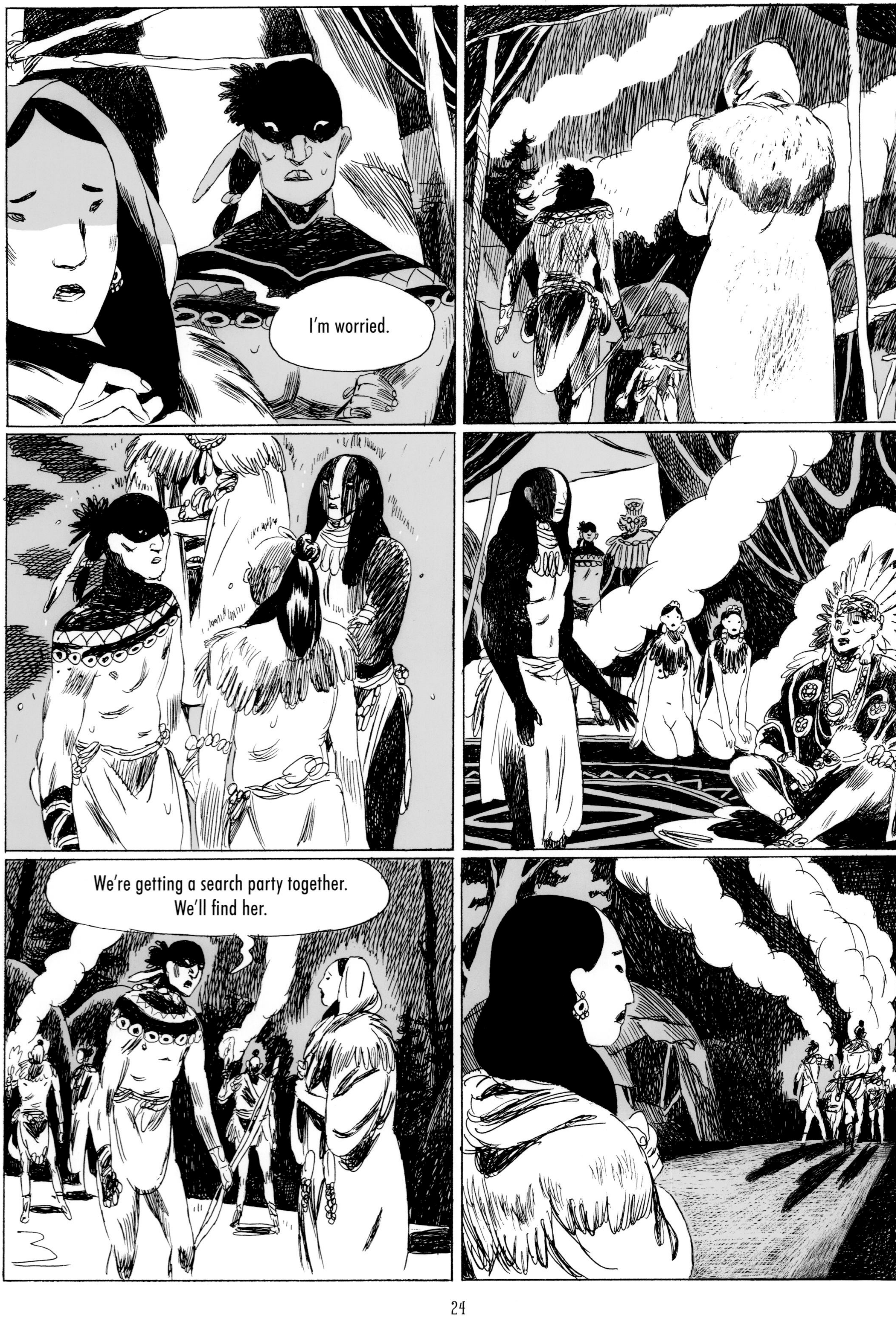
I'm worried.
We're getting a search party together.
We'll find her.

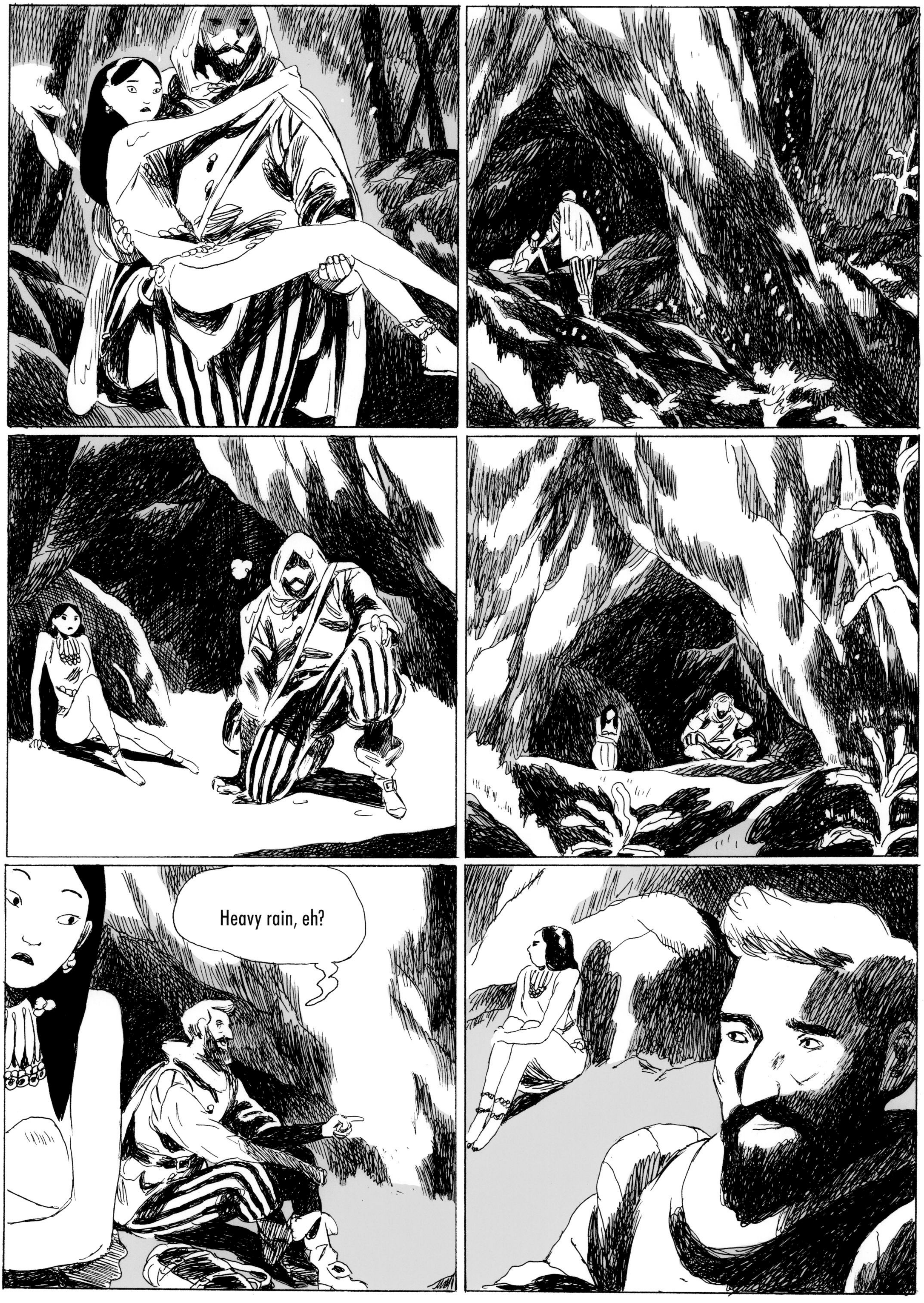
Heavy rain, eh?

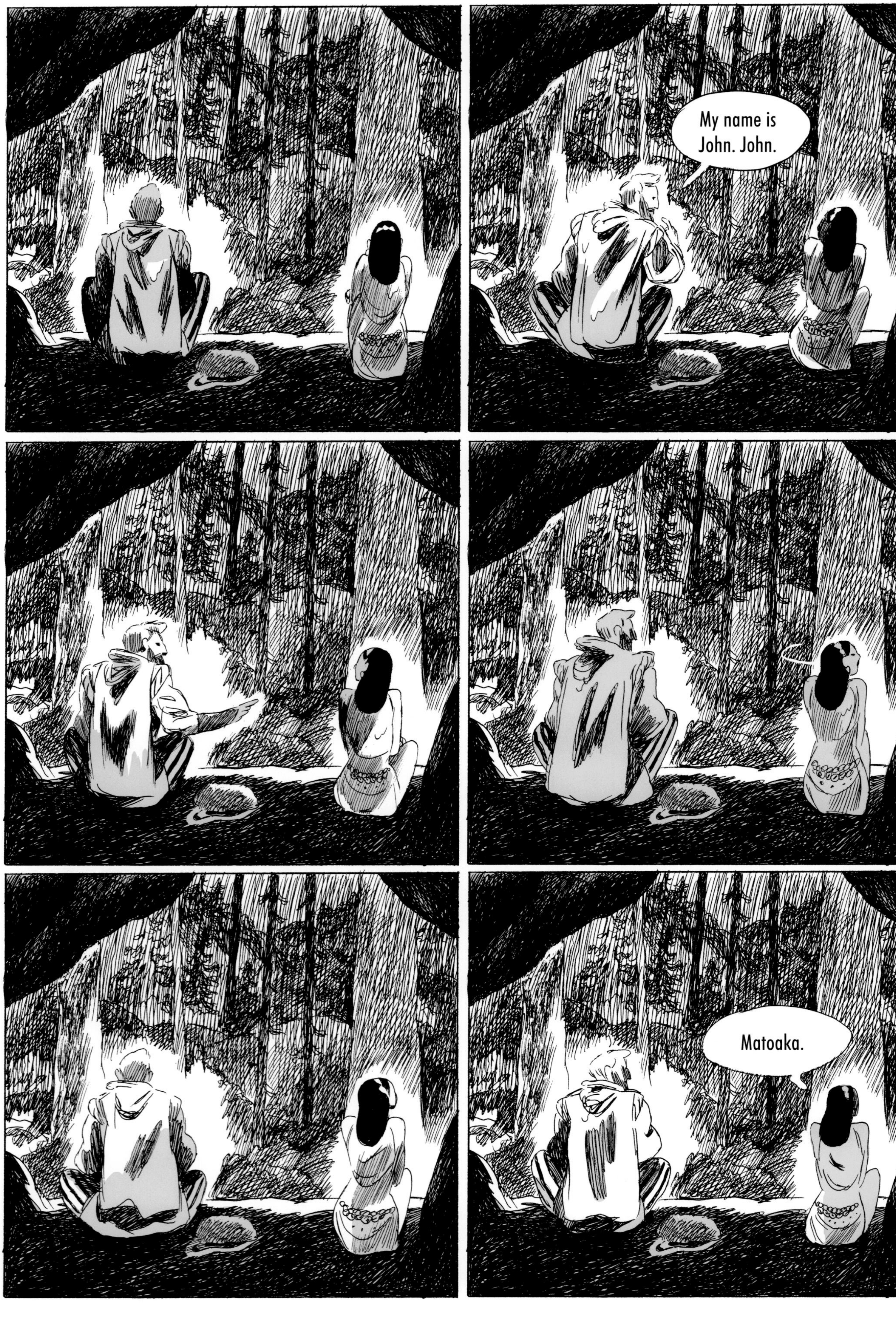
My name is John. John.
Matoaka.

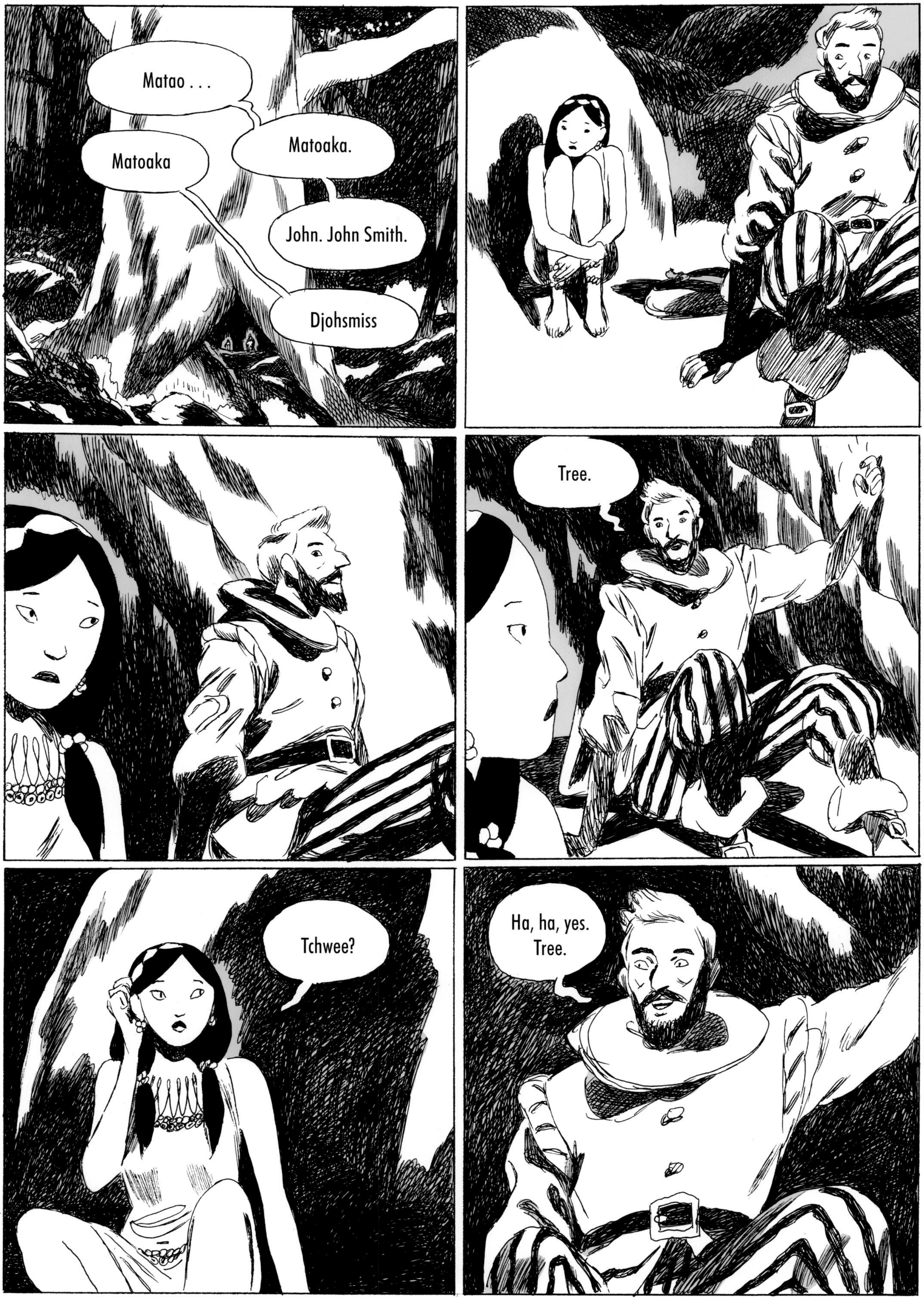
Matao . . .
Matoaka.
Matoaka
John. John Smith.
Djohsmiss
Tree.
Tchwee?
Ha, ha, yes.
Tree.

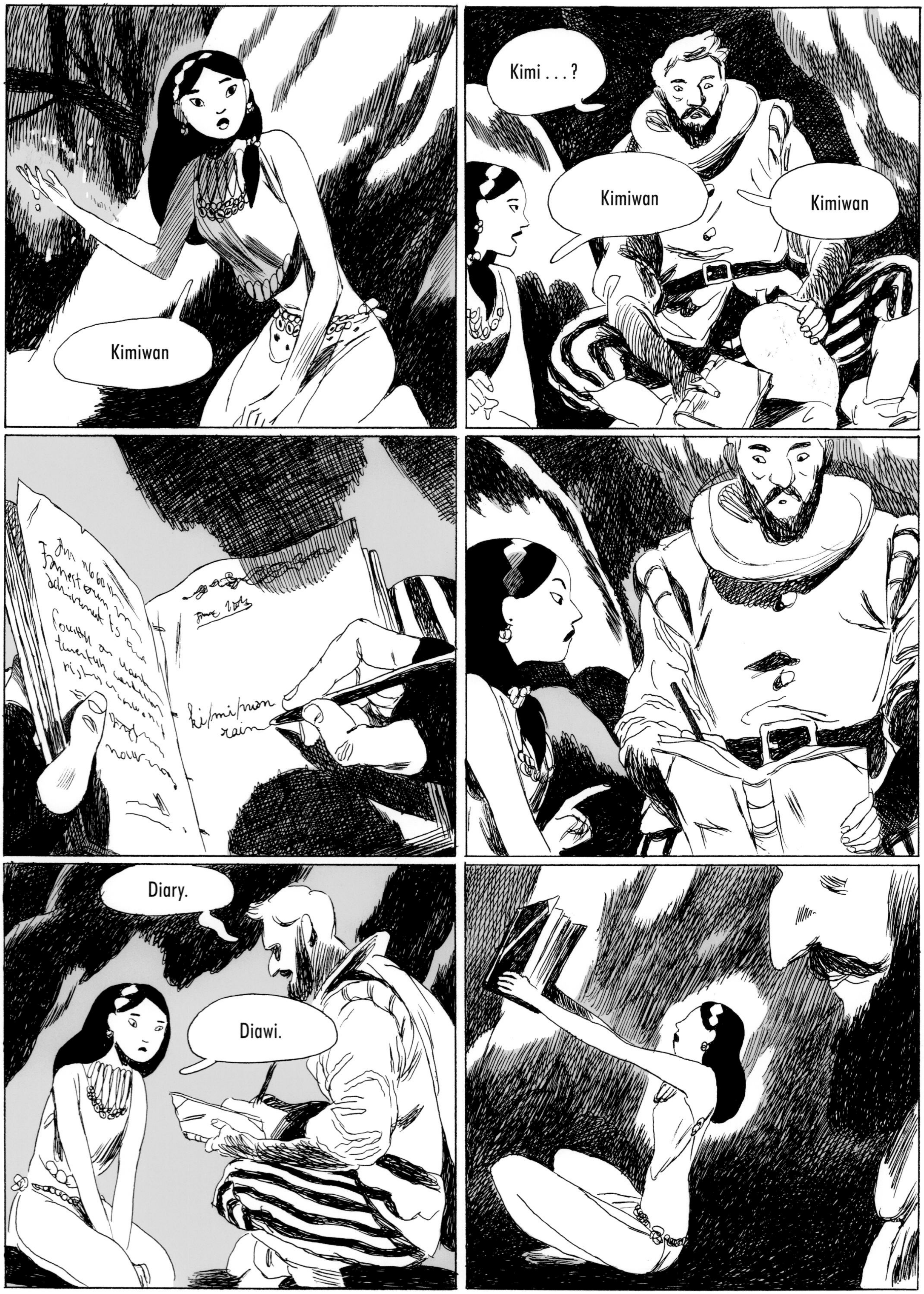
Kimiwan
Kimi . . . ?
Kimiwan
Kimiwan
Diary.
Diawi.

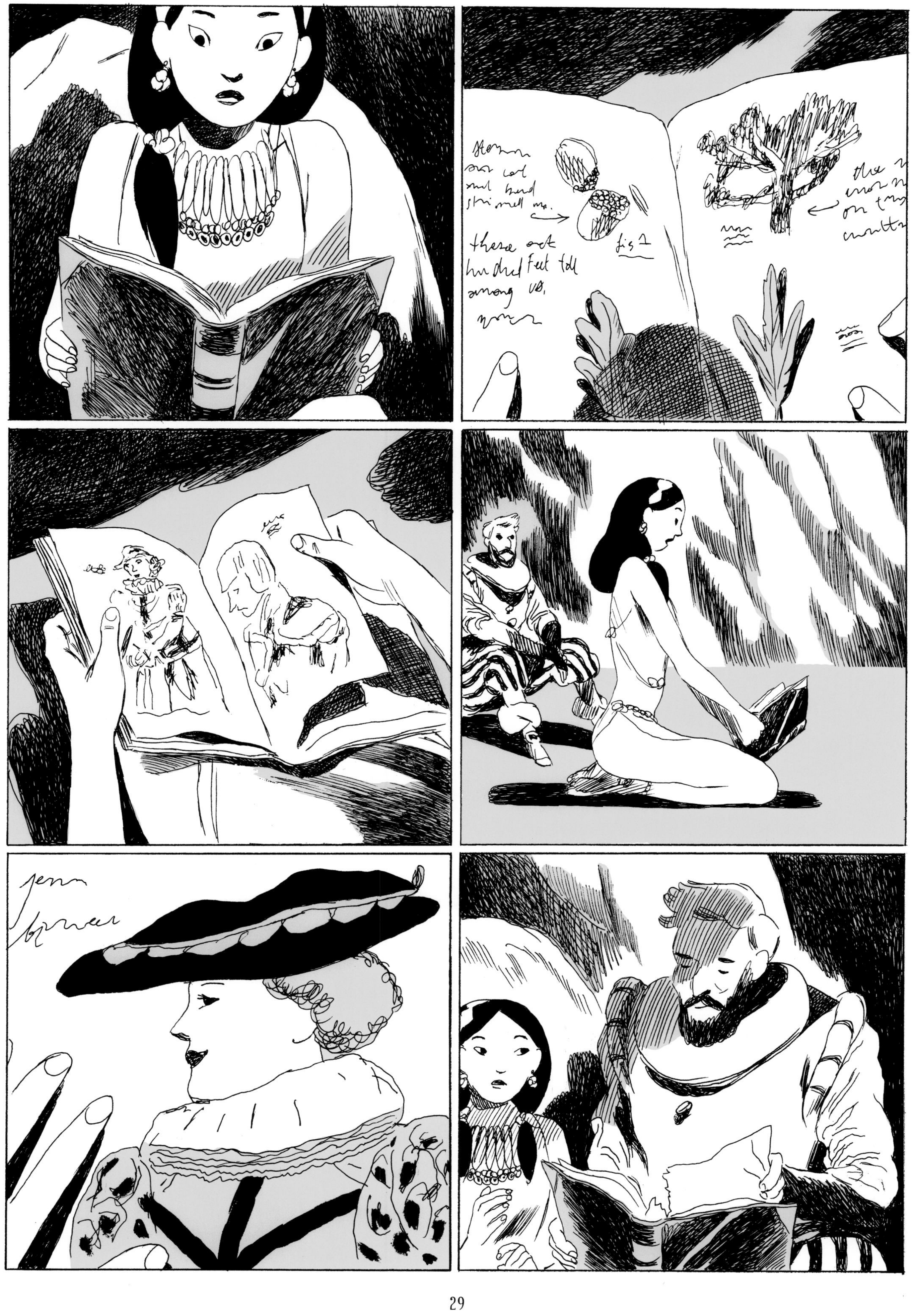

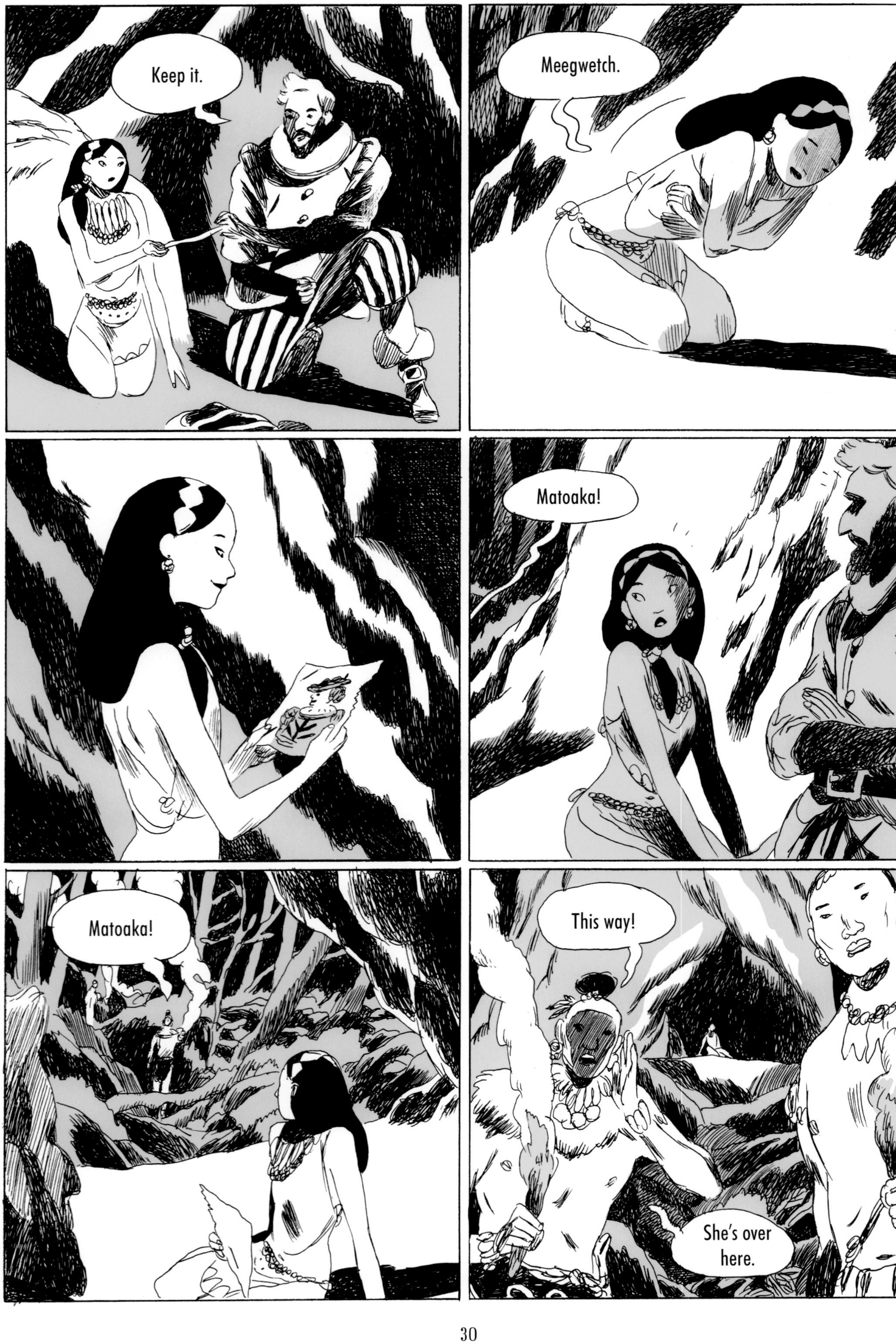
Keep it.
Meegwetch.
Matoaka!
Matoaka!
This way!
She's over here.

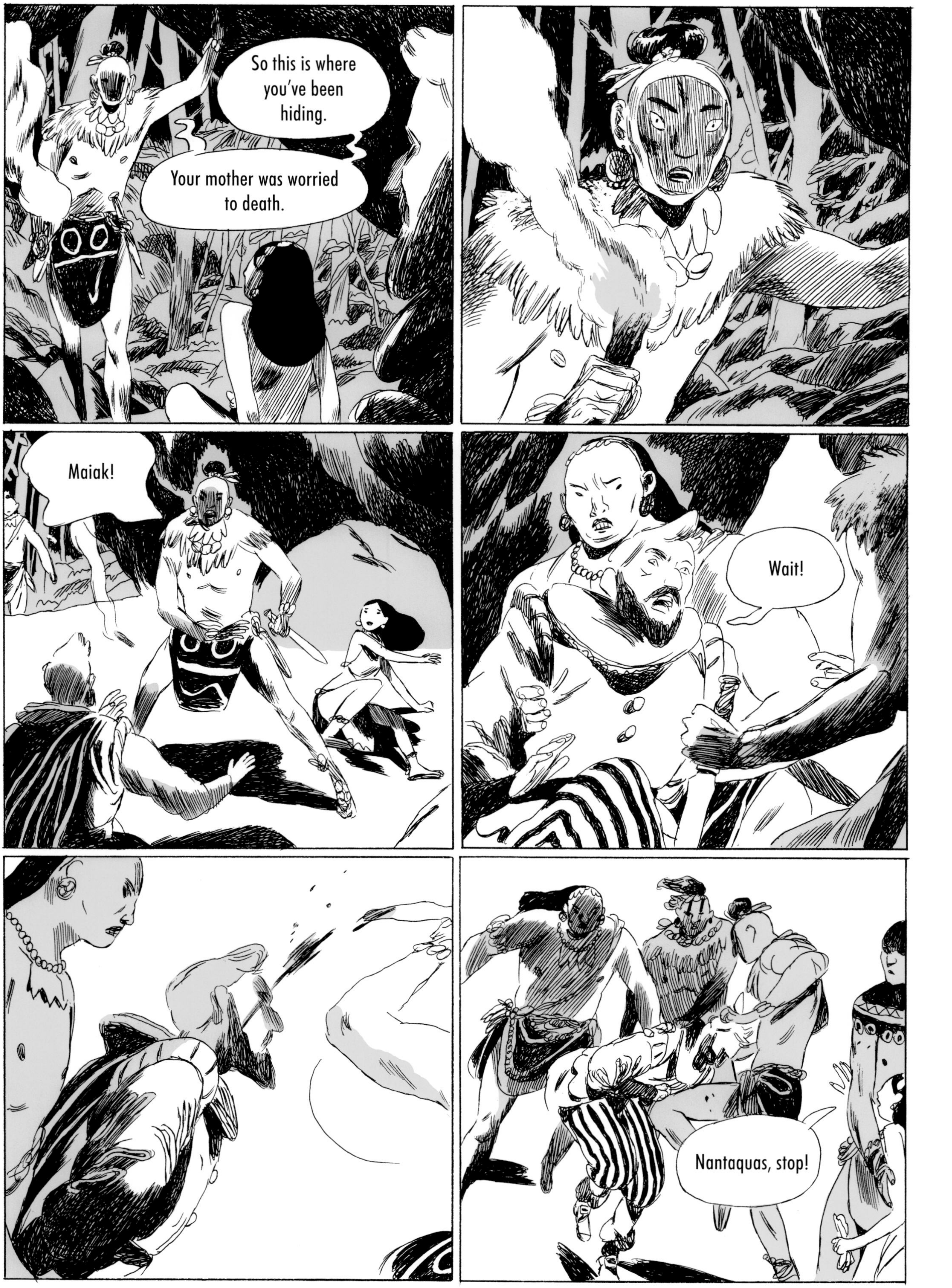
So this is where you've been hiding.
Your mother was worried to death.
Maiak!
Wait!
Nantaquas, stop!

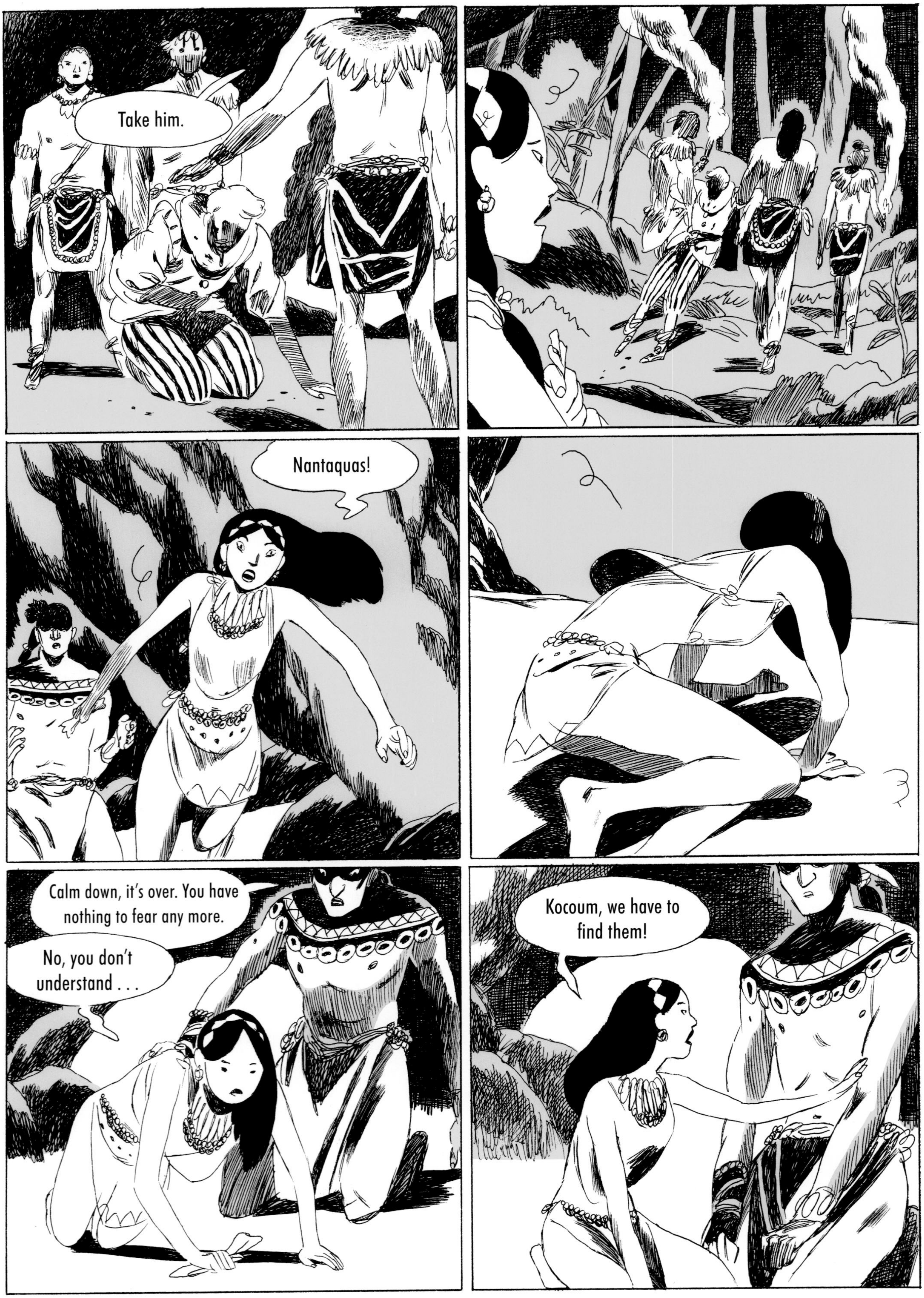
Take him.
Nantaquas!
Calm down, it's over. You have nothing to fear any more.
No, you don't understand . . .
Kocoum, we have to find them!

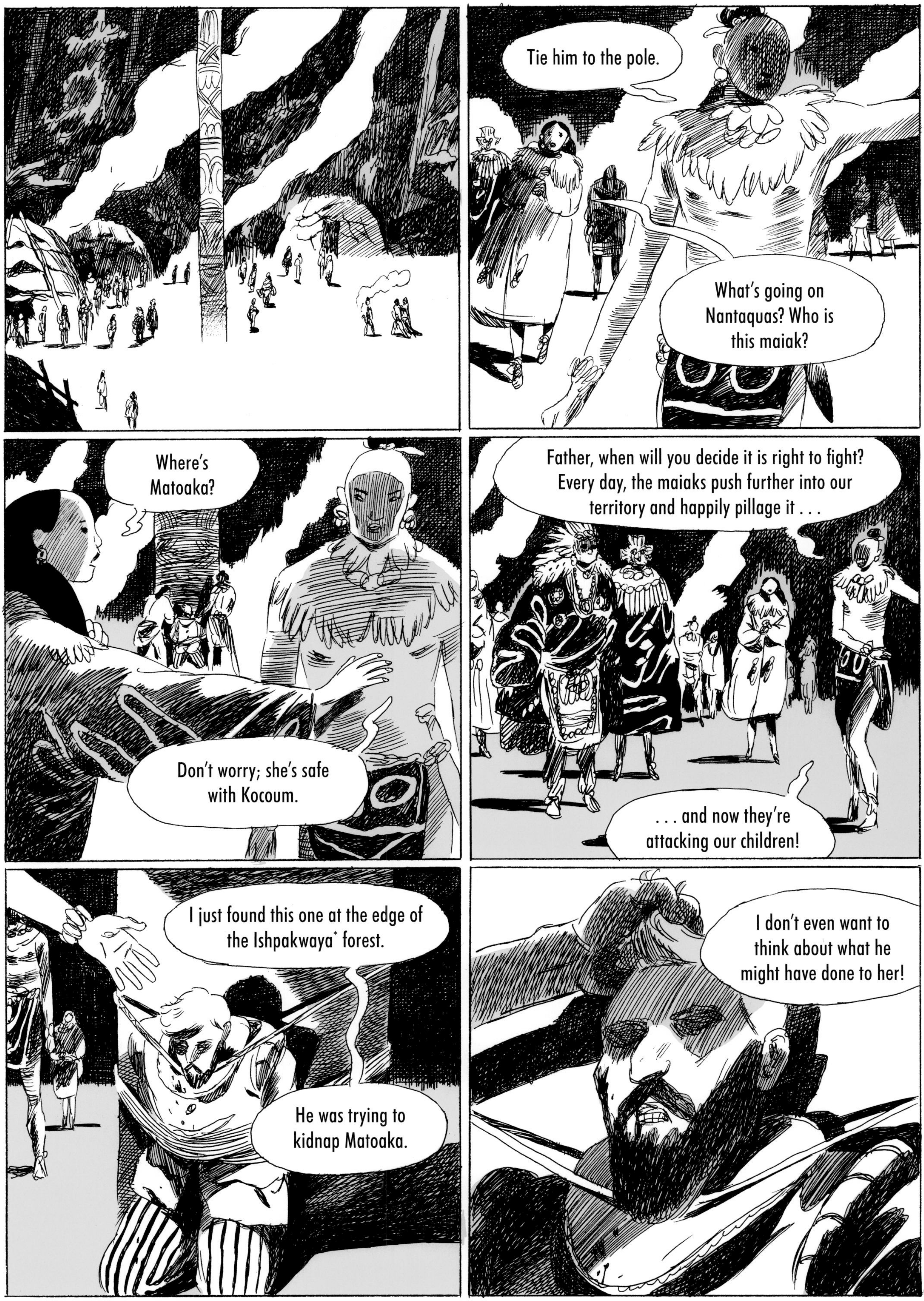
Tie him to the pole.
What's going on Nantaquas? Who is this maiak?
Where's Matoaka?
Don't worry; she's safe with Kocoum.
Father, when will you decide it is right to fight? Every day, the maiaks push further into our territory and happily pillage it . . .
. . . and now they're attacking our children!
I just found this one at the edge of the Ishpakwaya* forest.
He was trying to kidnap Matoaka.
I don't even want to think about what he might have done to her!

* the forest of tall trees

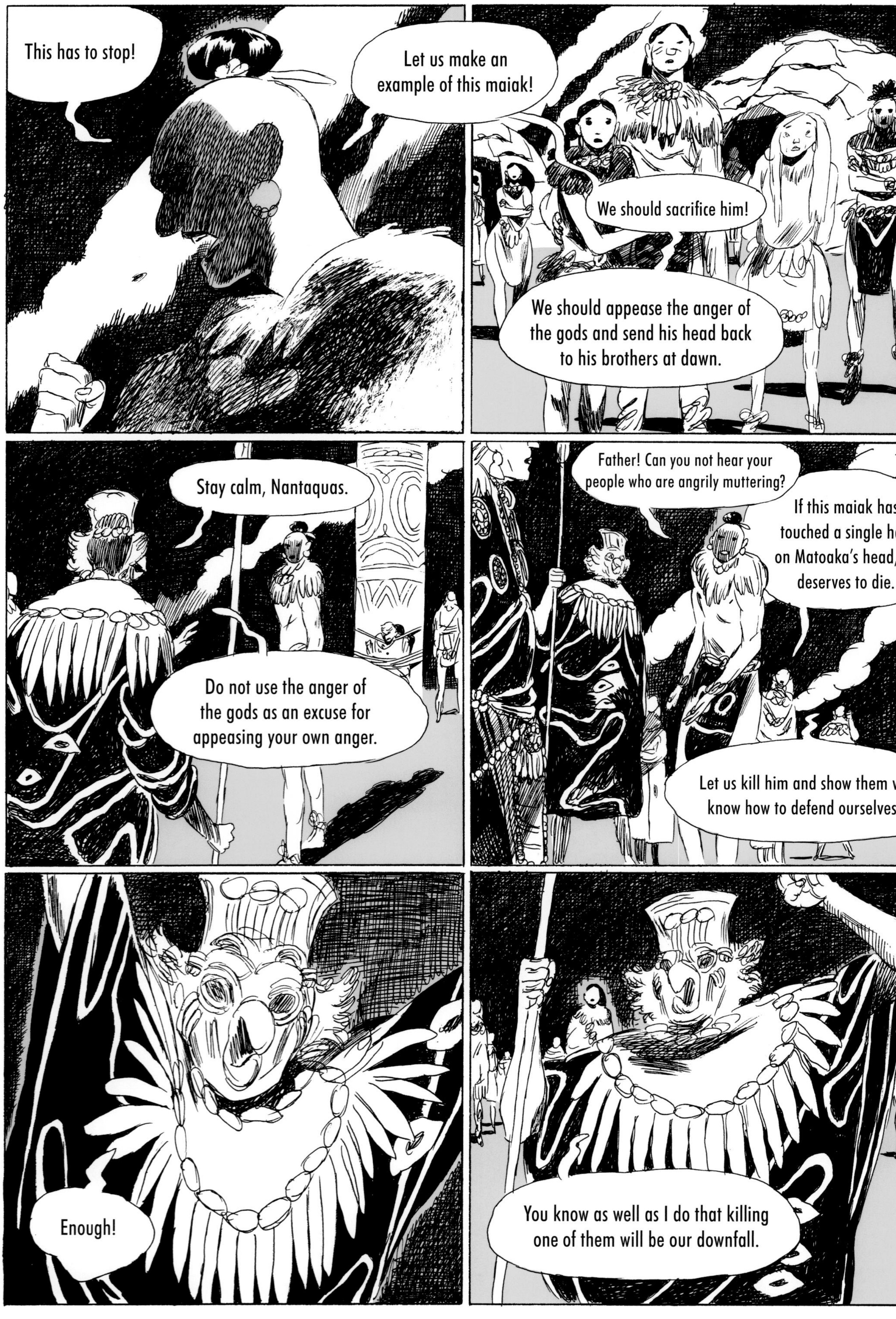
This has to stop!
Let us make an example of this maiak!
We should sacrifice him!
We should appease the anger of the gods and send his head back to his brothers at dawn.
Stay calm, Nantaquas.
Do not use the anger of the gods as an excuse for appeasing your own anger.
Father! Can you not hear your people who are angrily muttering?
If this maiak has touched a single hair on Matoaka's head, he deserves to die.
Let us kill him and show them we know how to defend ourselves.
Enough!
You know as well as I do that killing one of them will be our downfall.

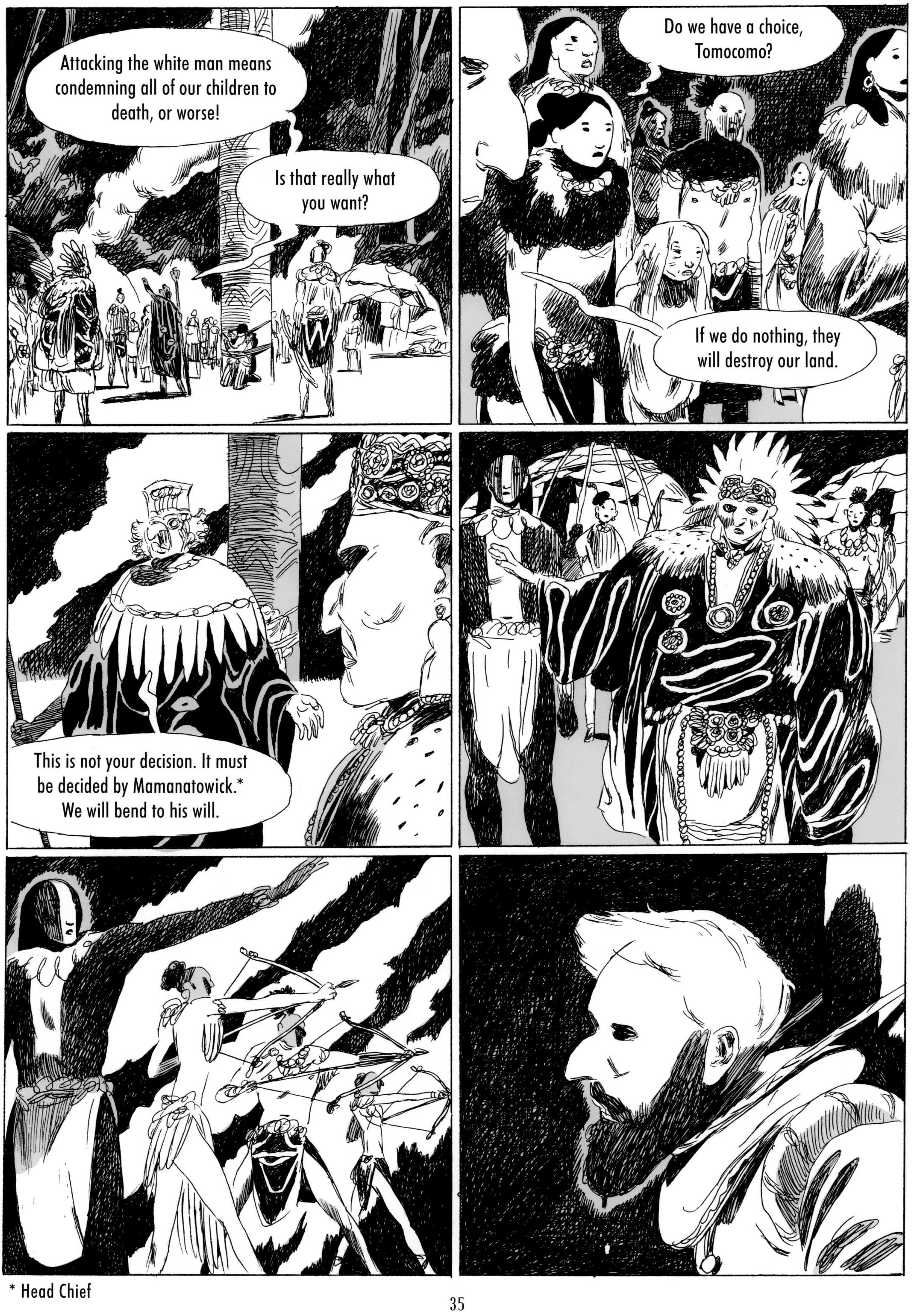
Attacking the white man means condemning all of our children to death, or worse!
Is that really what you want?
Do we have a choice, Tomocomo?
If we do nothing, they will destroy our land.
This is not your decision. It must be decided by Mamanatowick.* We will bend to his will.

* Head Chief

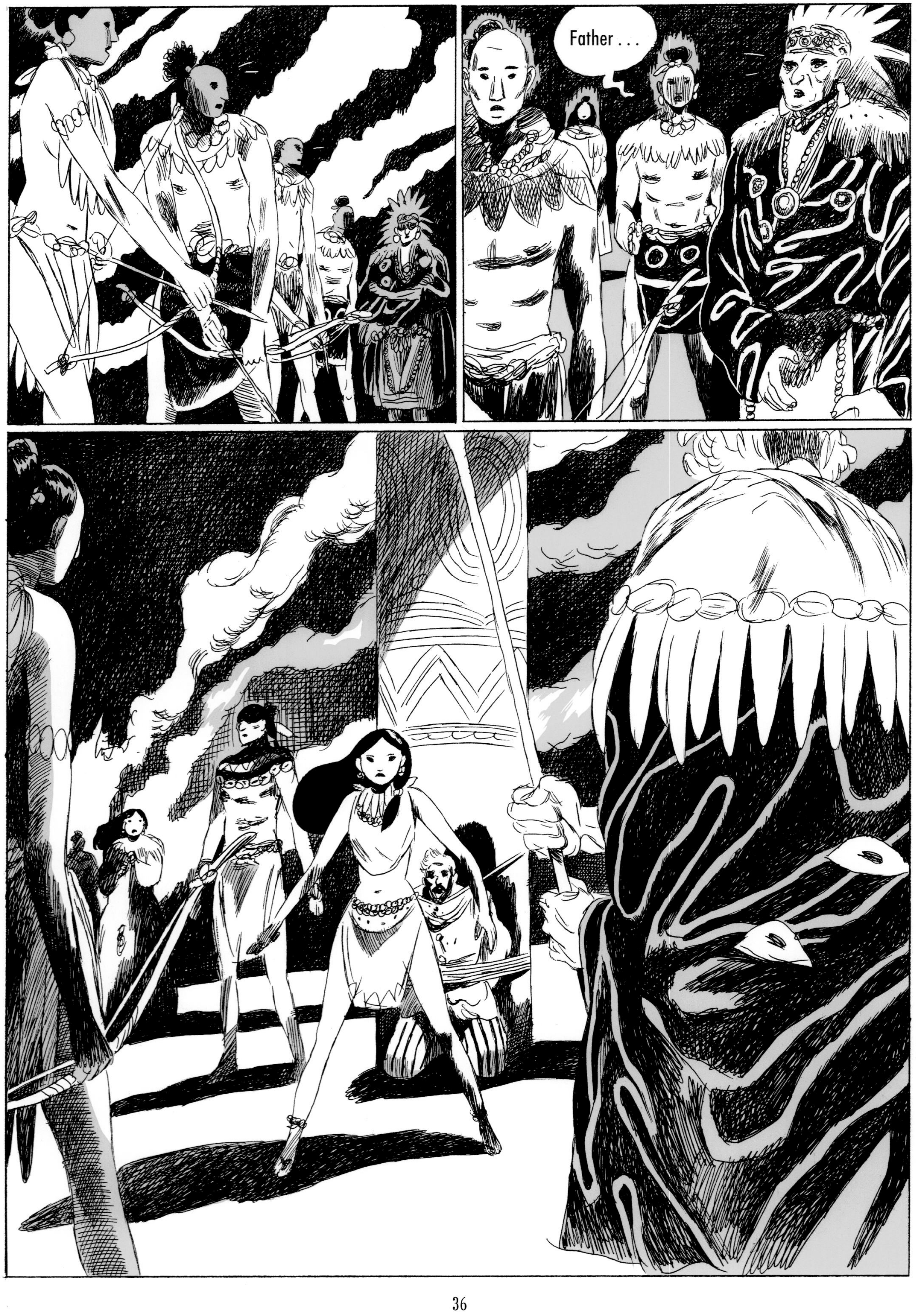
Father . . .

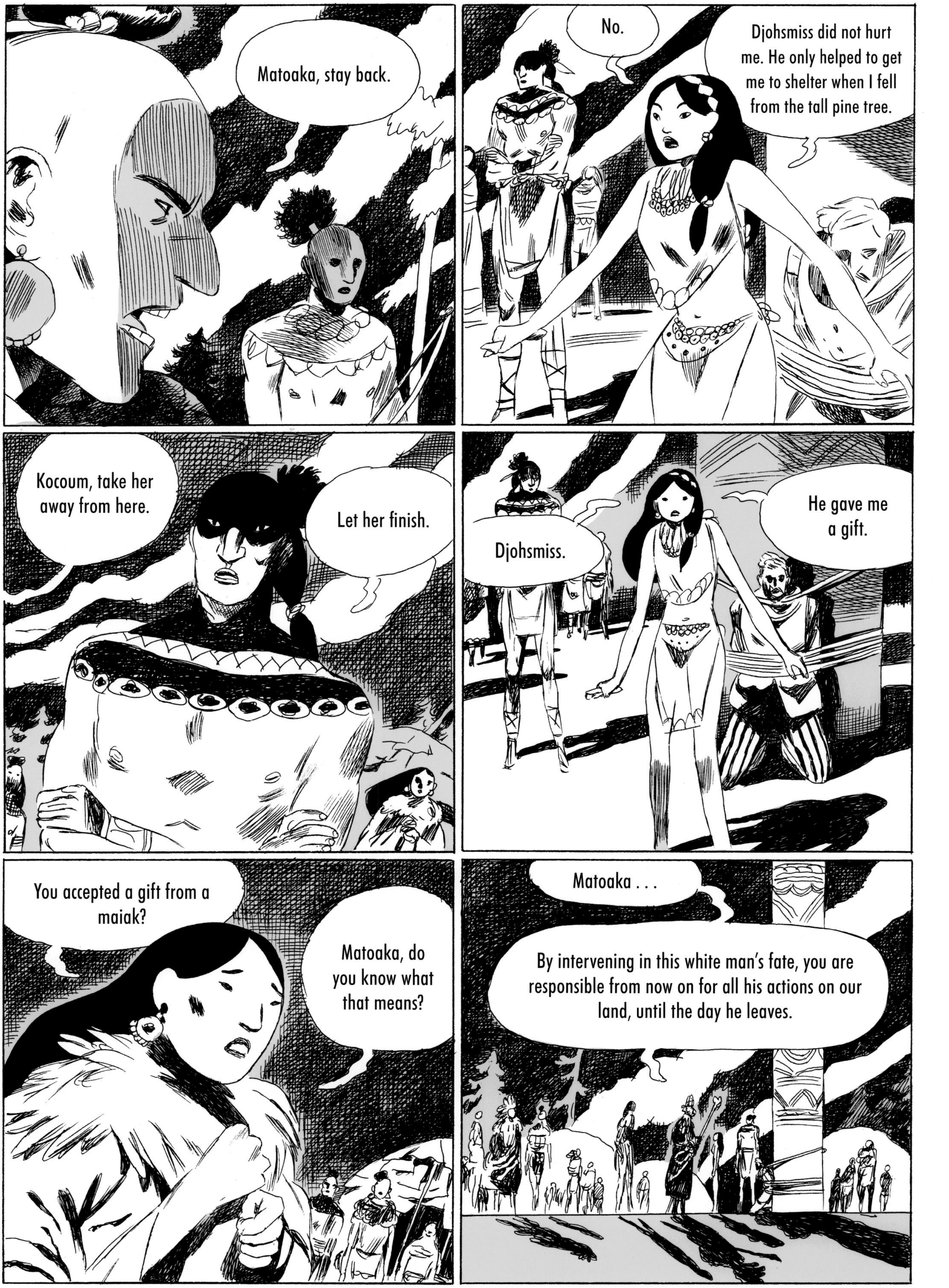

Matoaka, stay back.
No.
Djohsmiss did not hurt me. He only helped to get me to shelter when I fell from the tall pine tree.
Kocoum, take her away from here.
Let her finish.
Djohsmiss.
He gave me a gift.
You accepted a gift from a maiak?
Matoaka, do you know what that means?
Matoaka . . .
By intervening in this white man's fate, you are responsible from now on for all his actions on our land, until the day he leaves.

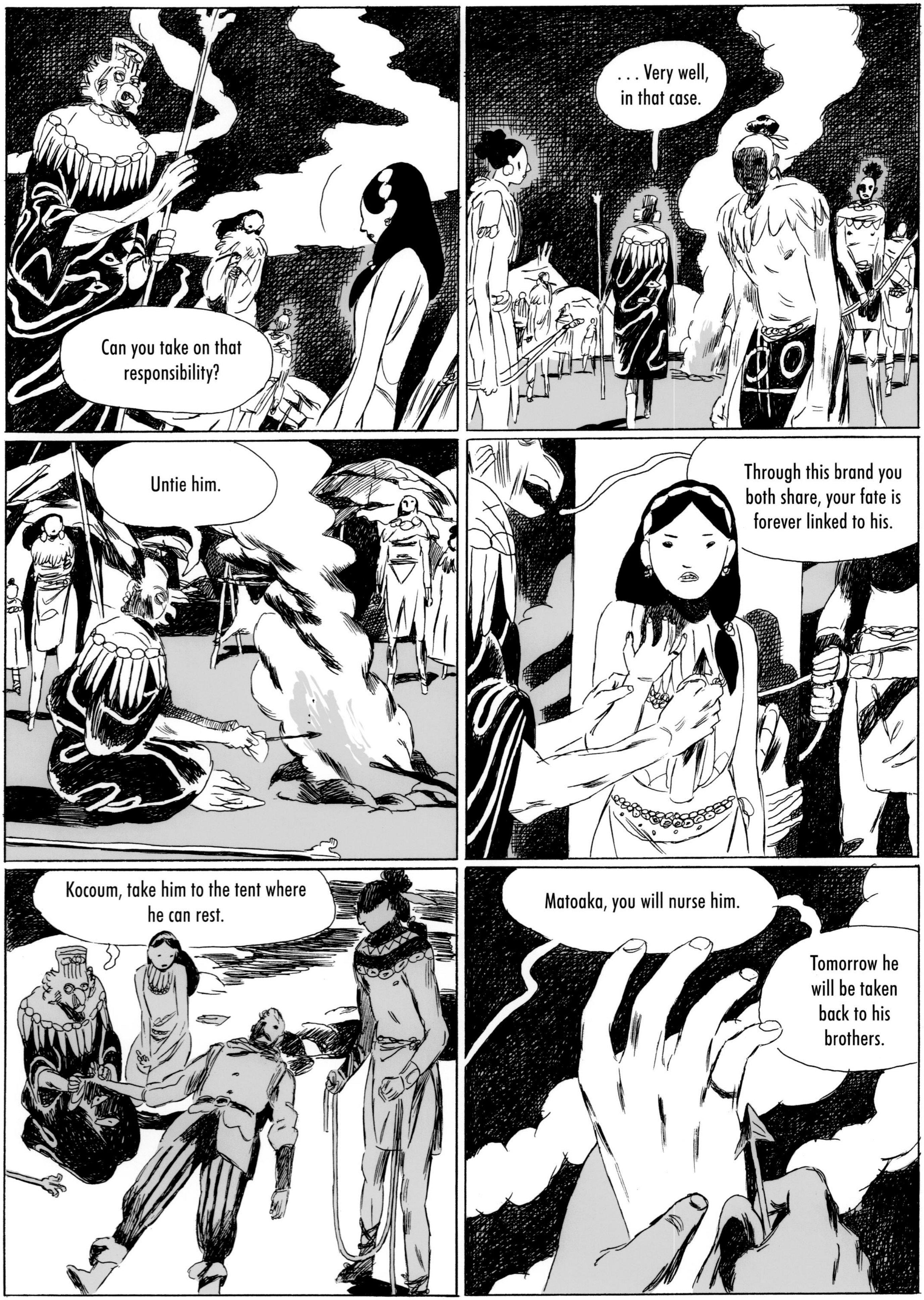
Can you take on that responsibility?
. . . Very well, in that case.
Untie him.
Through this brand you both share, your fate is forever linked to his.
Kocoum, take him to the tent where he can rest.
Matoaka, you will nurse him.
Tomorrow he will be taken back to his brothers.

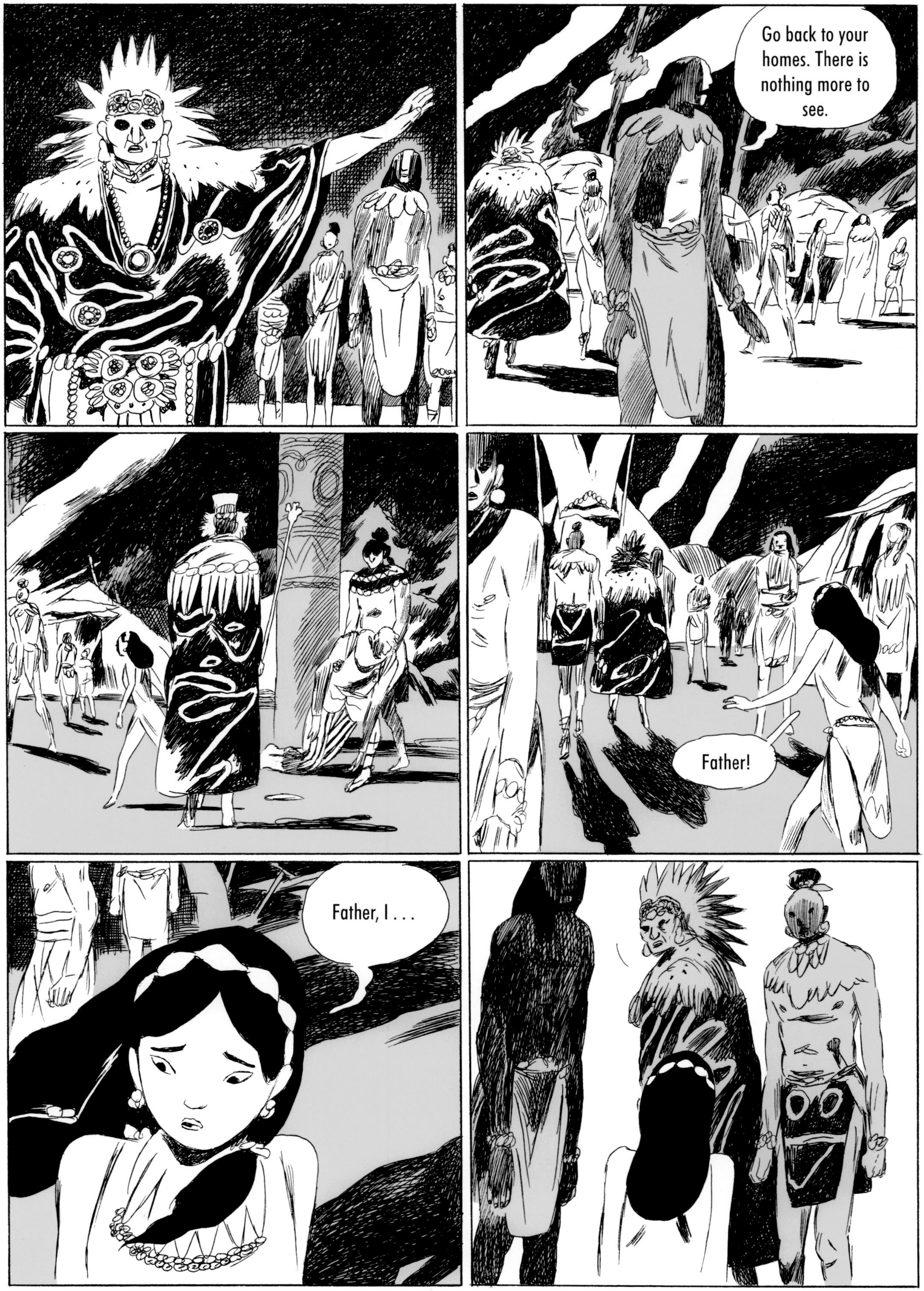
Go back to your homes. There is nothing more to see.
Father!
Father, I . . .

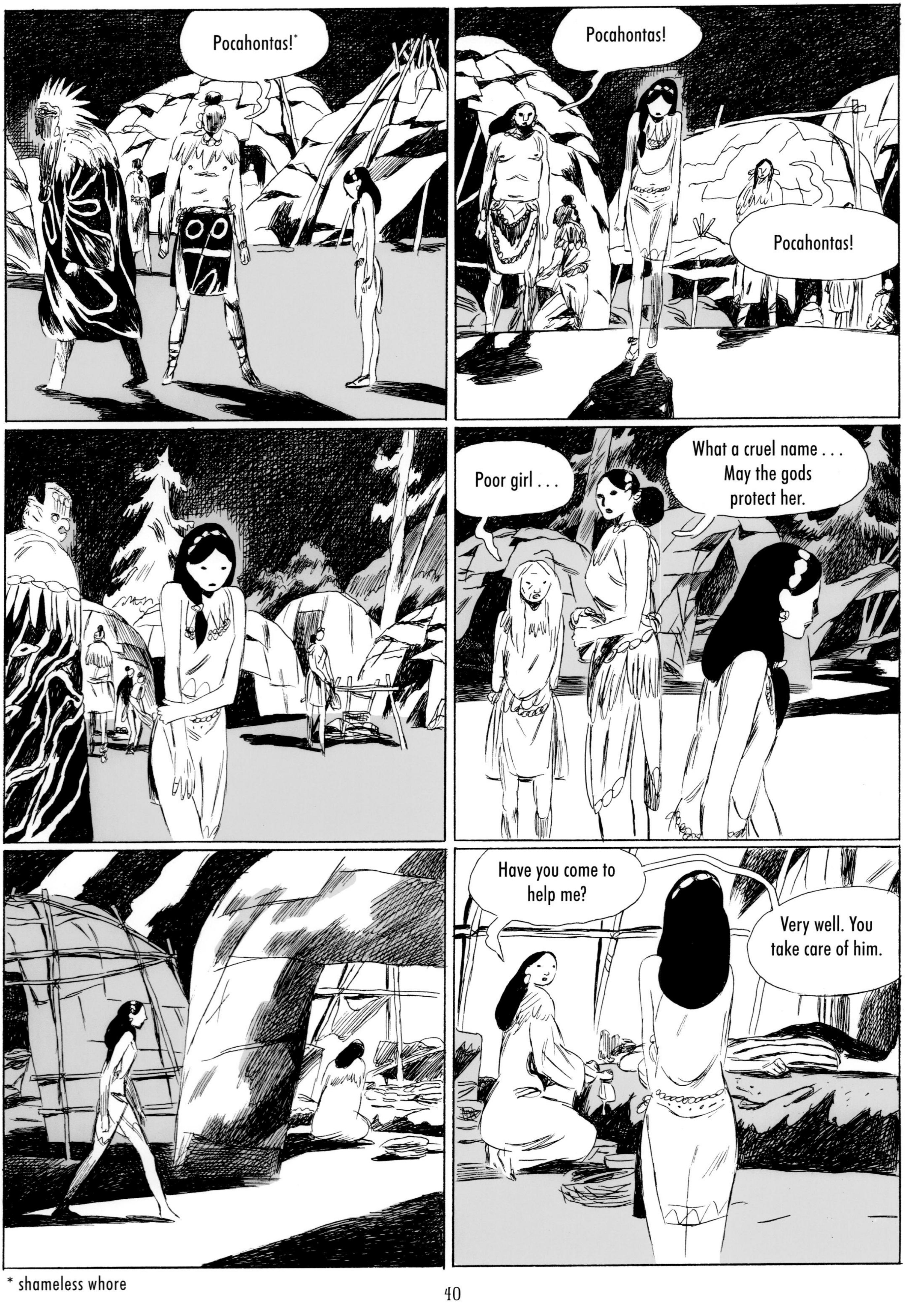
Pocahontas!*
Pocahontas!
Pocahontas!
Poor girl . . .
What a cruel name . . . May the gods protect her.
Have you come to help me?
Very well. You take care of him.

* shameless whore

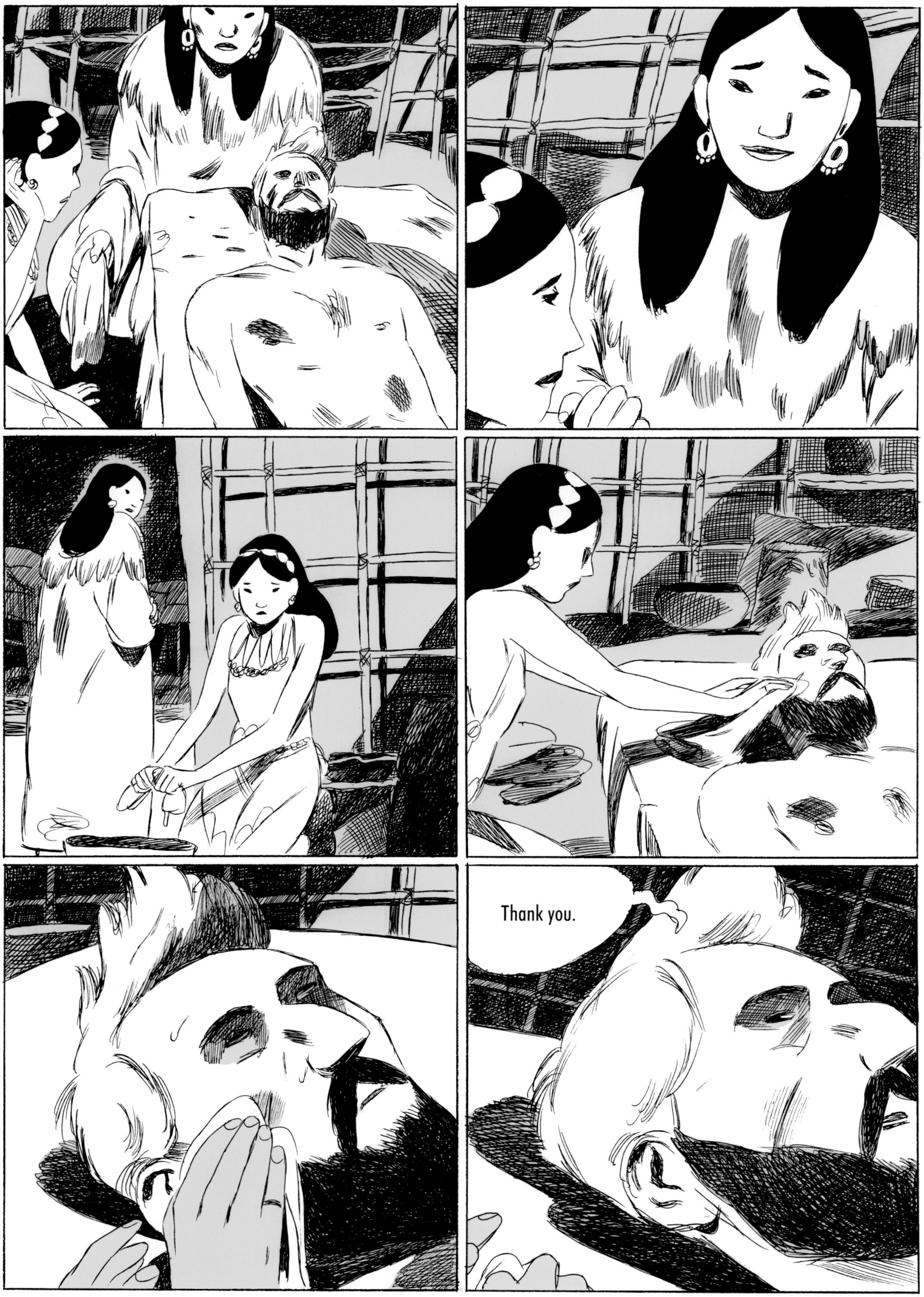
Thank you.

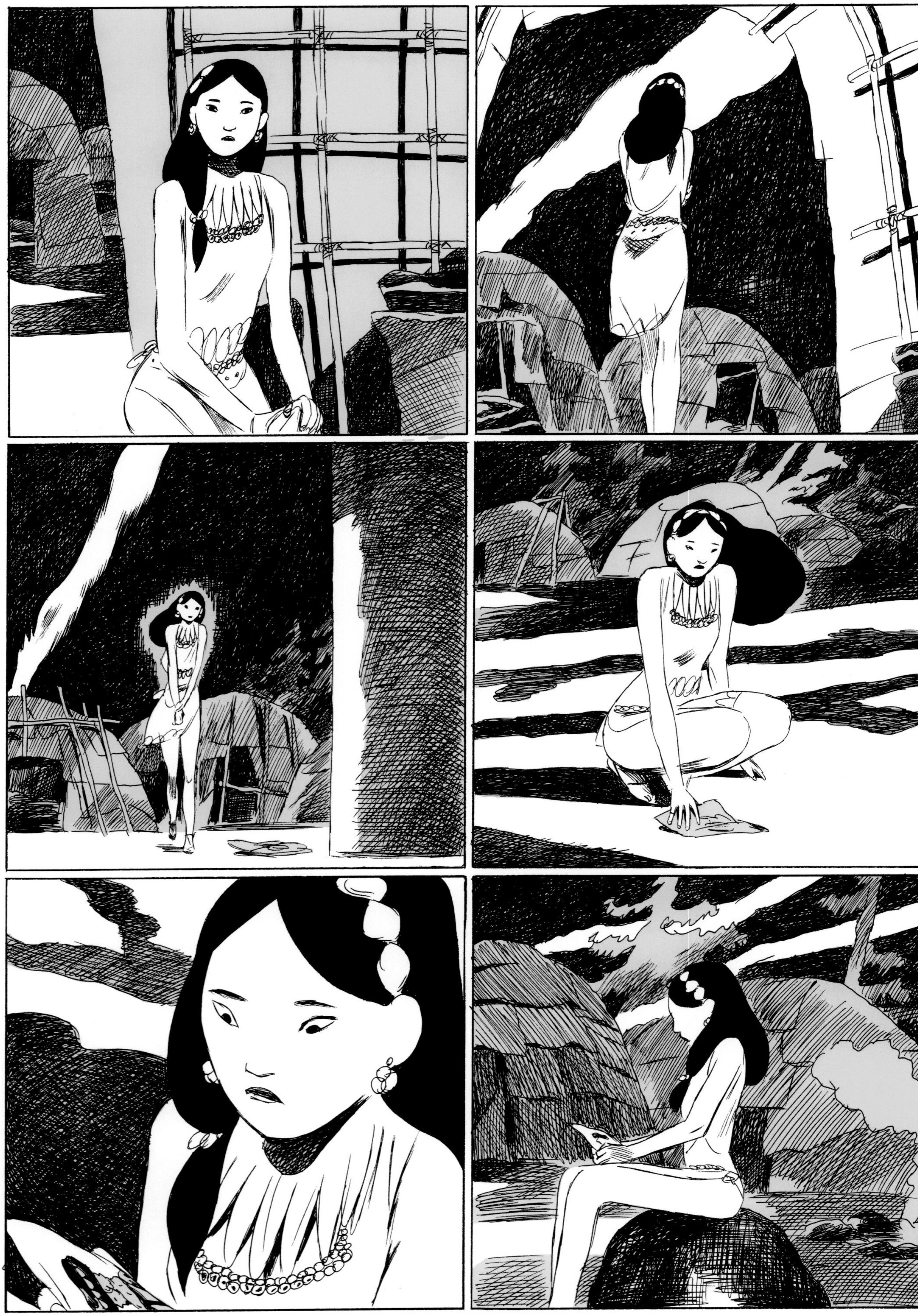

A few months later . . .

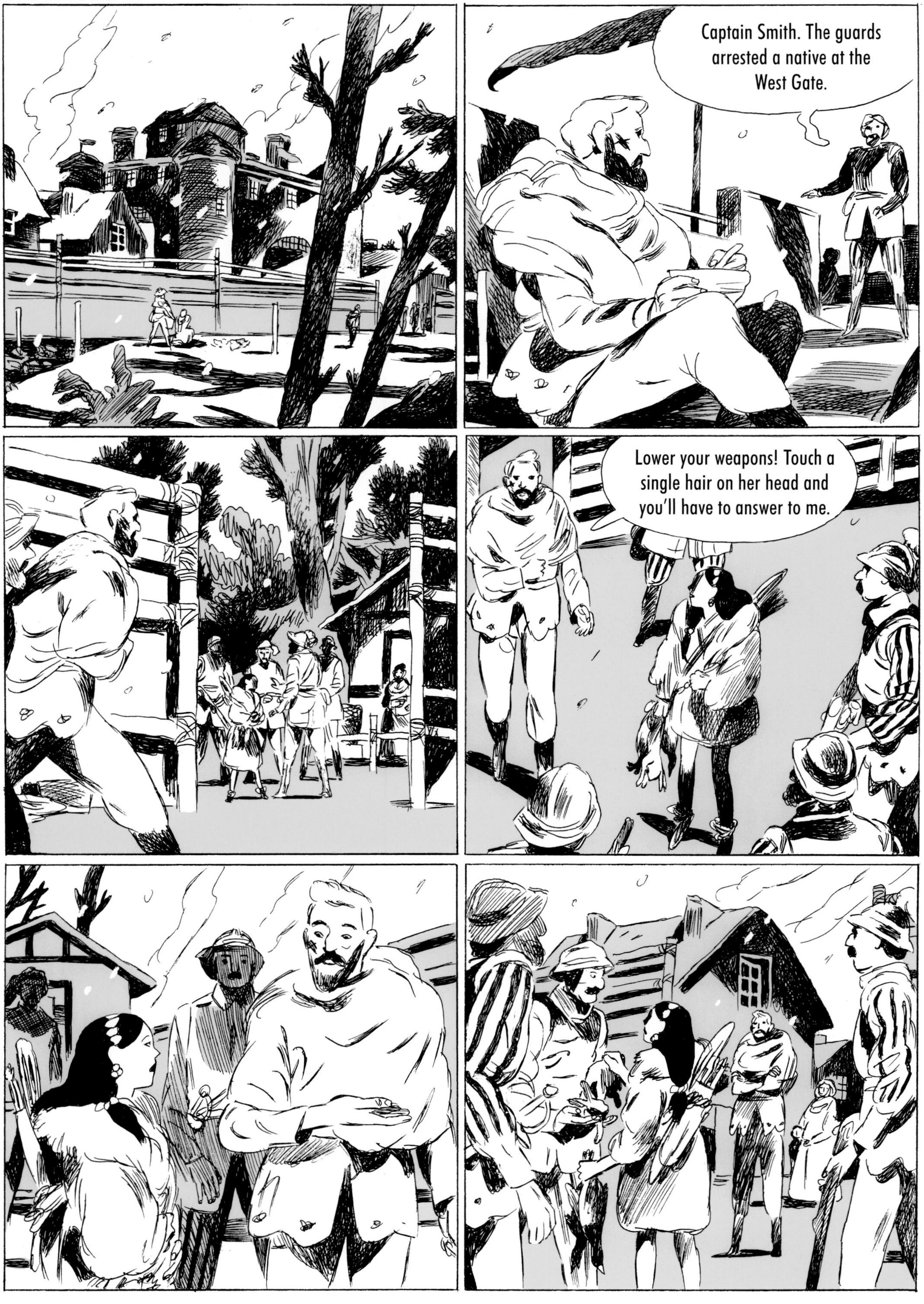
Captain Smith. The guards arrested a native at the West Gate.
Lower your weapons! Touch a single hair on her head and you'll have to answer to me.

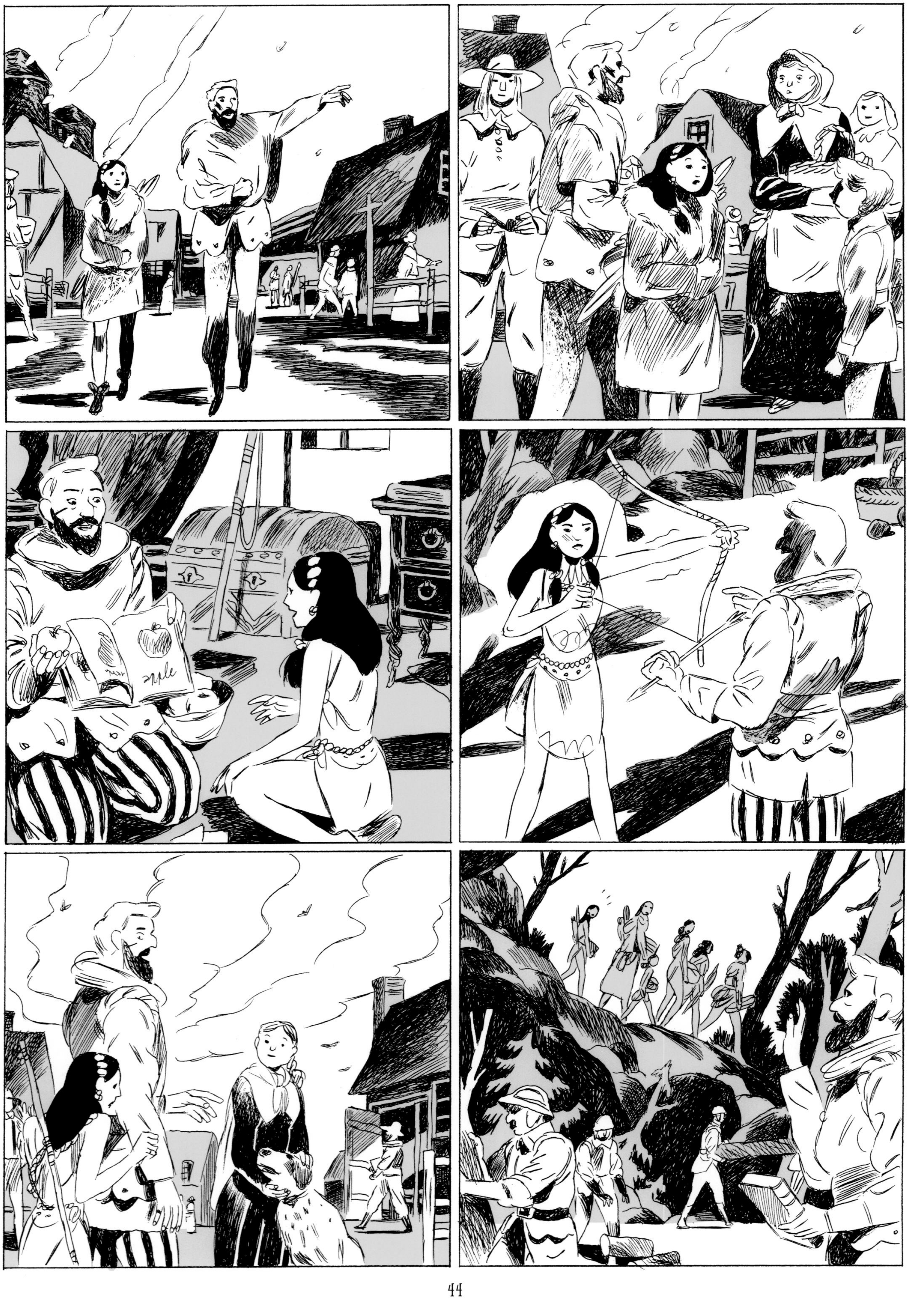
apple

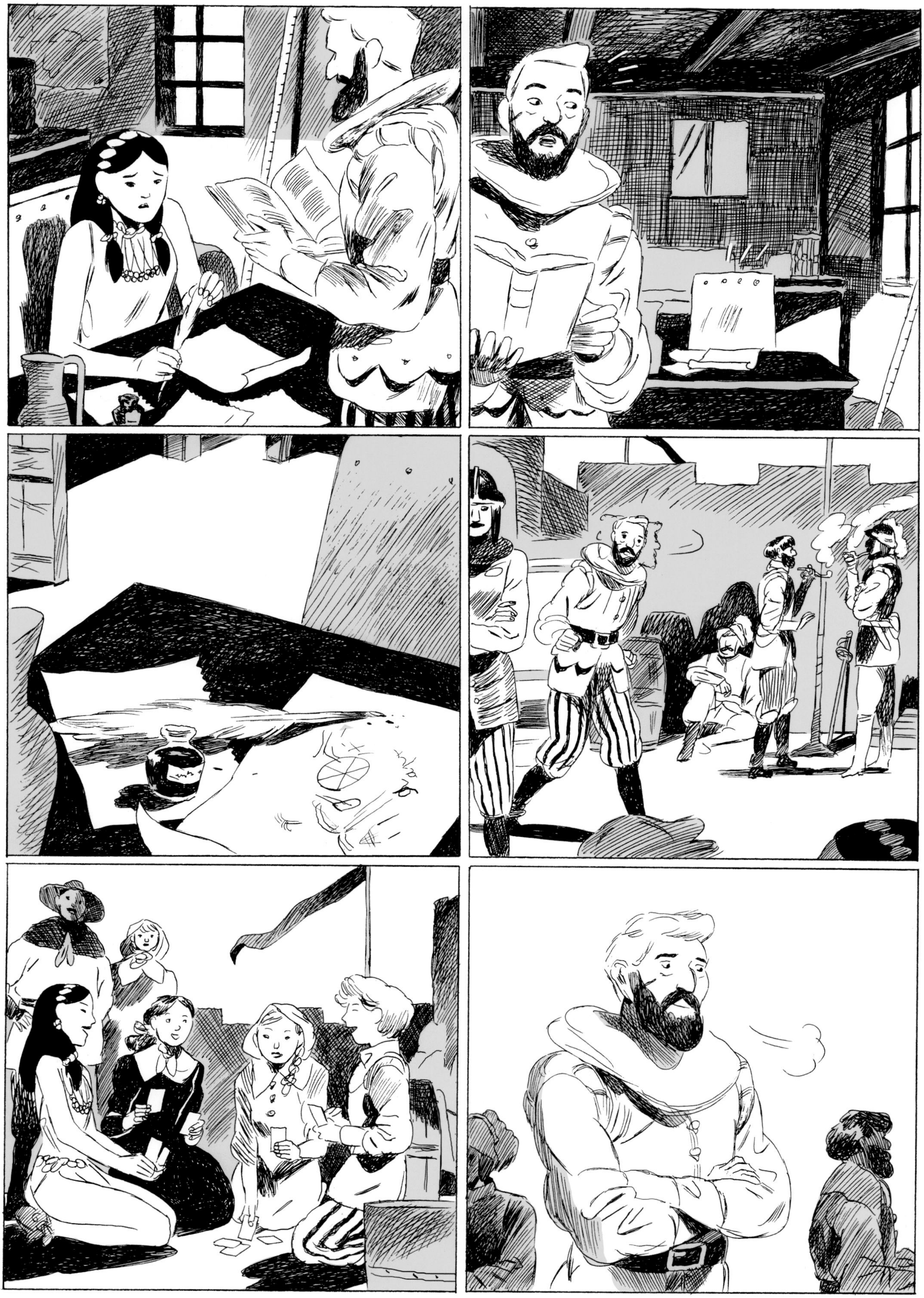

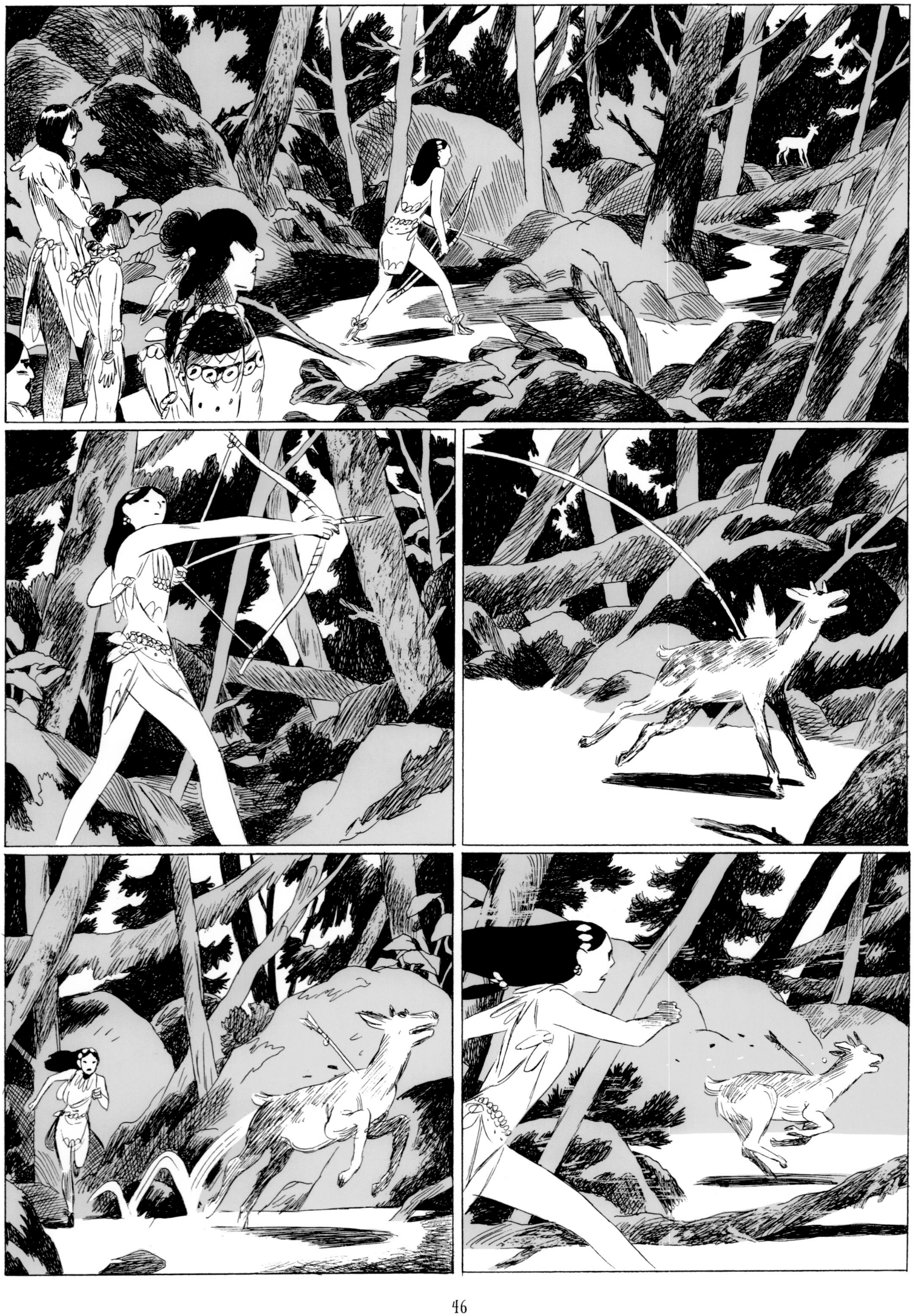

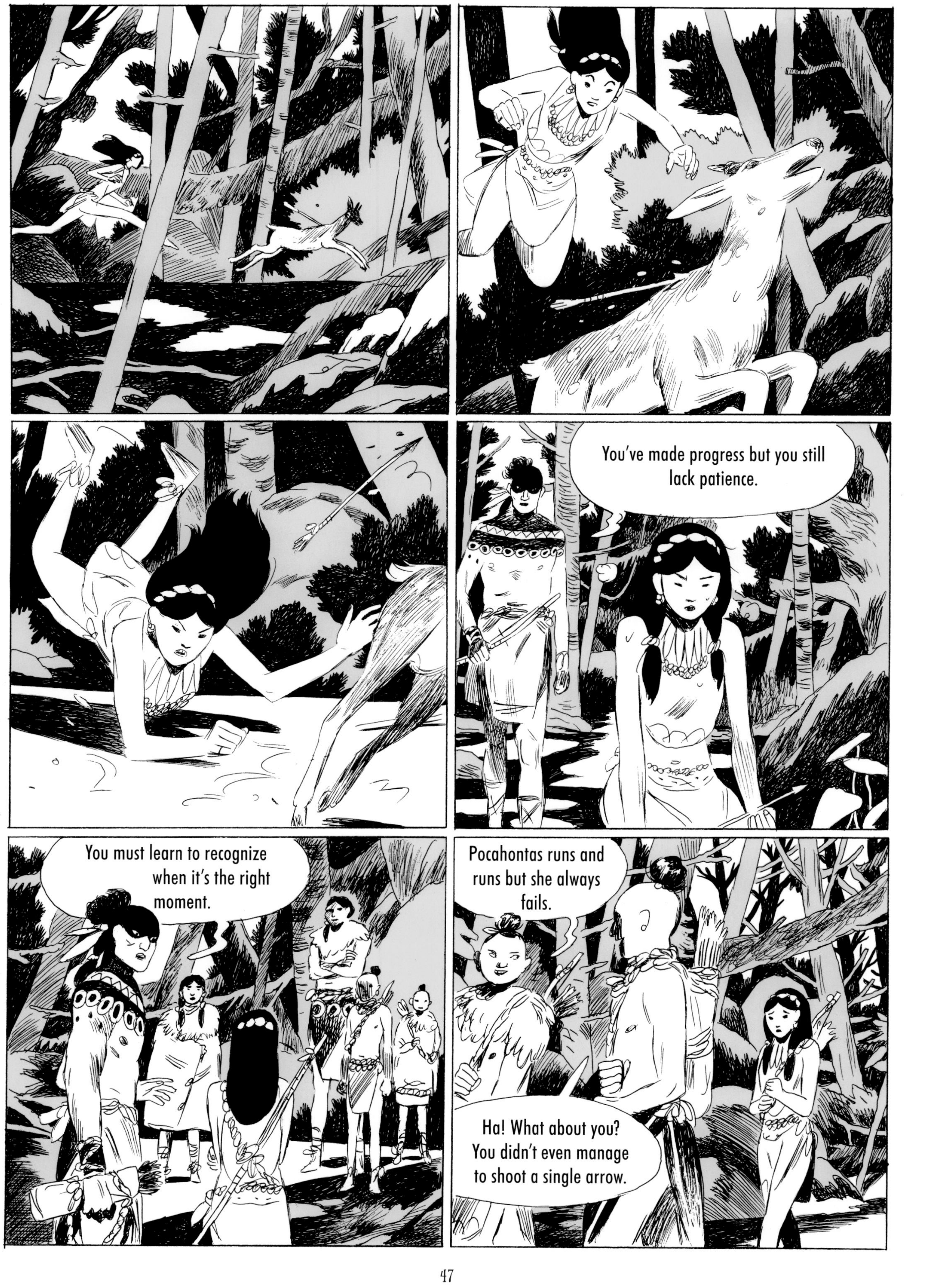
You've made progress but you still lack patience.
You must learn to recognize when it's the right moment.
Pocahontas runs and runs but she always fails.
Ha! What about you? You didn't even manage to shoot a single arrow.

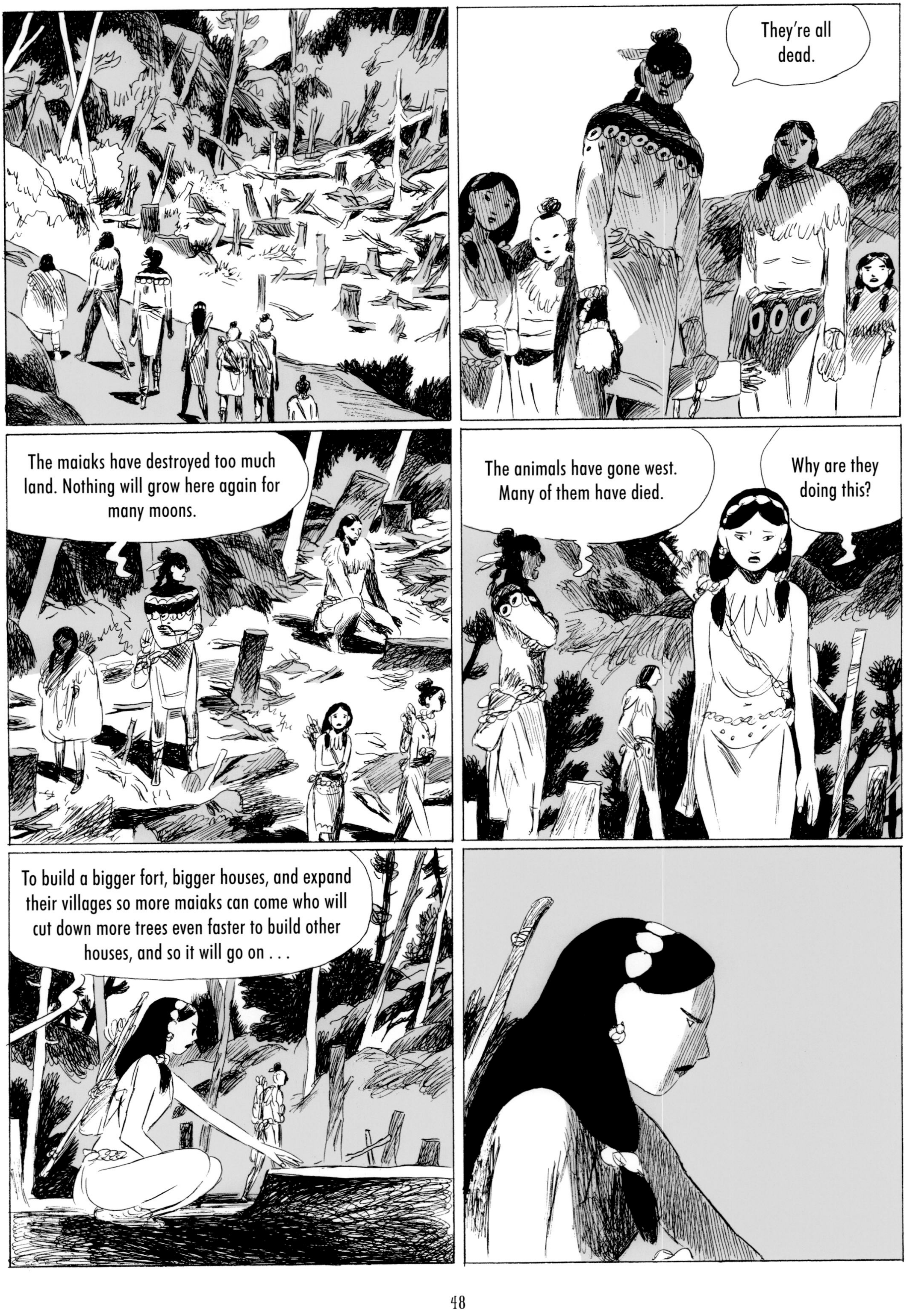
They're all dead.
The maiaks have destroyed too much land. Nothing will grow here again for many moons.
The animals have gone west. Many of them have died.
Why are they doing this?
To build a bigger fort, bigger houses, and expand their villages so more maiaks can come who will cut down more trees even faster to build other houses, and so it will go on . . .

Pocahontas

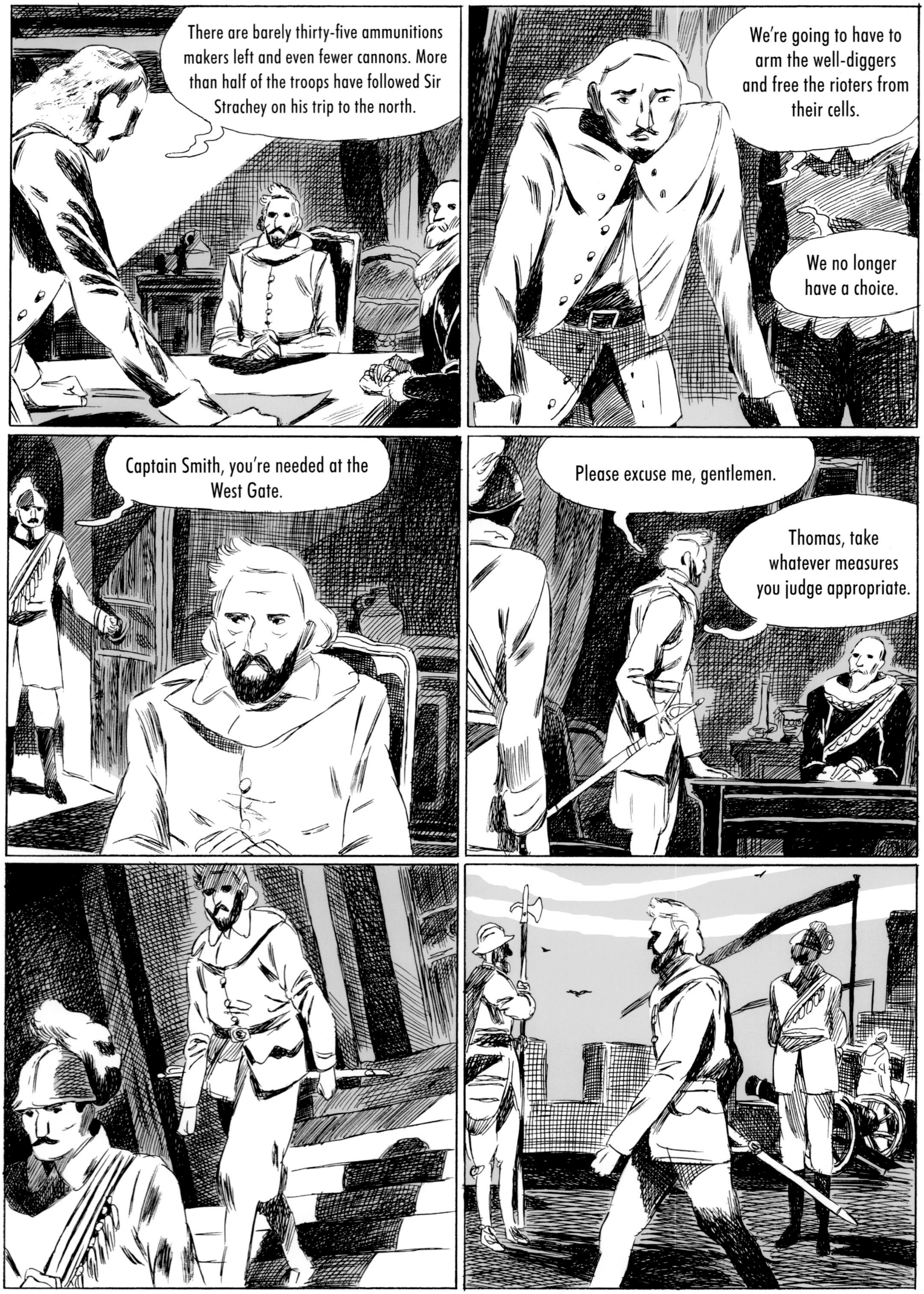
There are barely thirty-five ammunitions makers left and even fewer cannons. More than half of the troops have followed Sir Strachey on his trip to the north.
We're going to have to arm the well-diggers and free the rioters from their cells.
We no longer have a choice.
Captain Smith, you're needed at the West Gate.
Please excuse me, gentlemen.
Thomas, take whatever measures you judge appropriate.

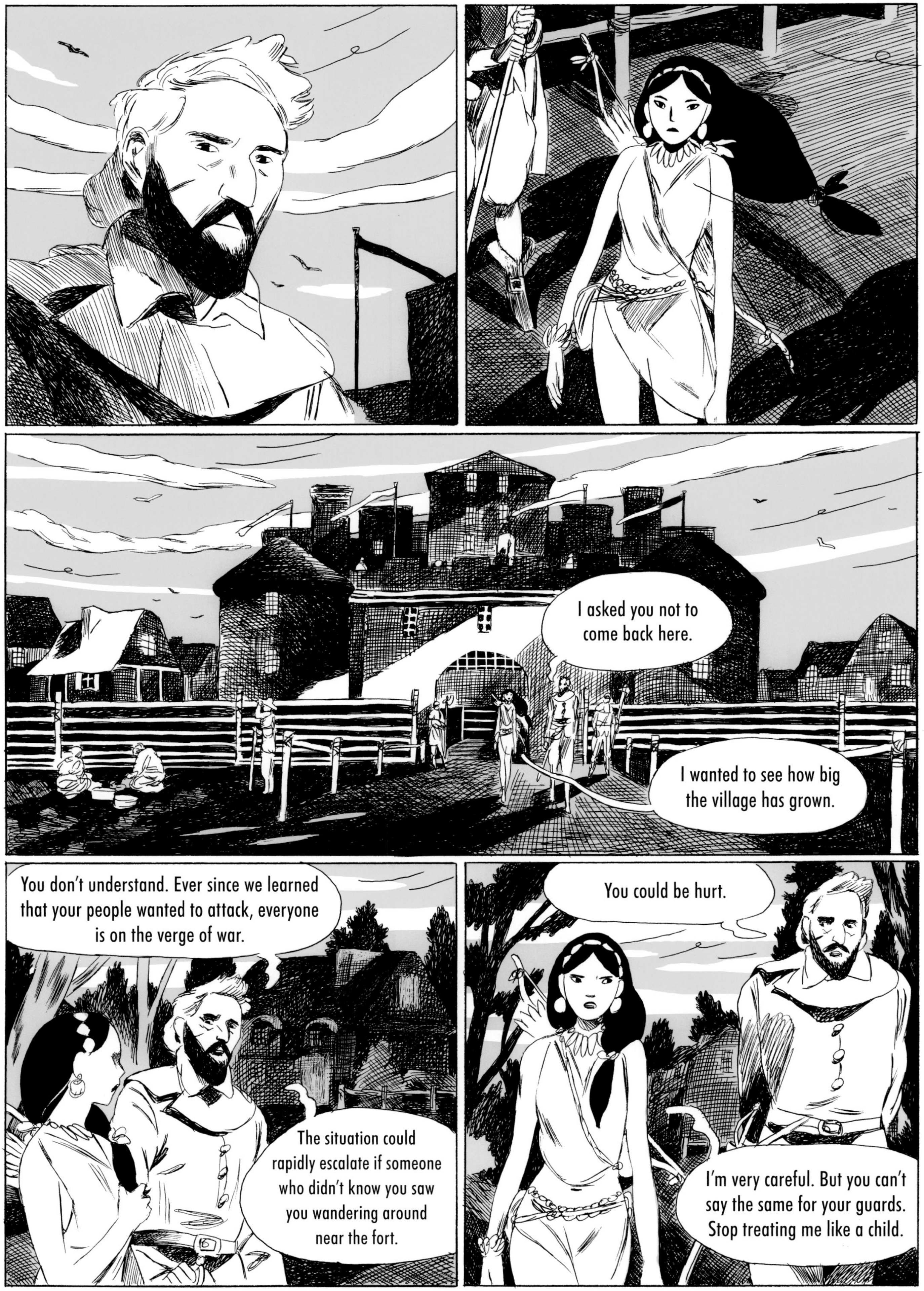
I asked you not to come back here.
I wanted to see how big the village has grown.
You don't understand. Ever since we learned that your people wanted to attack, everyone is on the verge of war.
The situation could rapidly escalate if someone who didn't know you saw you wandering around near the fort.
You could be hurt.
I'm very careful. But you can't say the same for your guards. Stop treating me like a child.

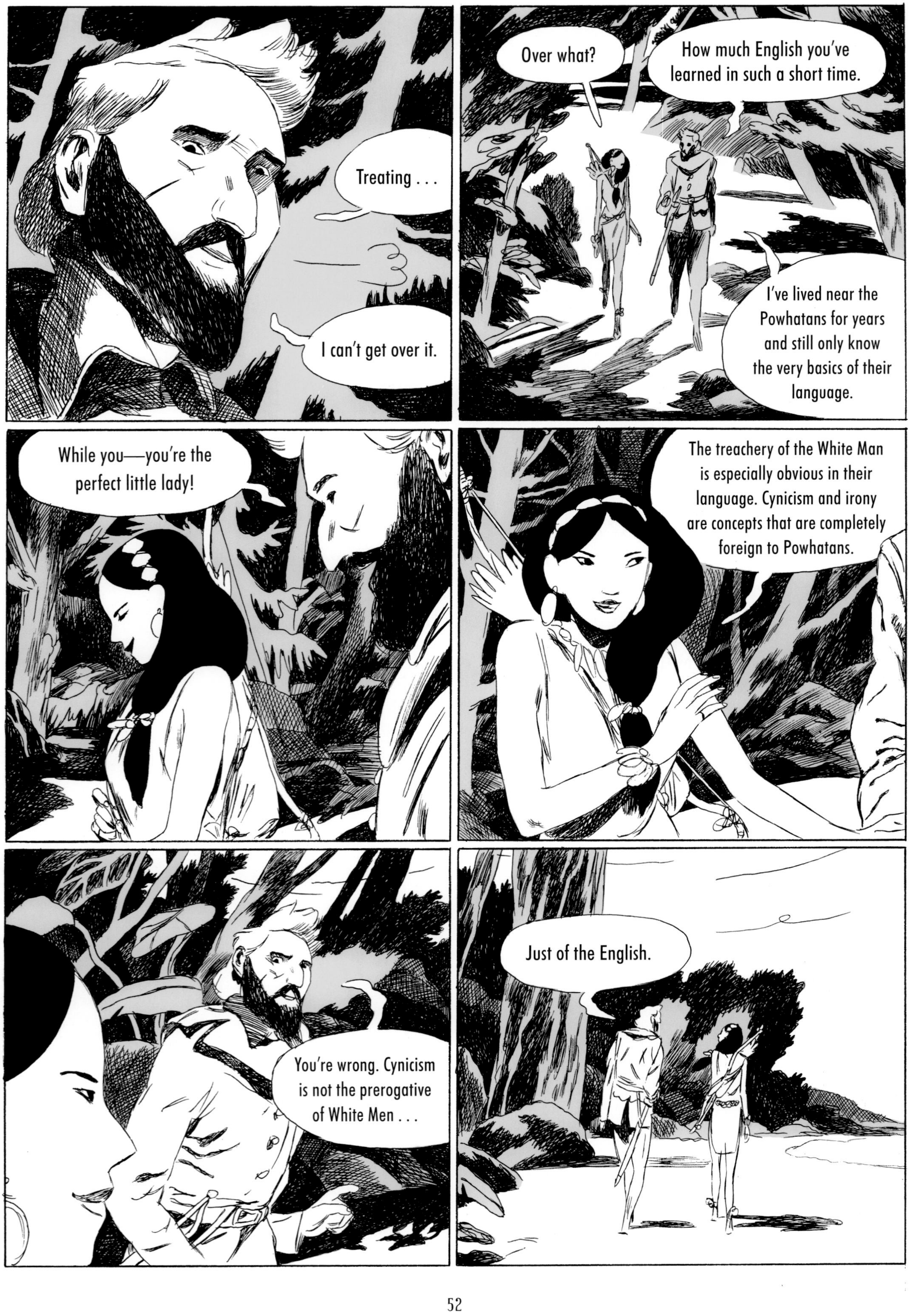
Treating . . .
I can't get over it.
Over what?
How much English you've learned in such a short time.
I've lived near the Powhatans for years and still only know the very basics of their language.
While you—you're the perfect little lady!
The treachery of the White Man is especially obvious in their language. Cynicism and irony are concepts that are completely foreign to Powhatans.
You're wrong. Cynicism is not the prerogative of White Men . . .
Just of the English.

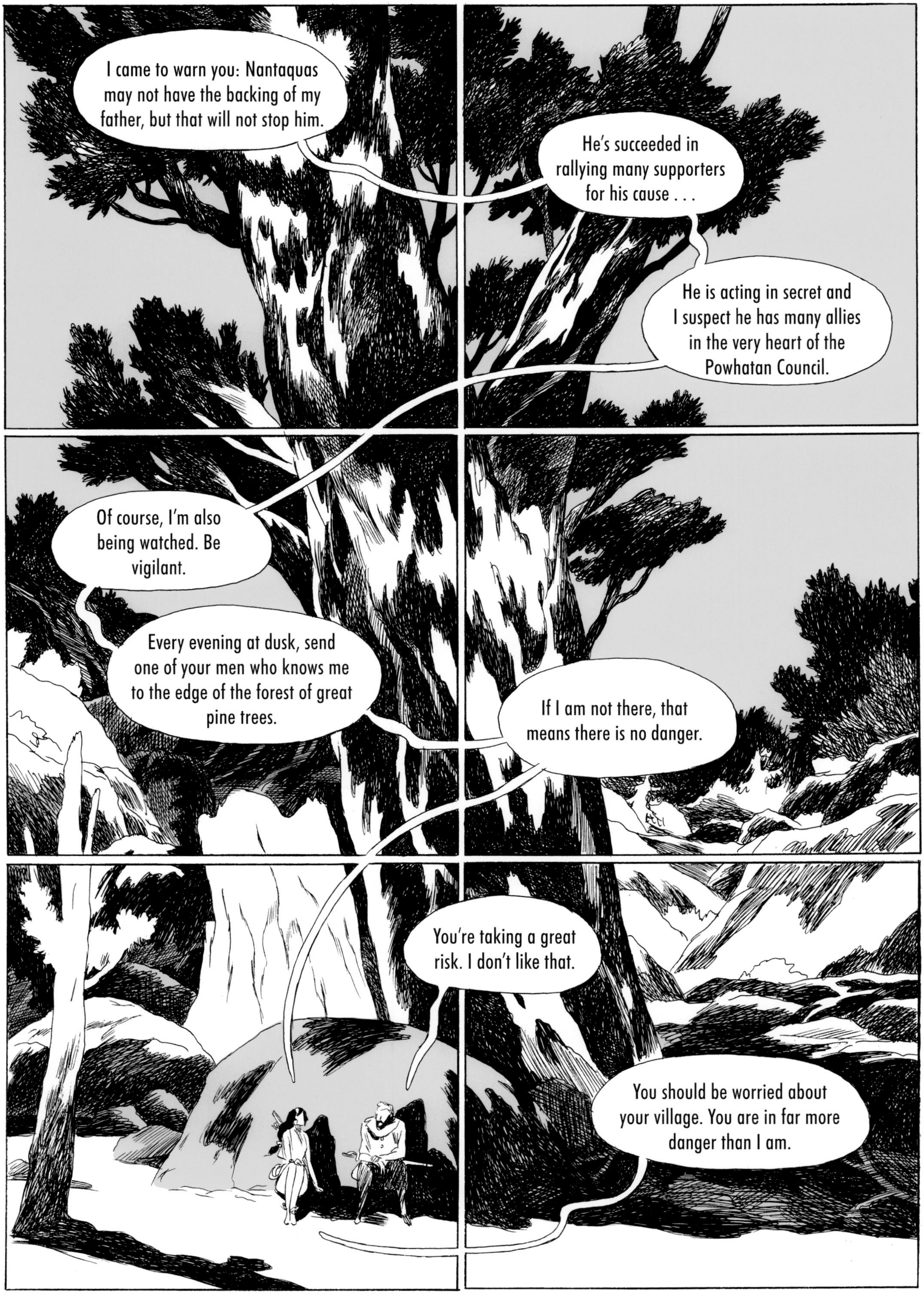
I came to warn you: Nantaquas may not have the backing of my father, but that will not stop him.
He's succeeded in rallying many supporters for his cause . . .
He is acting in secret and I suspect he has many allies in the very heart of the Powhatan Council.
Of course, I'm also being watched. Be vigilant.
Every evening at dusk, send one of your men who knows me to the edge of the forest of great pine trees.
If I am not there, that means there is no danger.
You're taking a great risk. I don't like that.
You should be worried about your village. You are in far more danger than I am.

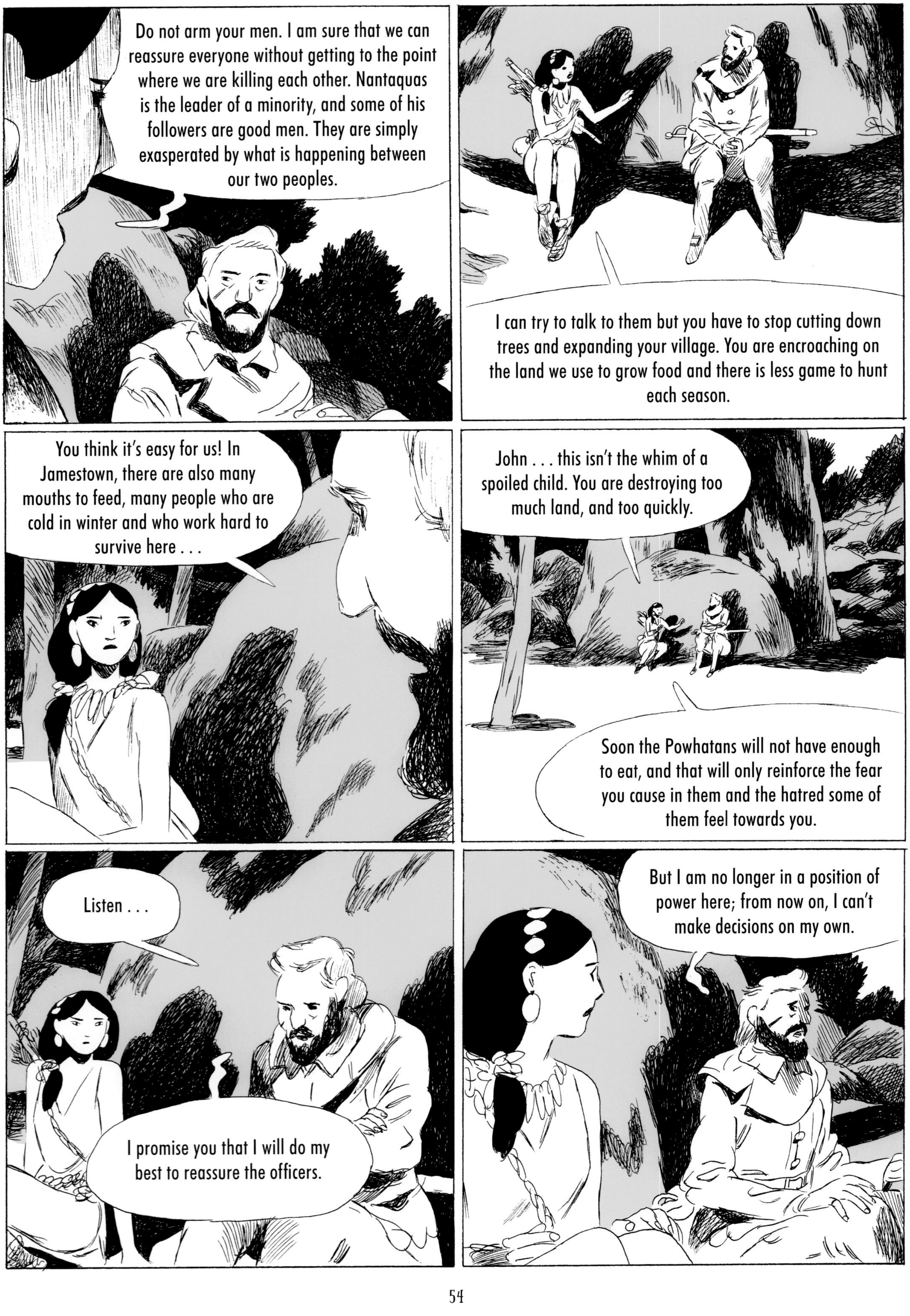
Do not arm your men. I am sure that we can reassure everyone without getting to the point where we are killing each other. Nantaquas is the leader of a minority, and some of his followers are good men. They are simply exasperated by what is happening between our two peoples.
I can try to talk to them but you have to stop cutting down trees and expanding your village. You are encroaching on the land we use to grow food and there is less game to hunt each season.
You think it's easy for us! In Jamestown, there are also many mouths to feed, many people who are cold in winter and who work hard to survive here . . .
John . . . this isn't the whim of a spoiled child. You are destroying too much land, and too quickly.
Soon the Powhatans will not have enough to eat, and that will only reinforce the fear you cause in them and the hatred some of them feel towards you.
Listen . . .
I promise you that I will do my best to reassure the officers.
But I am no longer in a position of power here; from now on, I can't make decisions on my own.

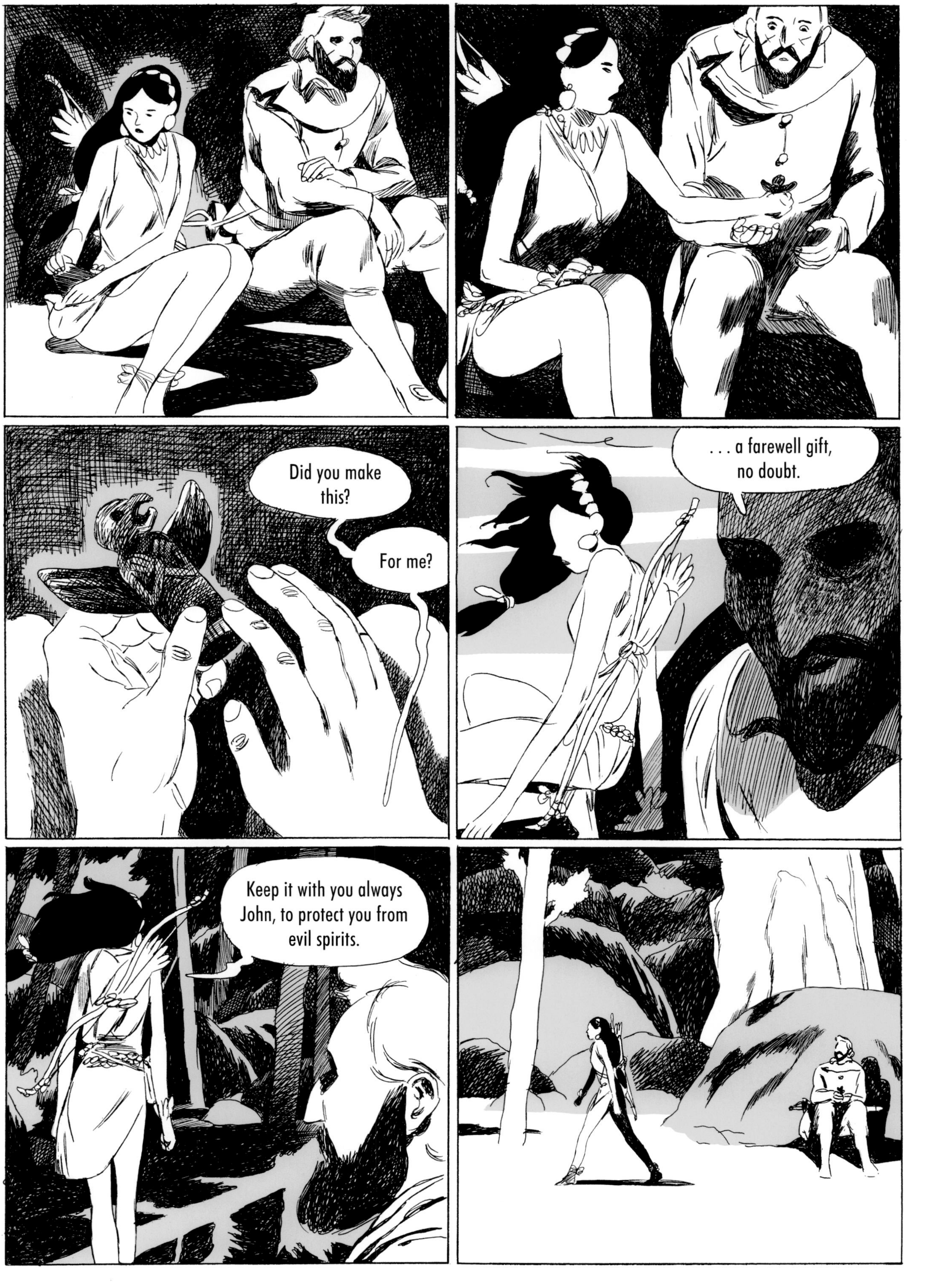
Did you make this?
For me?
. . . a farewell gift, no doubt.
Keep it with you always John, to protect you from evil spirits.

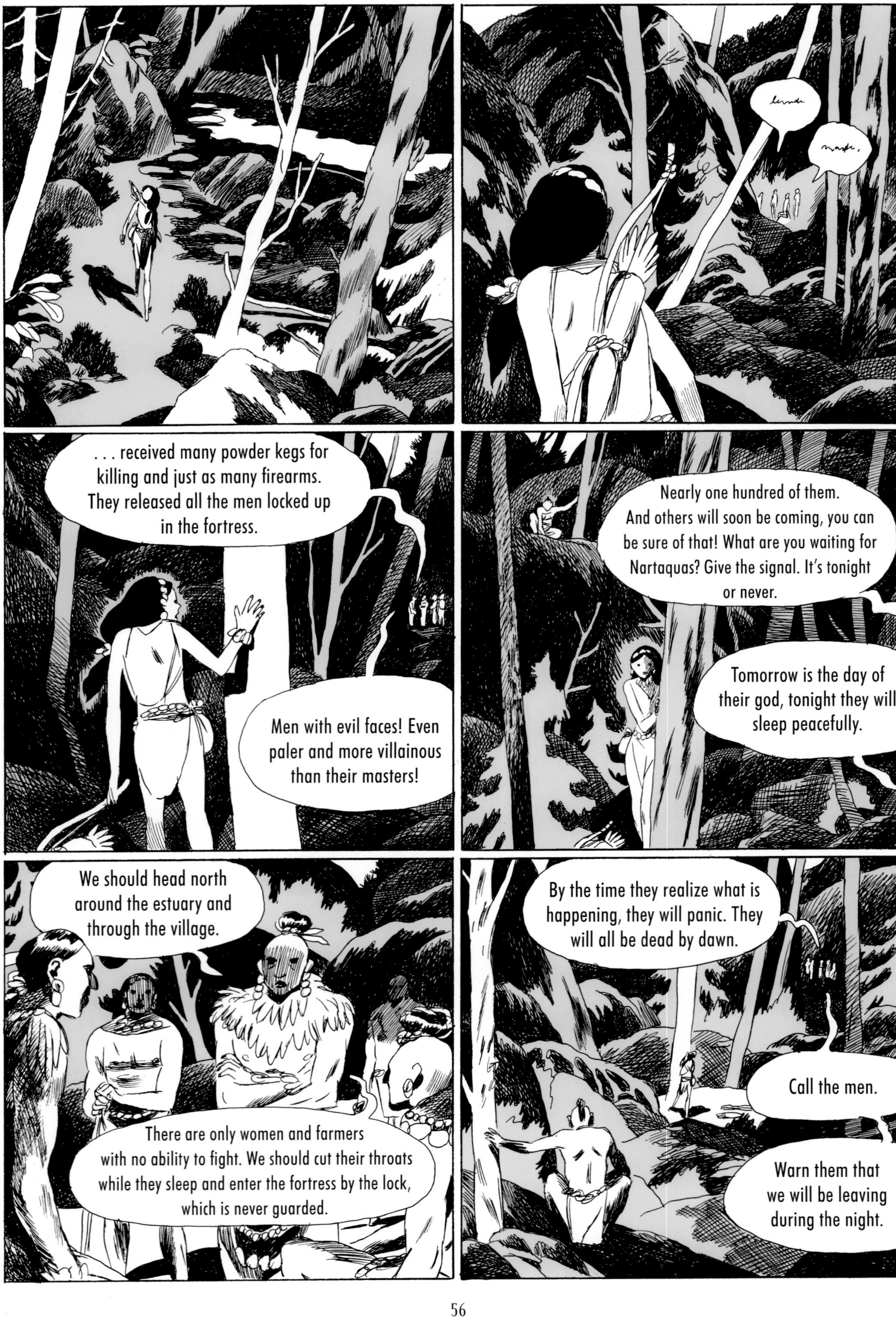
. . . received many powder kegs for killing and just as many firearms. They released all the men locked up in the fortress.
Men with evil faces! Even paler and more villainous than their masters!
Nearly one hundred of them. And others will soon be coming, you can be sure of that! What are you waiting for Nartaquas? Give the signal. It's tonight or never.
Tomorrow is the day of their god, tonight they will sleep peacefully.
We should head north around the estuary and through the village.
There are only women and farmers with no ability to fight. We should cut their throats while they sleep and enter the fortress by the lock, which is never guarded.
By the time they realize what is happening, they will panic. They will all be dead by dawn.
Call the men.
Warn them that we will be leaving during the night.

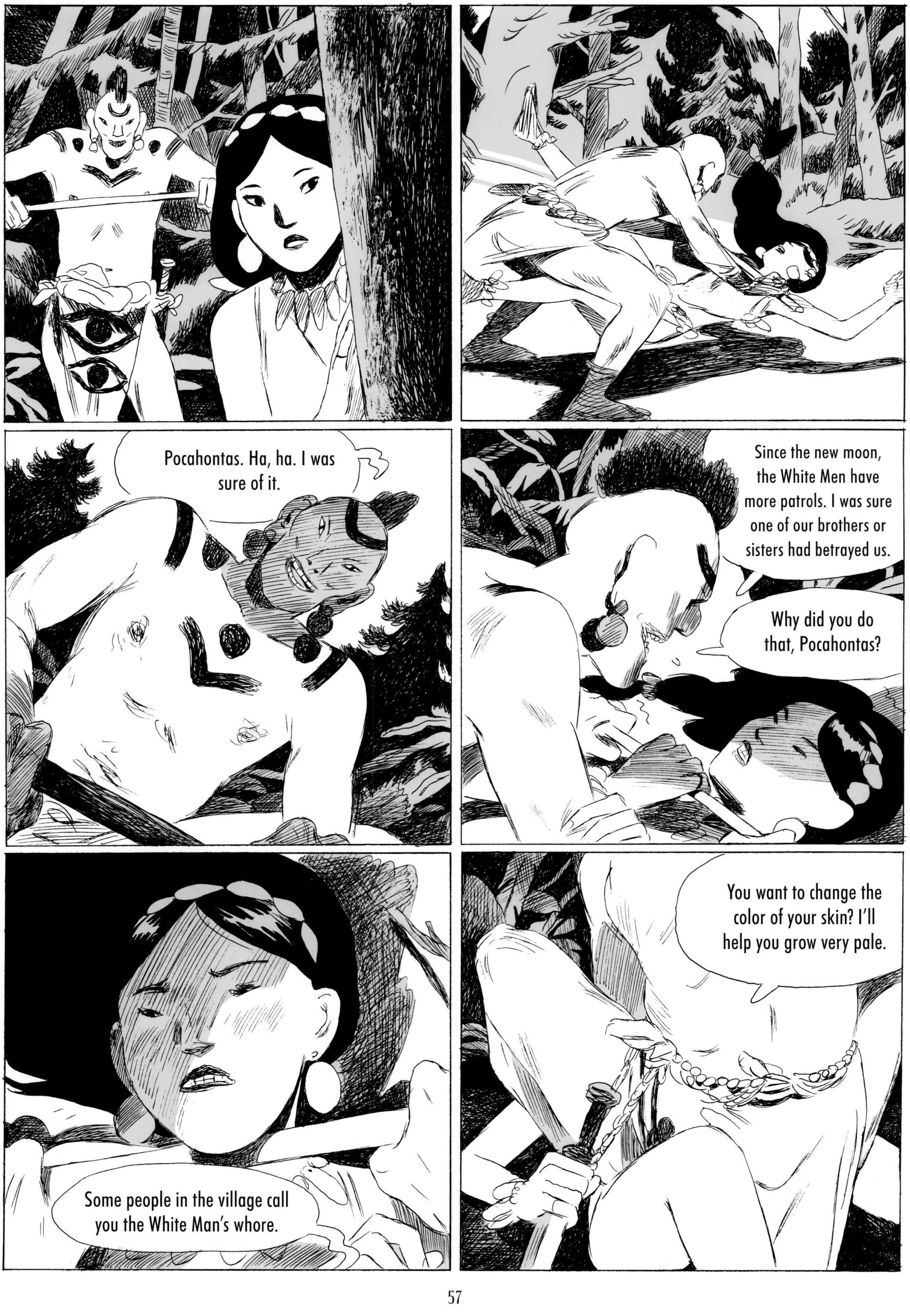

Pocahontas. Ha, ha. I was sure of it.
Since the new moon, the White Men have more patrols. I was sure one of our brothers or sisters had betrayed us.
Why did you do that, Pocahontas?
Some people in the village call you the White Man's whore.
You want to change the color of your skin? I'll help you grow very pale.

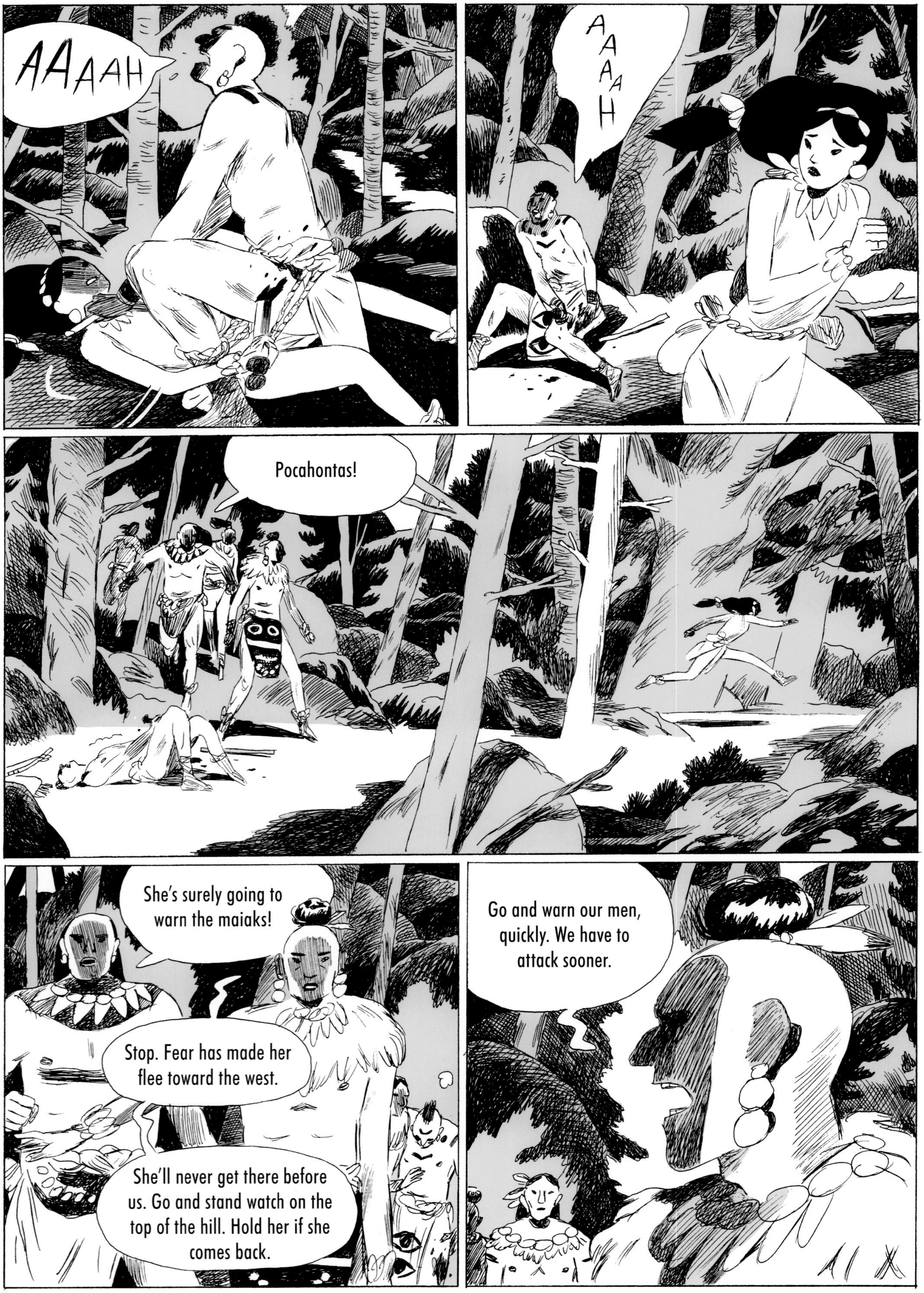
AAAAH
AAAAH
Pocahontas!
She's surely going to warn the maiaks!
Stop. Fear has made her flee toward the west.
She'll never get there before us. Go and stand watch on the top of the hill. Hold her if she comes back.
Go and warn our men, quickly. We have to attack sooner.

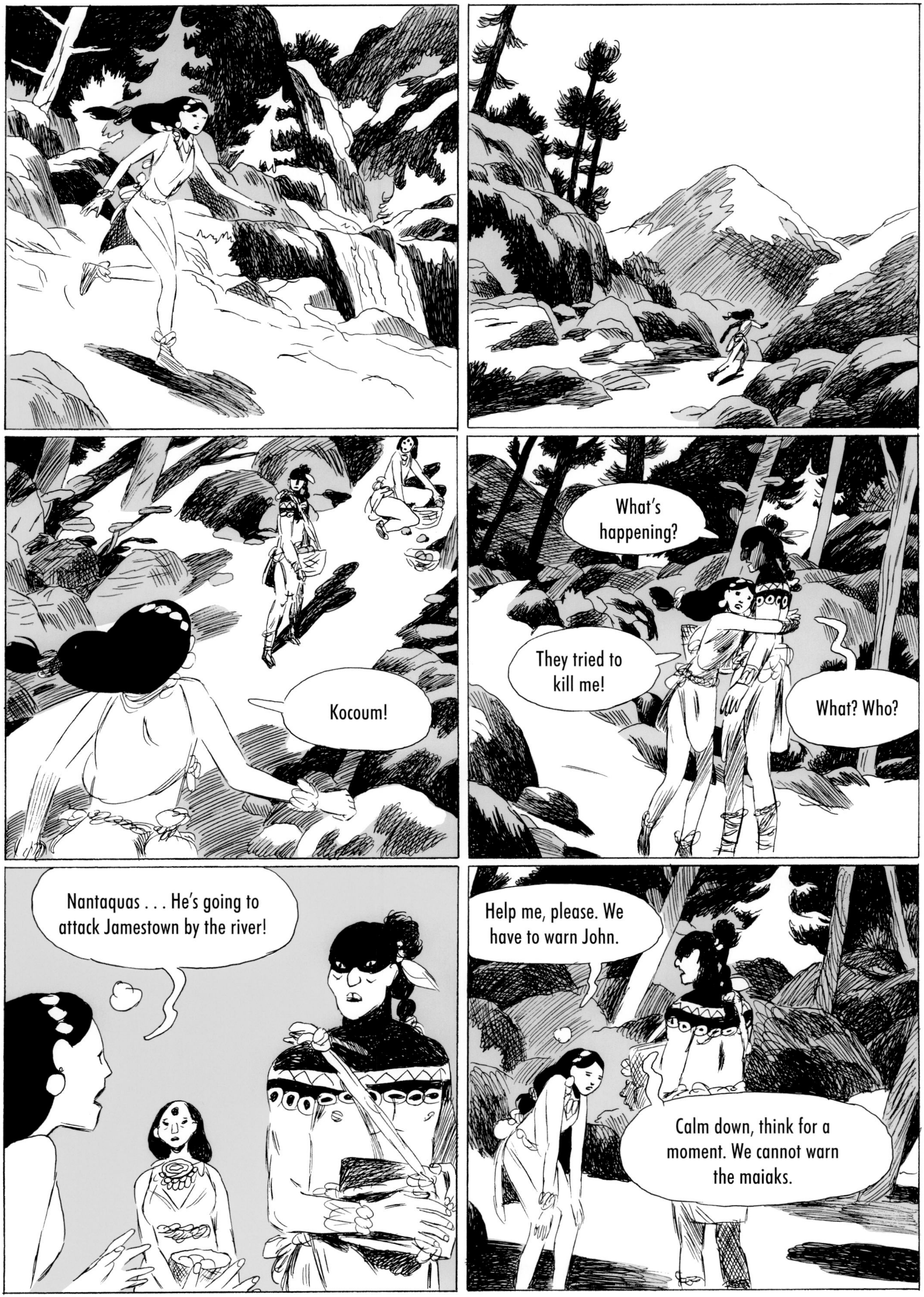

Kocoum!
What's happening?
They tried to kill me!
What? Who?
Nantaquas . . . He's going to attack Jamestown by the river!
Help me, please. We have to warn John.
Calm down, think for a moment. We cannot warn the maiaks.

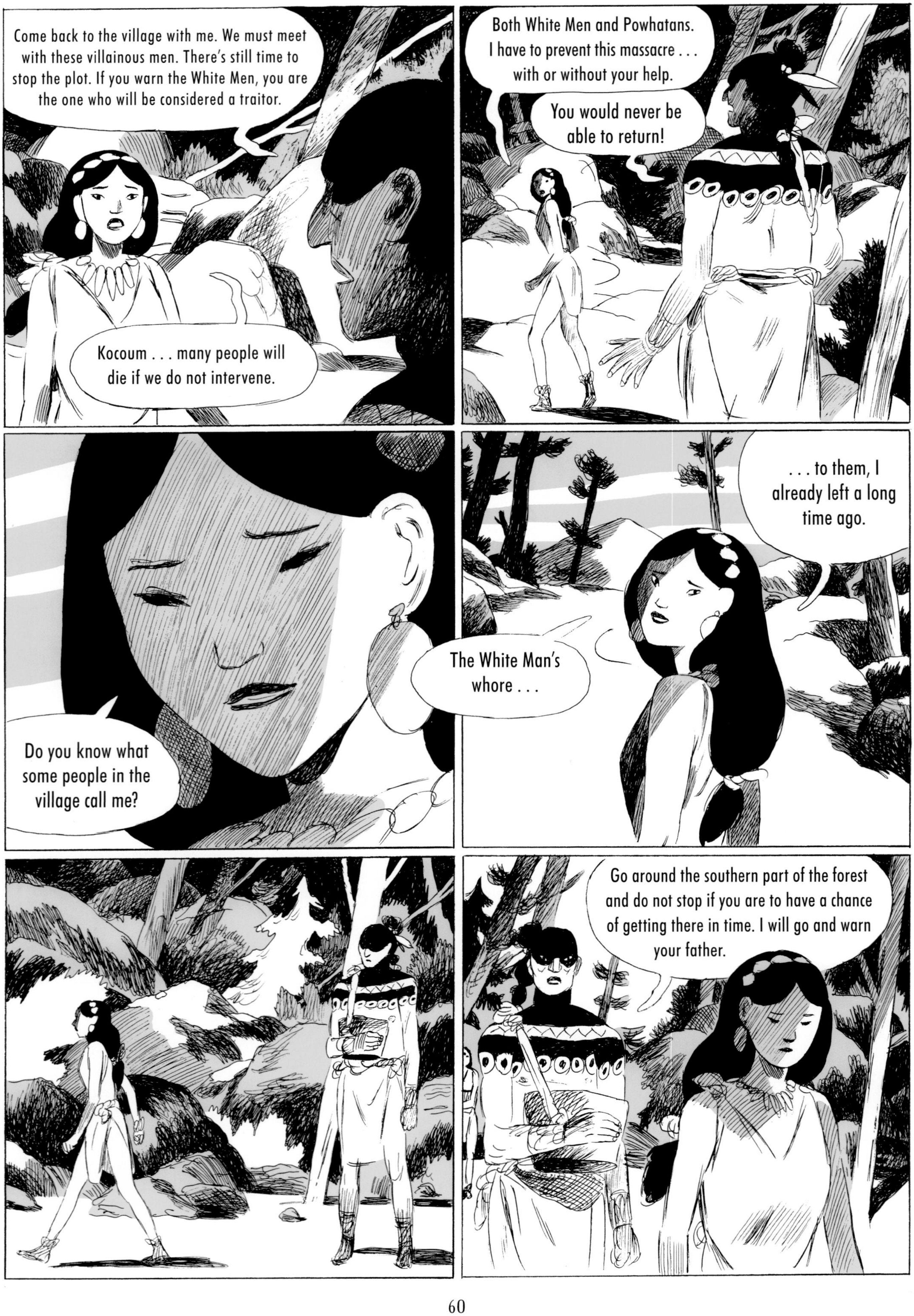
Come back to the village with me. We must meet with these villainous men. There's still time to stop the plot. If you warn the White Men, you are the one who will be considered a traitor.
Kocoum . . . many people will die if we do not intervene.
Both White Men and Powhatans. I have to prevent this massacre . . . with or without your help.
You would never be able to return!
Do you know what some people in the village call me?
The White Man's whore . . .
. . . to them, I already left a long time ago.
Go around the southern part of the forest and do not stop if you are to have a chance of getting there in time. I will go and warn your father.

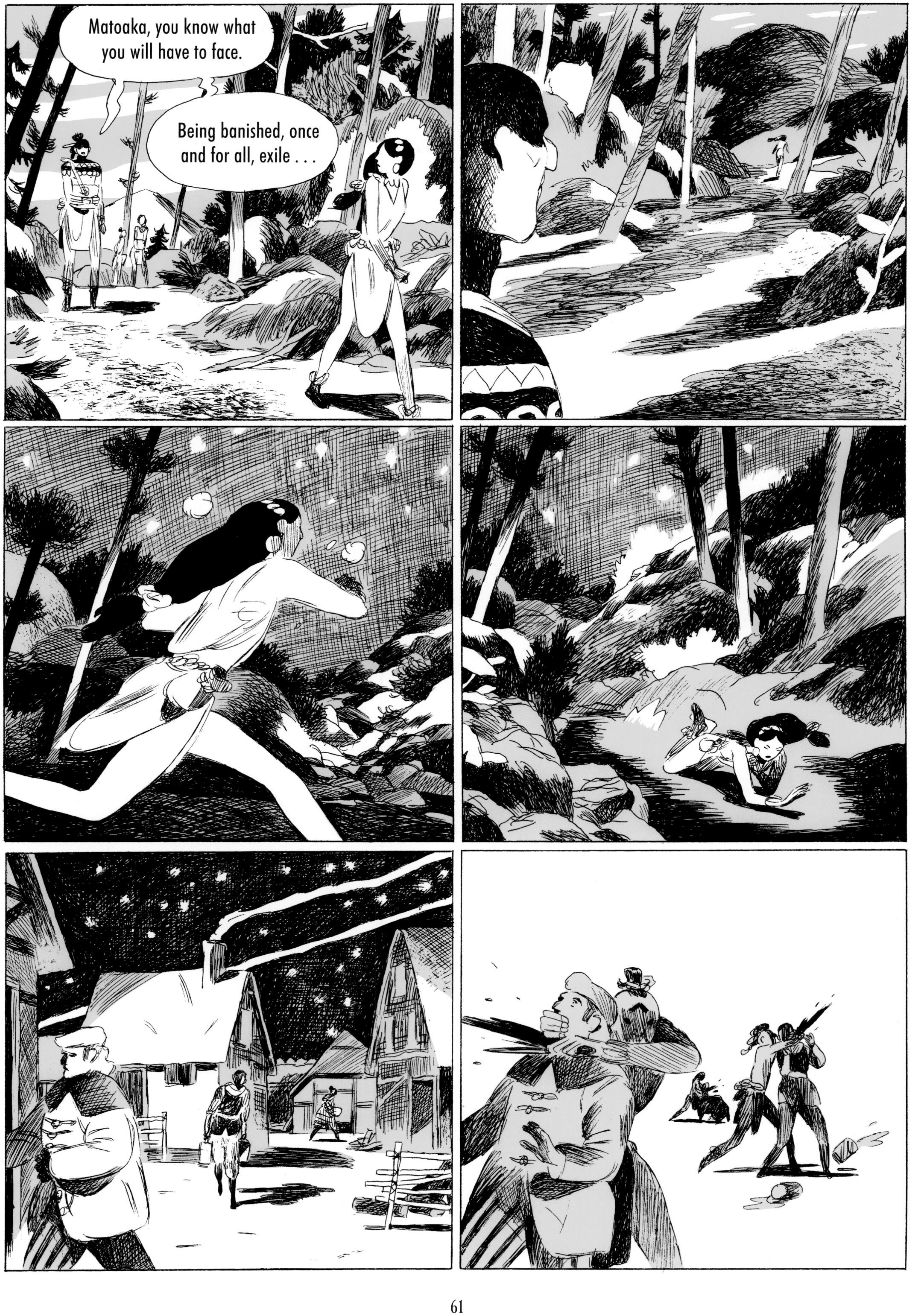
Matoaka, you know what you will have to face.
Being banished, once and for all, exile . . .

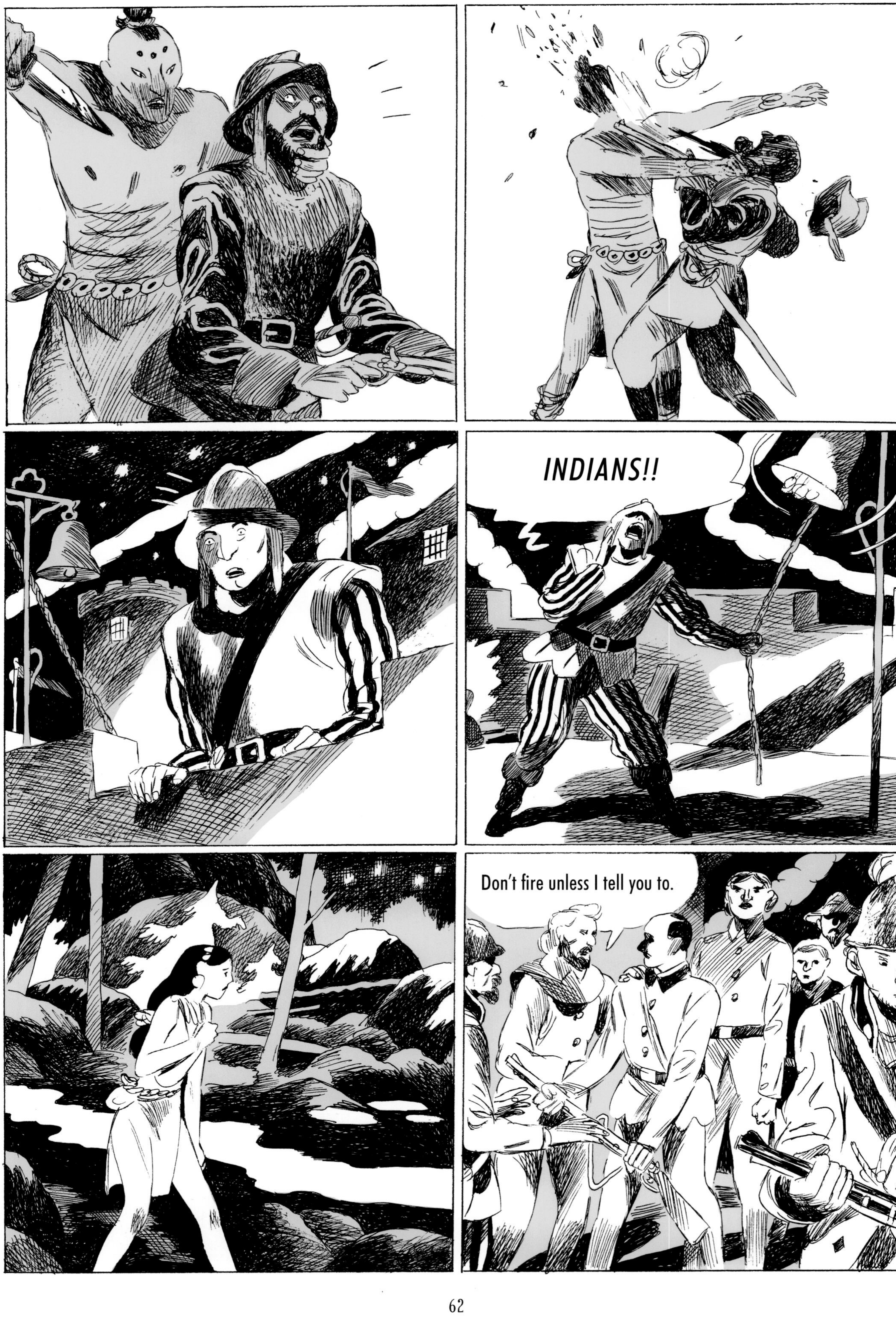
INDIANS!!
Don't fire unless I tell you to.

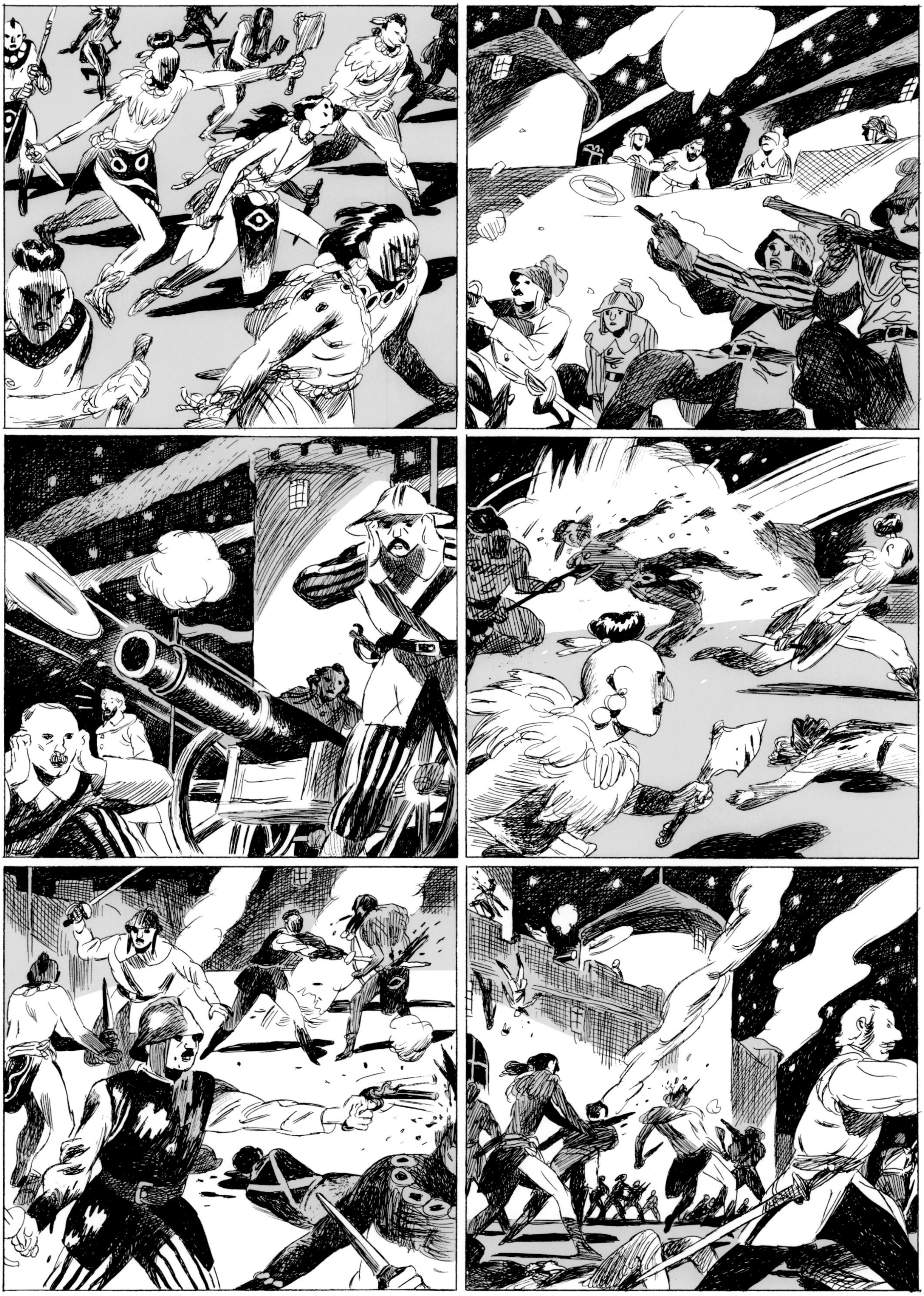

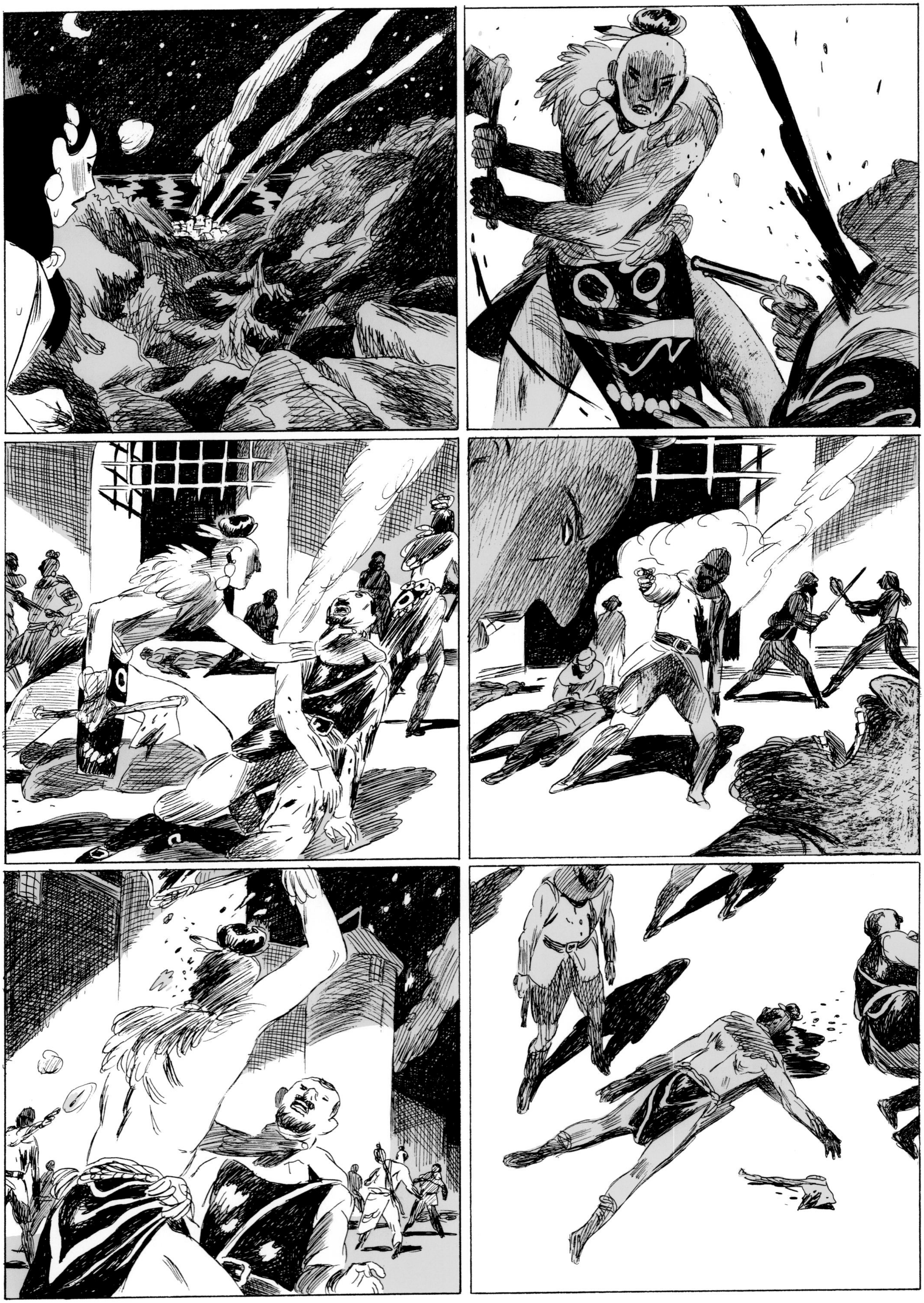

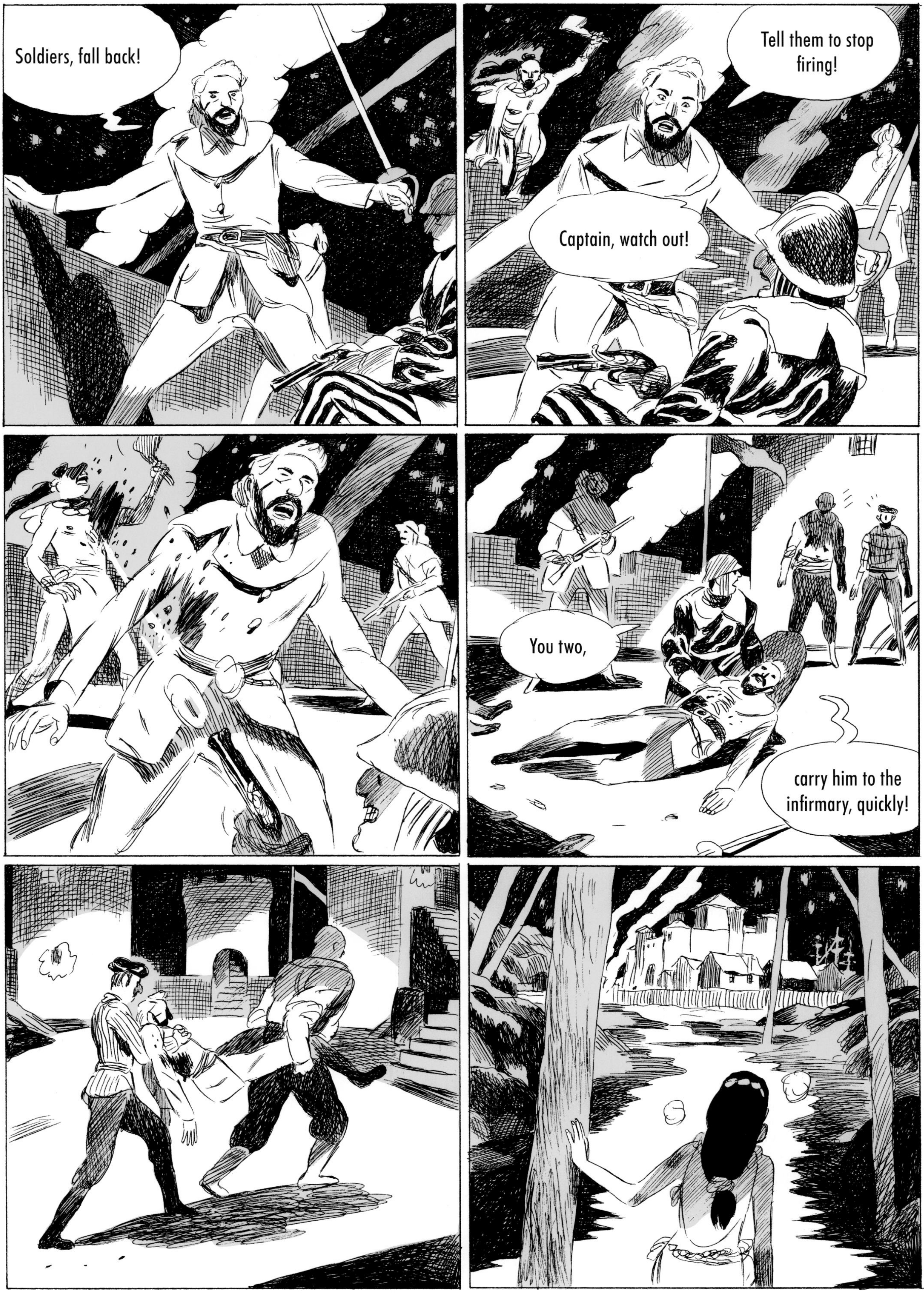
Soldiers, fall back!
Tell them to stop firing!
Captain, watch out!
You two,
carry him to the infirmary, quickly!

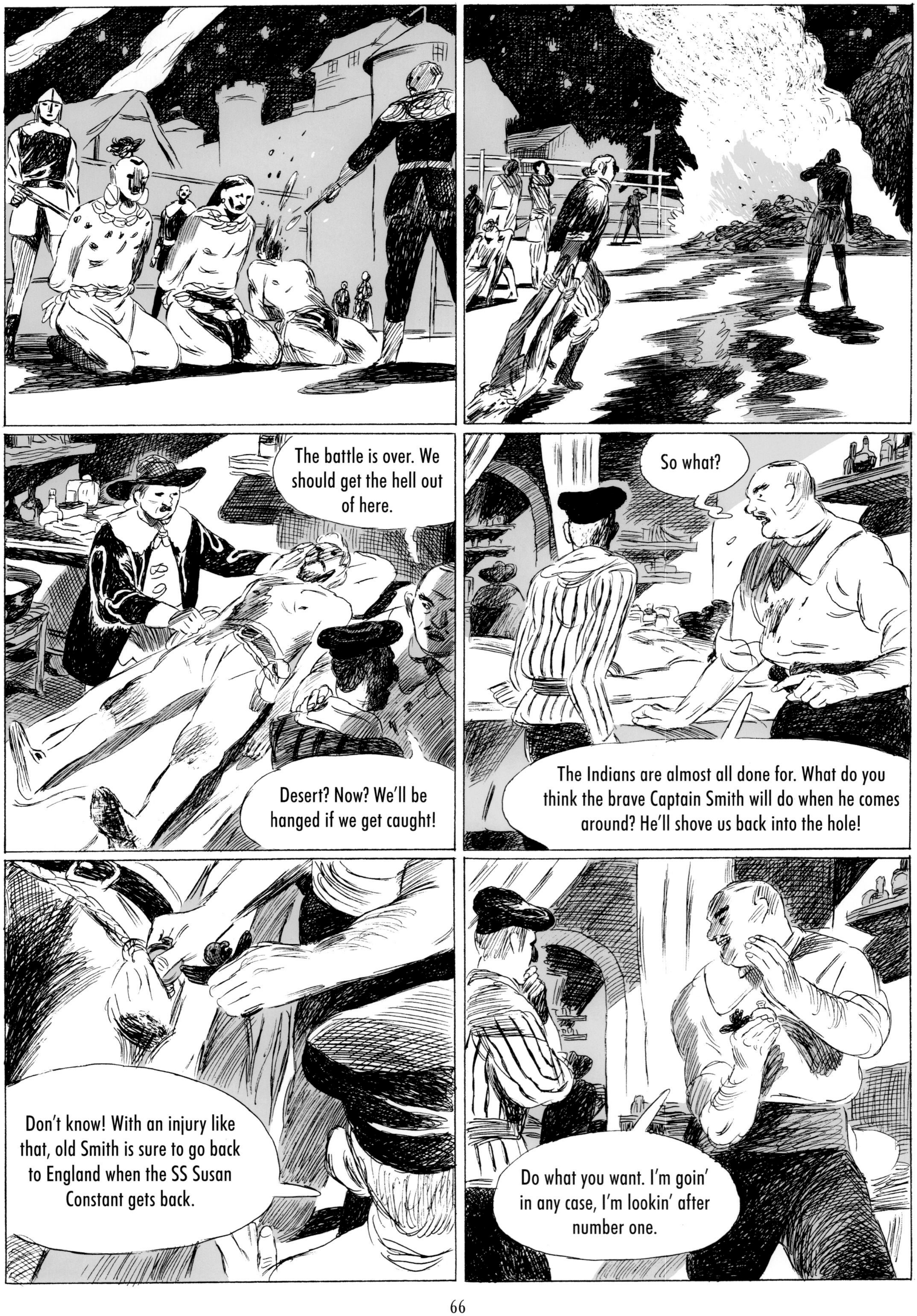
The battle is over. We should get the hell out of here.
Desert? Now? We'll be hanged if we get caught!
So what?
The Indians are almost all done for. What do you think the brave Captain Smith will do when he comes around? He'll shove us back into the hole!
Don't know! With an injury like that, old Smith is sure to go back to England when the SS Susan Constant gets back.
Do what you want. I'm goin' in any case, I'm lookin' after number one.

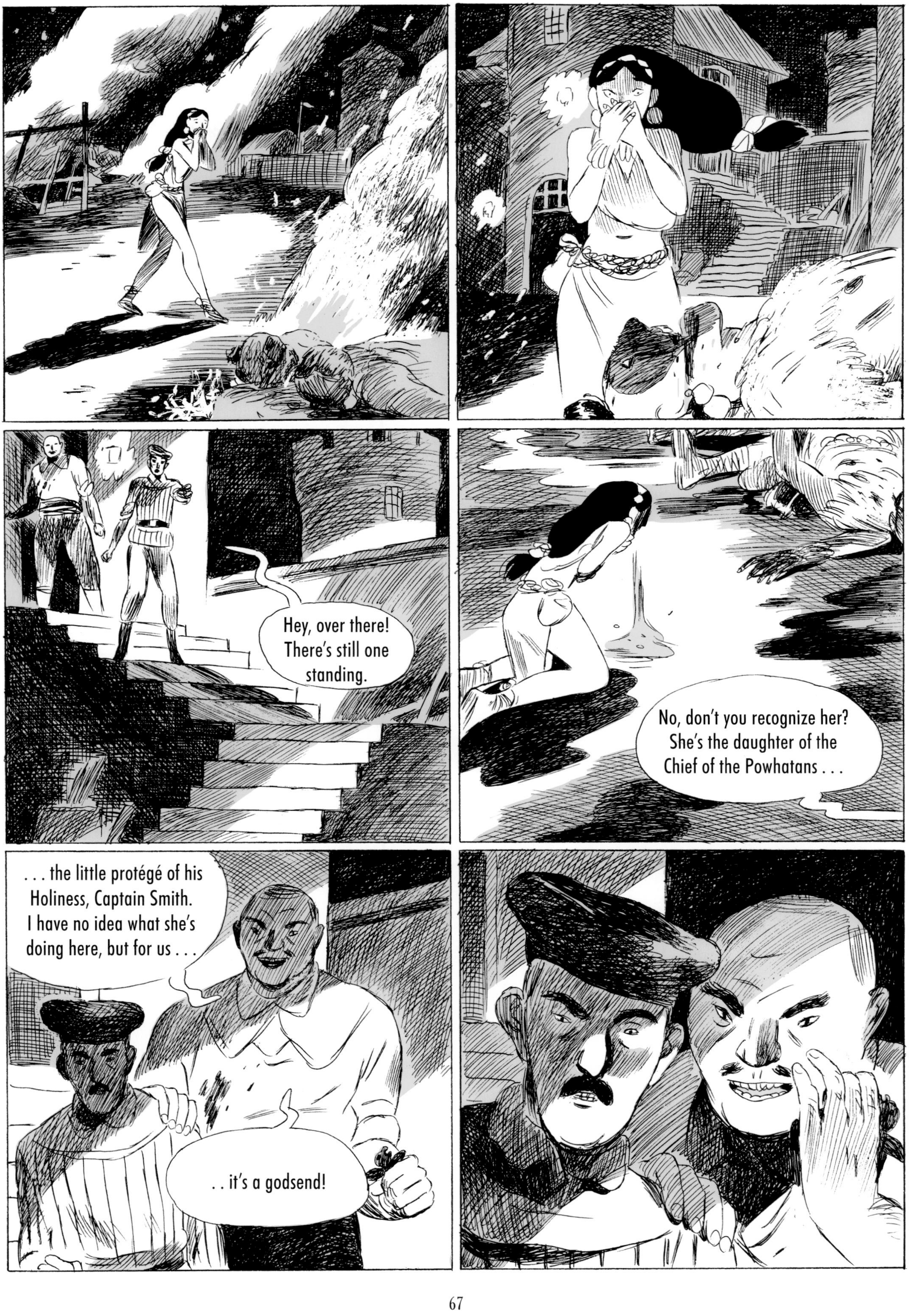
Hey, over there! There's still one standing.
No, don't you recognize her? She's the daughter of the Chief of the Powhatans . . .
. . . the little protégé of his Holiness, Captain Smith. I have no idea what she's doing here, but for us . . .
. . it's a godsend!

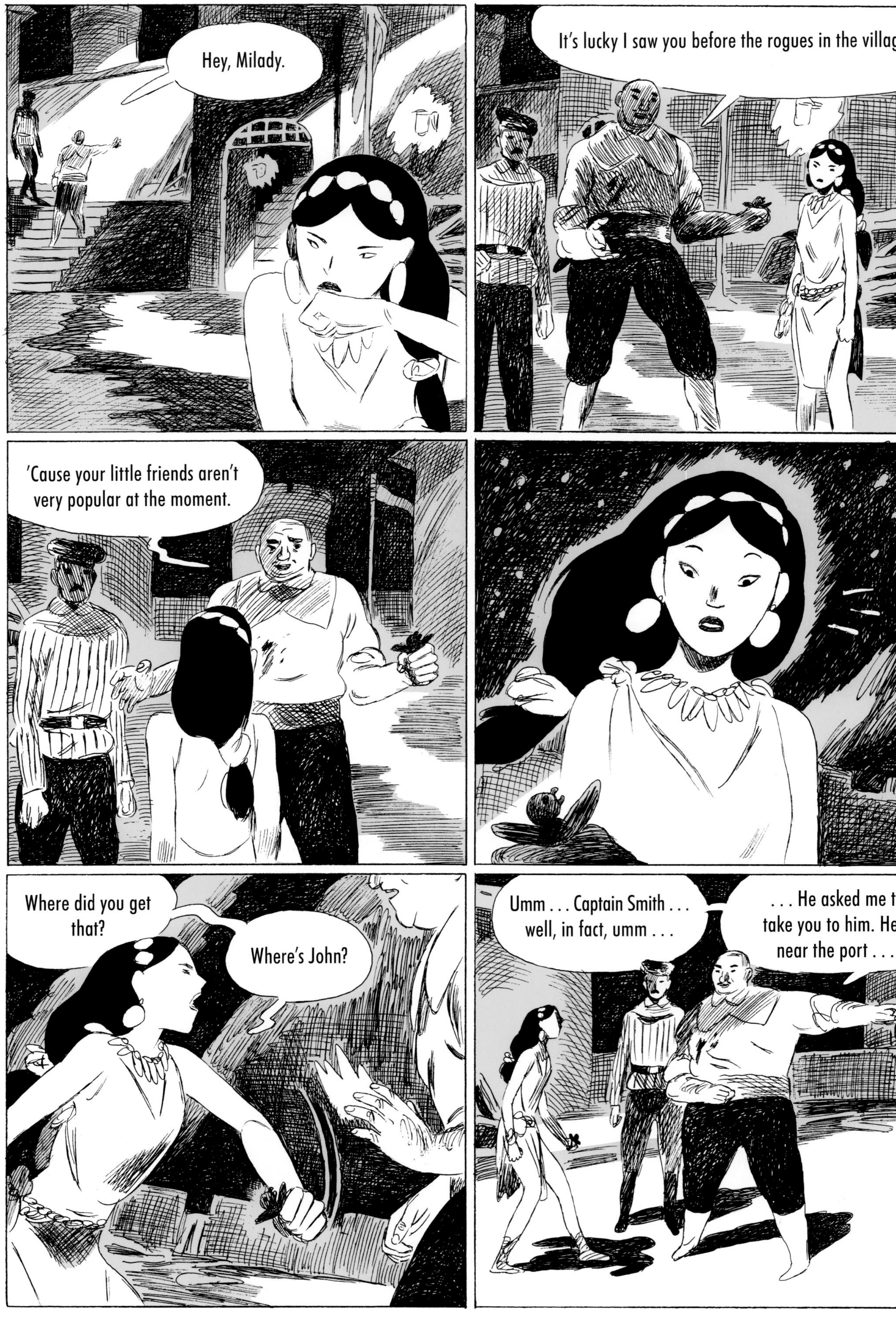

Hey, Milady.
It's lucky I saw you before the rogues in the village.
'Cause your little friends aren't very popular at the moment.
Where did you get that?
Where's John?
Umm . . . Captain Smith . . . well, in fact, umm . . .
. . . He asked me to take you to him. He's near the port . . .

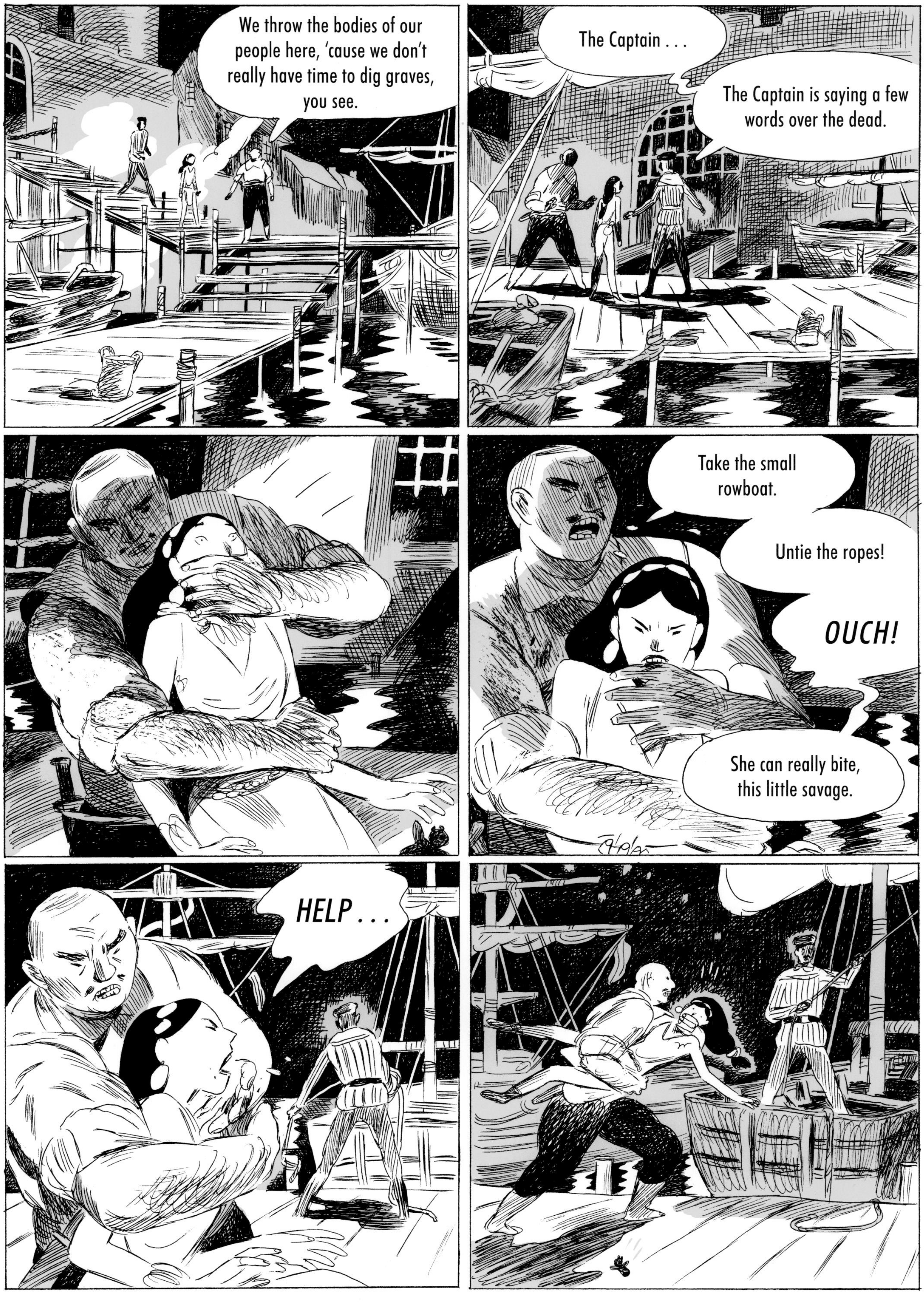
We throw the bodies of our people here, 'cause we don't really have time to dig graves, you see.
The Captain . . .
The Captain is saying a few words over the dead.
Take the small rowboat.
Untie the ropes!
OUCH!
She can really bite, this little savage.
HELP . . .

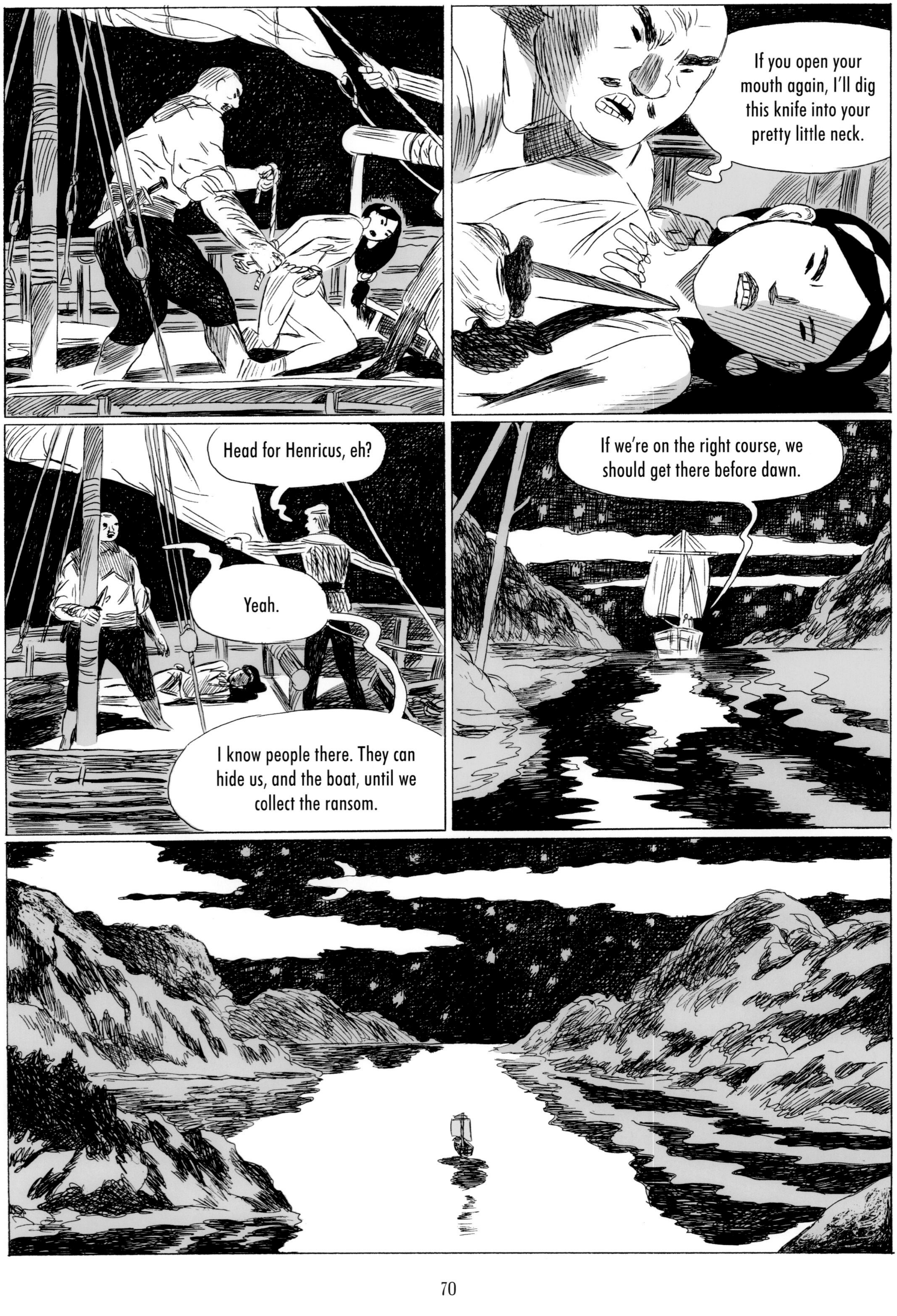

If you open your mouth again, I'll dig this knife into your pretty little neck.
Head for Henricus, eh?
Yeah.
I know people there. They can hide us, and the boat, until we collect the ransom.
If we're on the right course, we should get there before dawn.

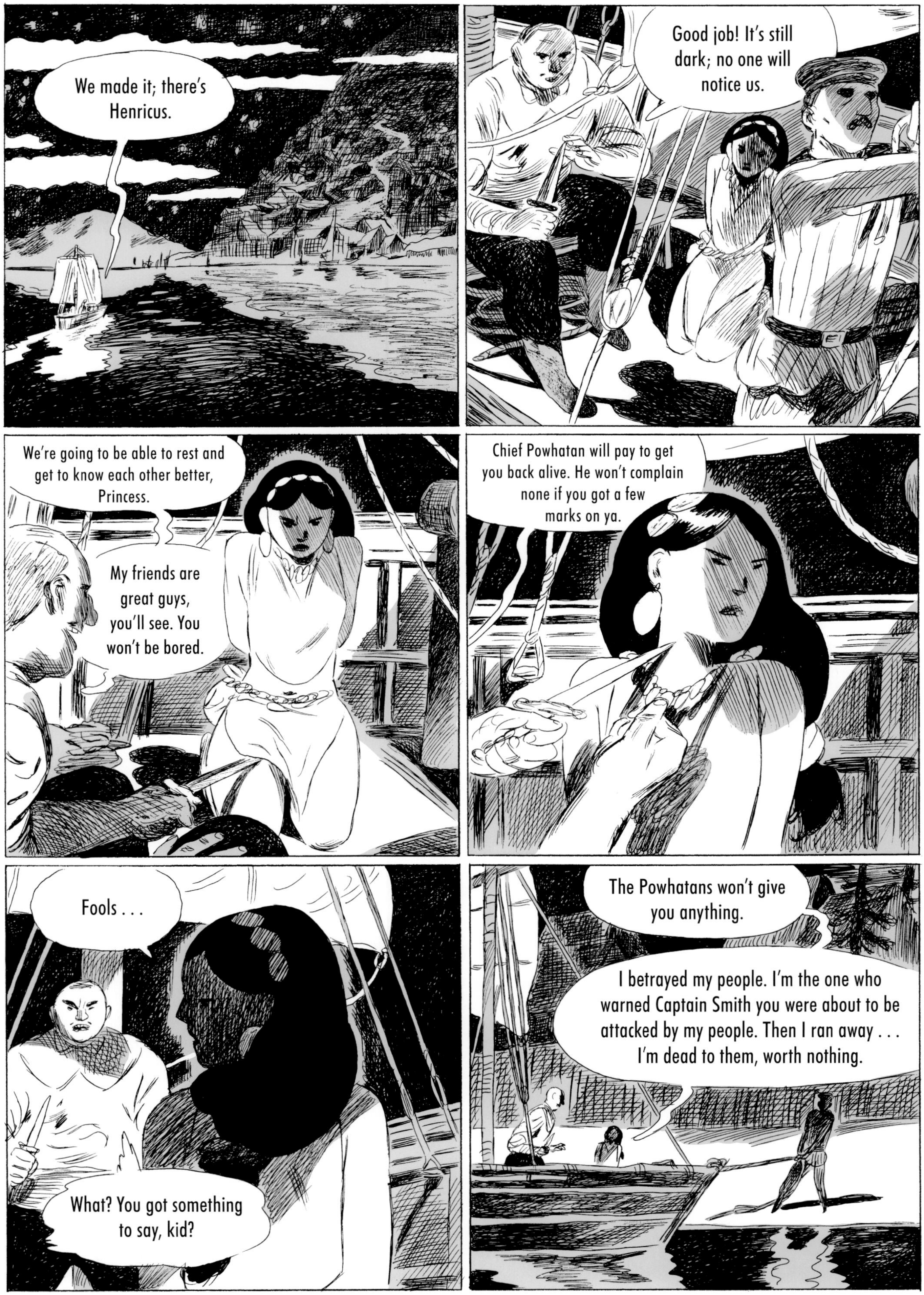
We made it; there's Henricus.
Good job! It's still dark; no one will notice us.
We're going to be able to rest and get to know each other better, Princess.
My friends are great guys, you'll see. You won't be bored.
Chief Powhatan will pay to get you back alive. He won't complain none if you got a few marks on ya.
Fools . . .
What? You got something to say, kid?
The Powhatans won't give you anything.
I betrayed my people. I'm the one who warned Captain Smith you were about to be attacked by my people. Then I ran away . . . I'm dead to them, worth nothing.

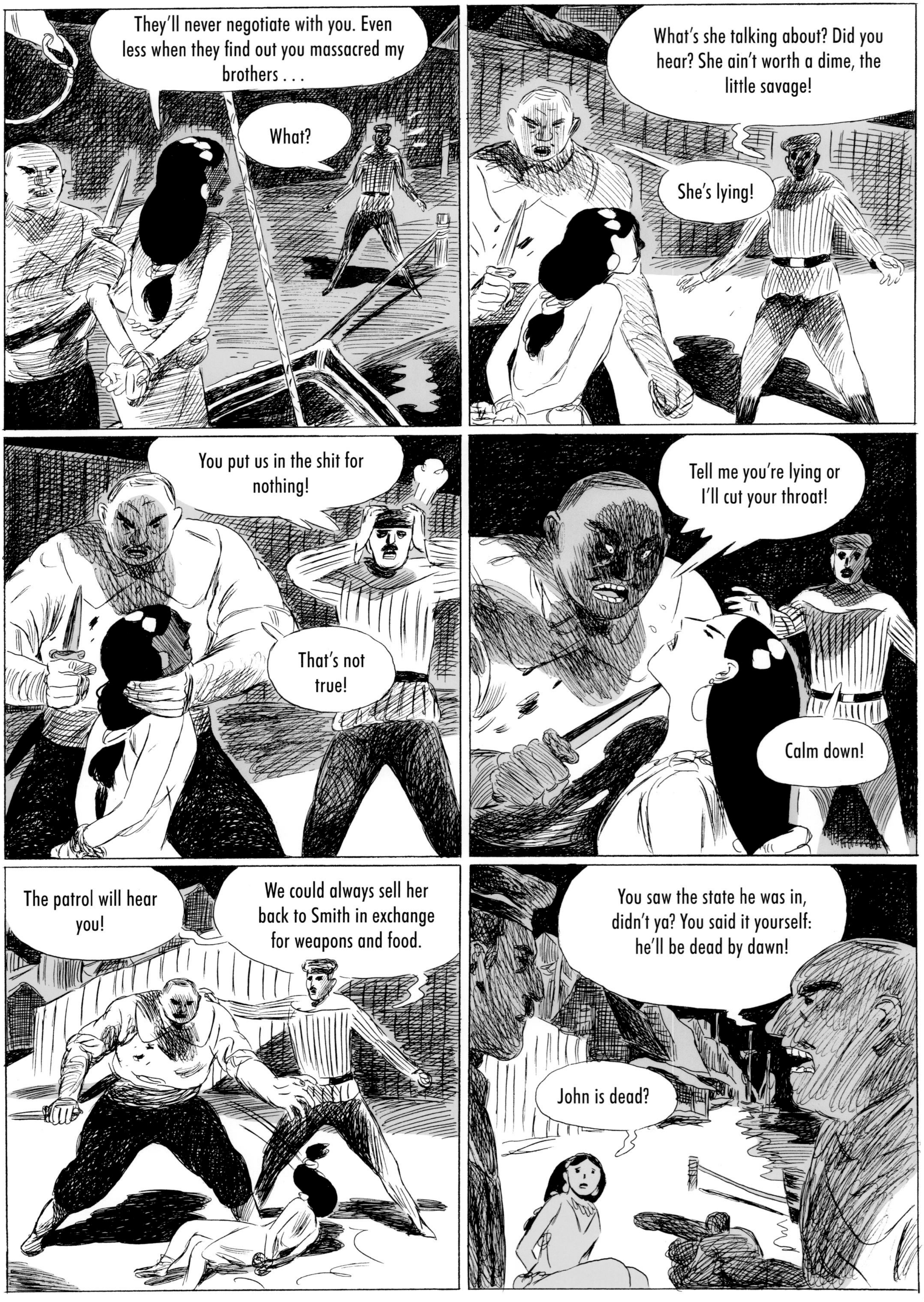
They'll never negotiate with you. Even less when they find out you massacred my brothers . . .
What?
What's she talking about? Did you hear? She ain't worth a dime, the little savage!
She's lying!
You put us in the shit for nothing!
That's not true!
Tell me you're lying or I'll cut your throat!
Calm down!
The patrol will hear you!
We could always sell her back to Smith in exchange for weapons and food.
You saw the state he was in, didn't ya? You said it yourself: he'll be dead by dawn!
John is dead?

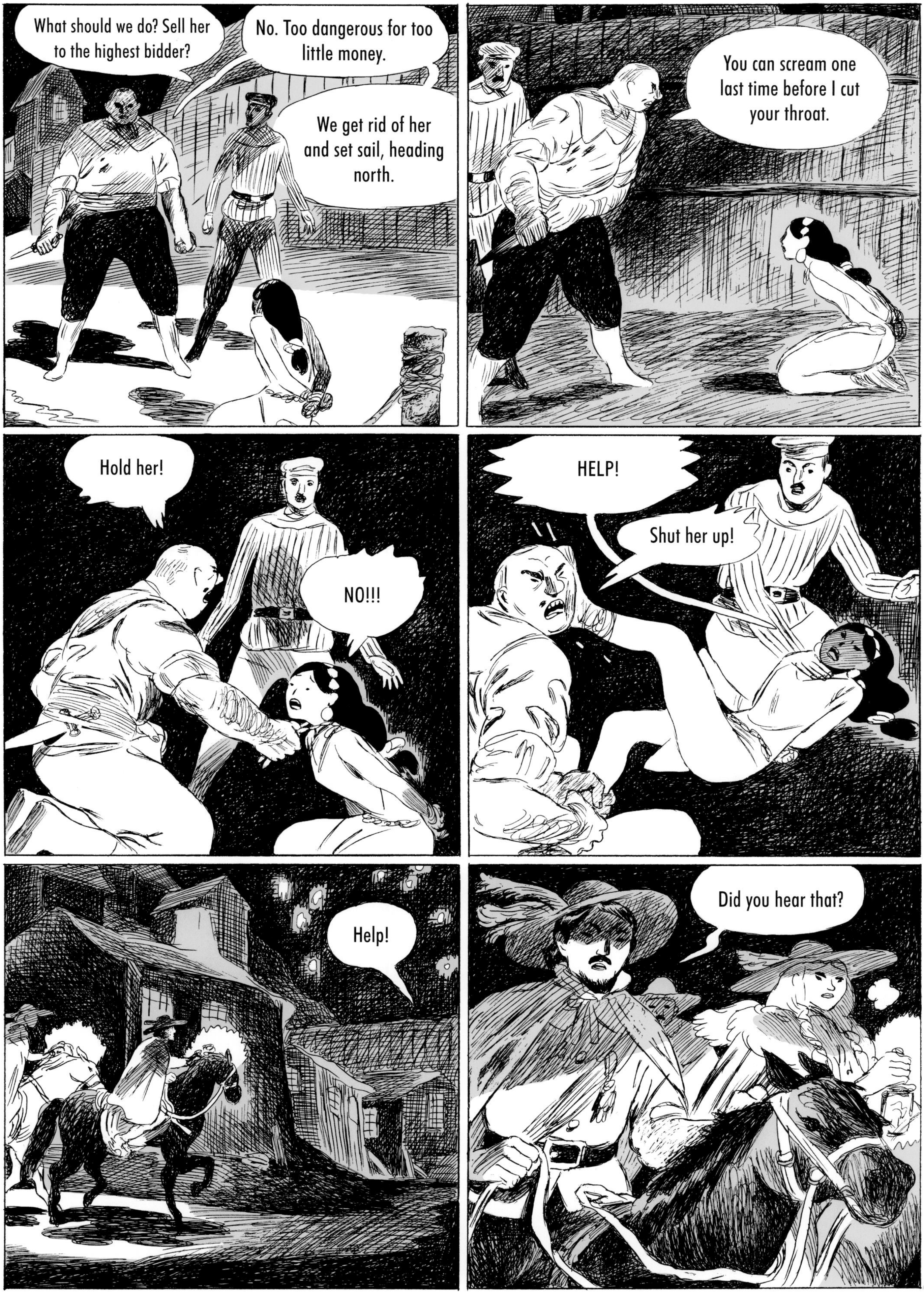
What should we do? Sell her to the highest bidder?
No. Too dangerous for too little money.
We get rid of her and set sail, heading north.
You can scream one last time before I cut your throat.
Hold her!
NO!!!
HELP!
Shut her up!
Help!
Did you hear that?

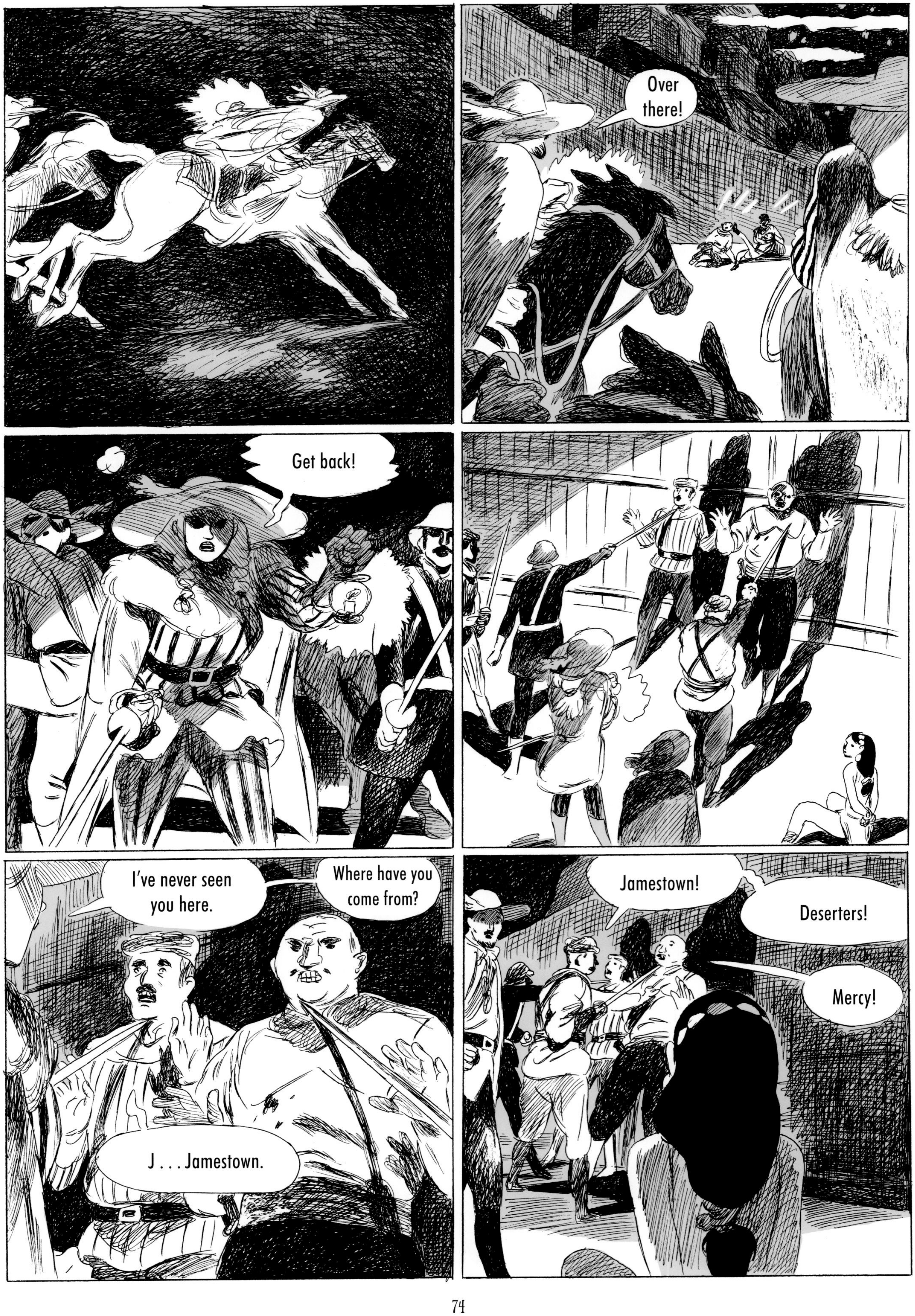
Over there!
Get back!
I've never seen you here.
Where have you come from?
J . . . Jamestown.
Jamestown!
Deserters!
Mercy!

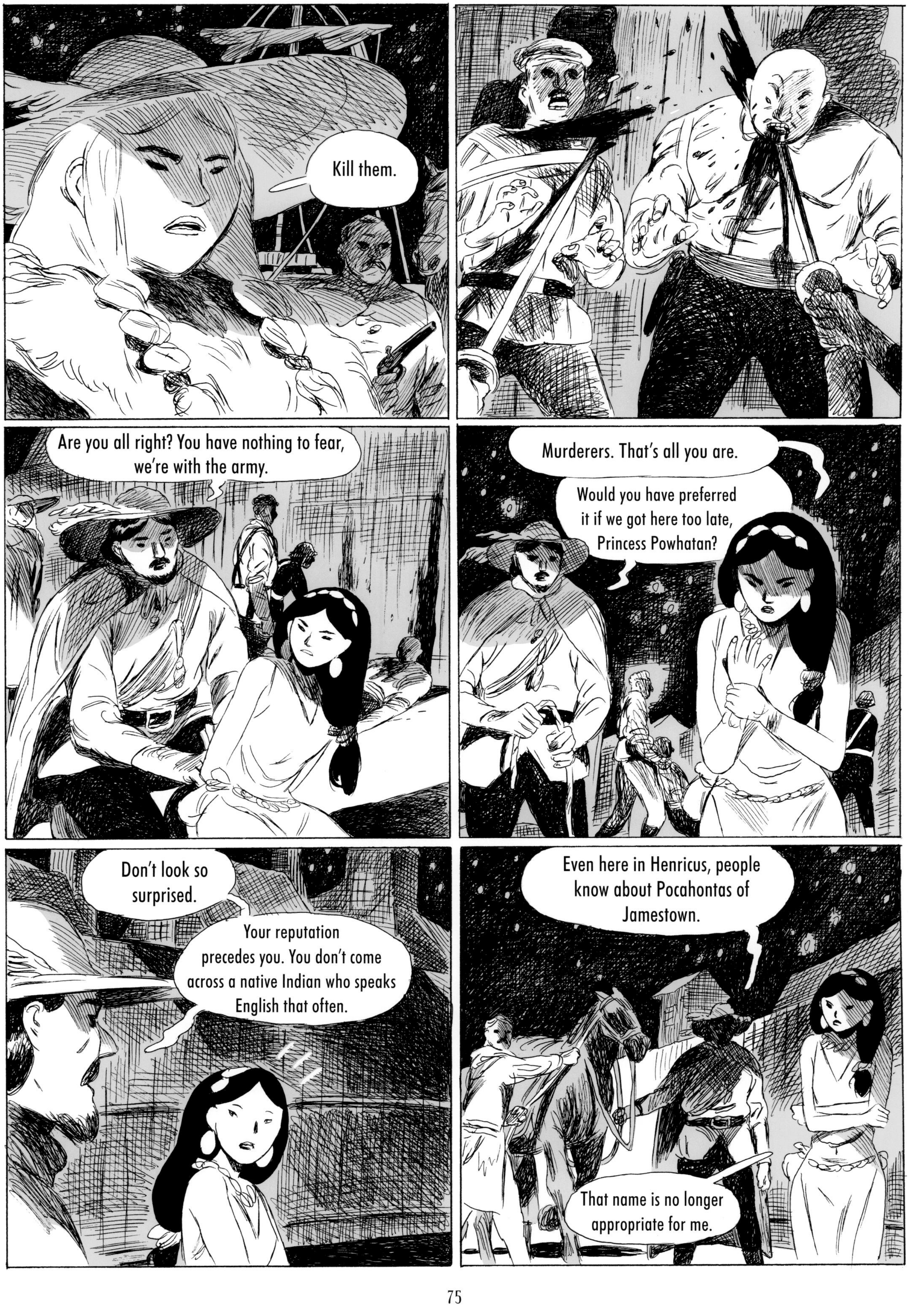
Kill them.
Are you all right? You have nothing to fear, we're with the army.
Murderers. That's all you are.
Would you have preferred it if we got here too late, Princess Powhatan?
Don't look so surprised.
Your reputation precedes you. You don't come across a native Indian who speaks English that often.
Even here in Henricus, people know about Pocahontas of Jamestown.
That name is no longer appropriate for me.

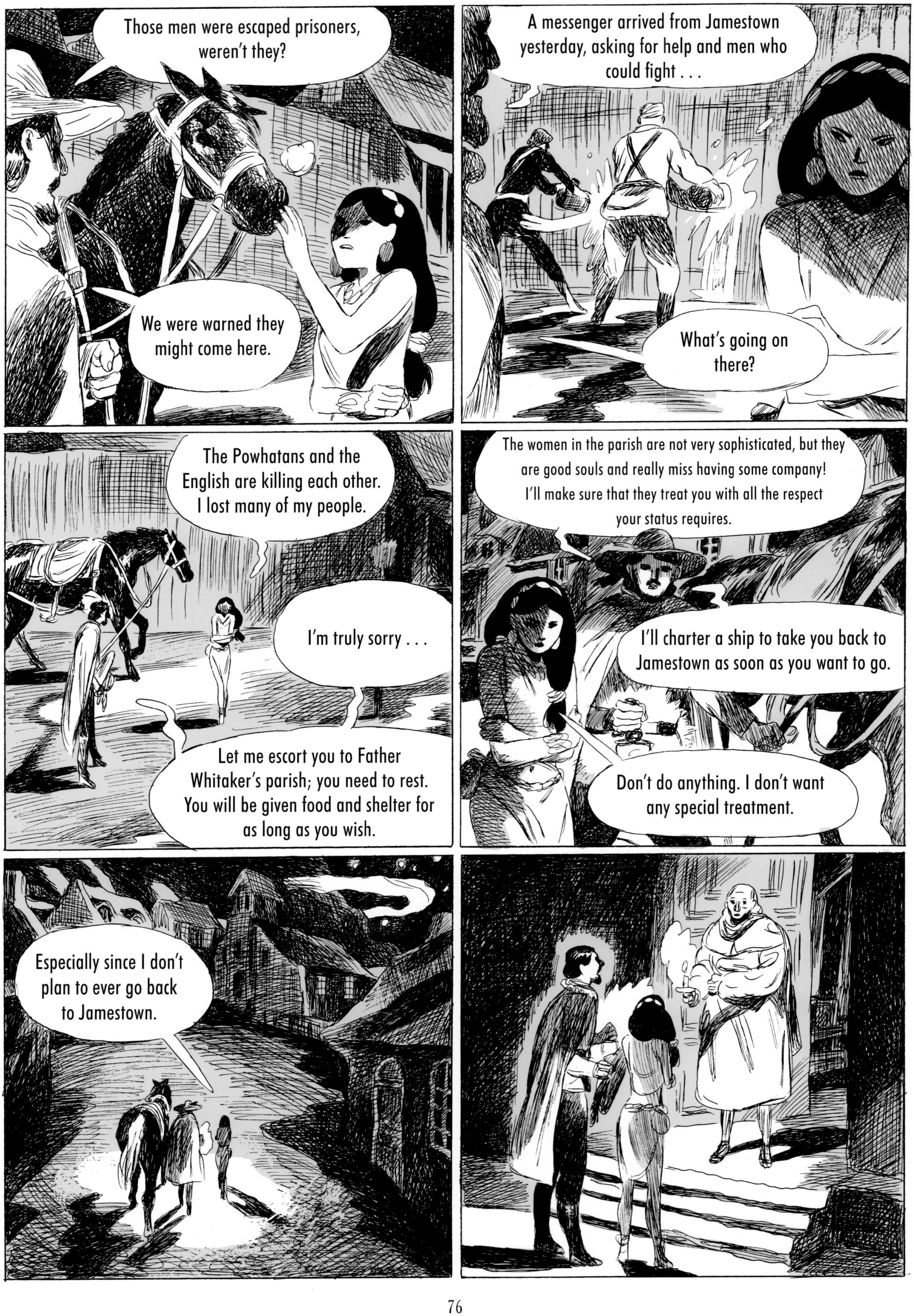
Those men were escaped prisoners, weren't they?
We were warned they might come here.
A messenger arrived from Jamestown yesterday, asking for help and men who could fight . . .
What's going on there?
The Powhatans and the English are killing each other. I lost many of my people.
I'm truly sorry . . .
Let me escort you to Father Whitaker's parish; you need to rest. You will be given food and shelter for as long as you wish.
The women in the parish are not very sophisticated, but they are good souls and really miss having some company! I'll make sure that they treat you with all the respect your status requires.
I'll charter a ship to take you back to Jamestown as soon as you want to go.
Don't do anything. I don't want any special treatment.
Especially since I don't plan to ever go back to Jamestown.

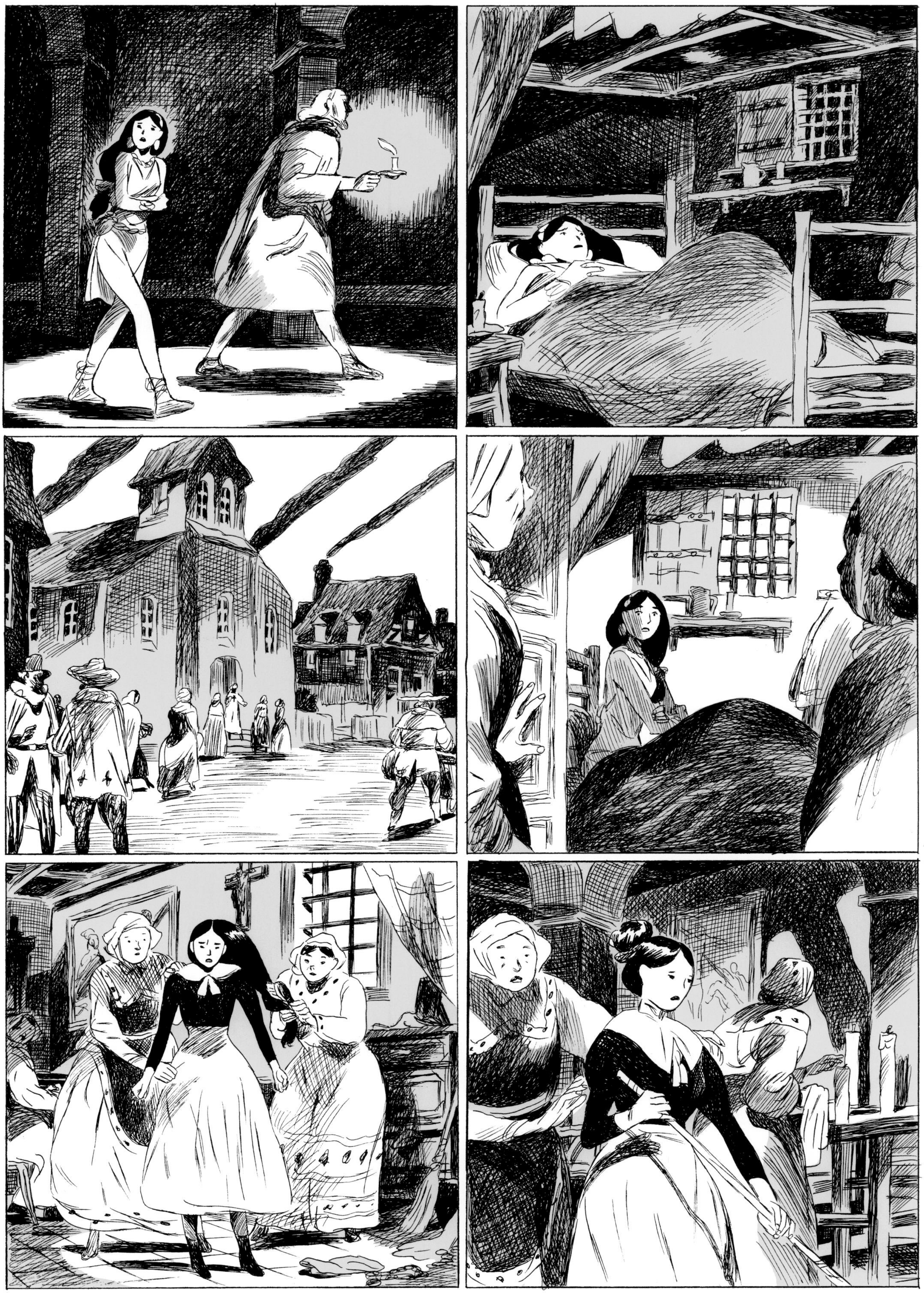

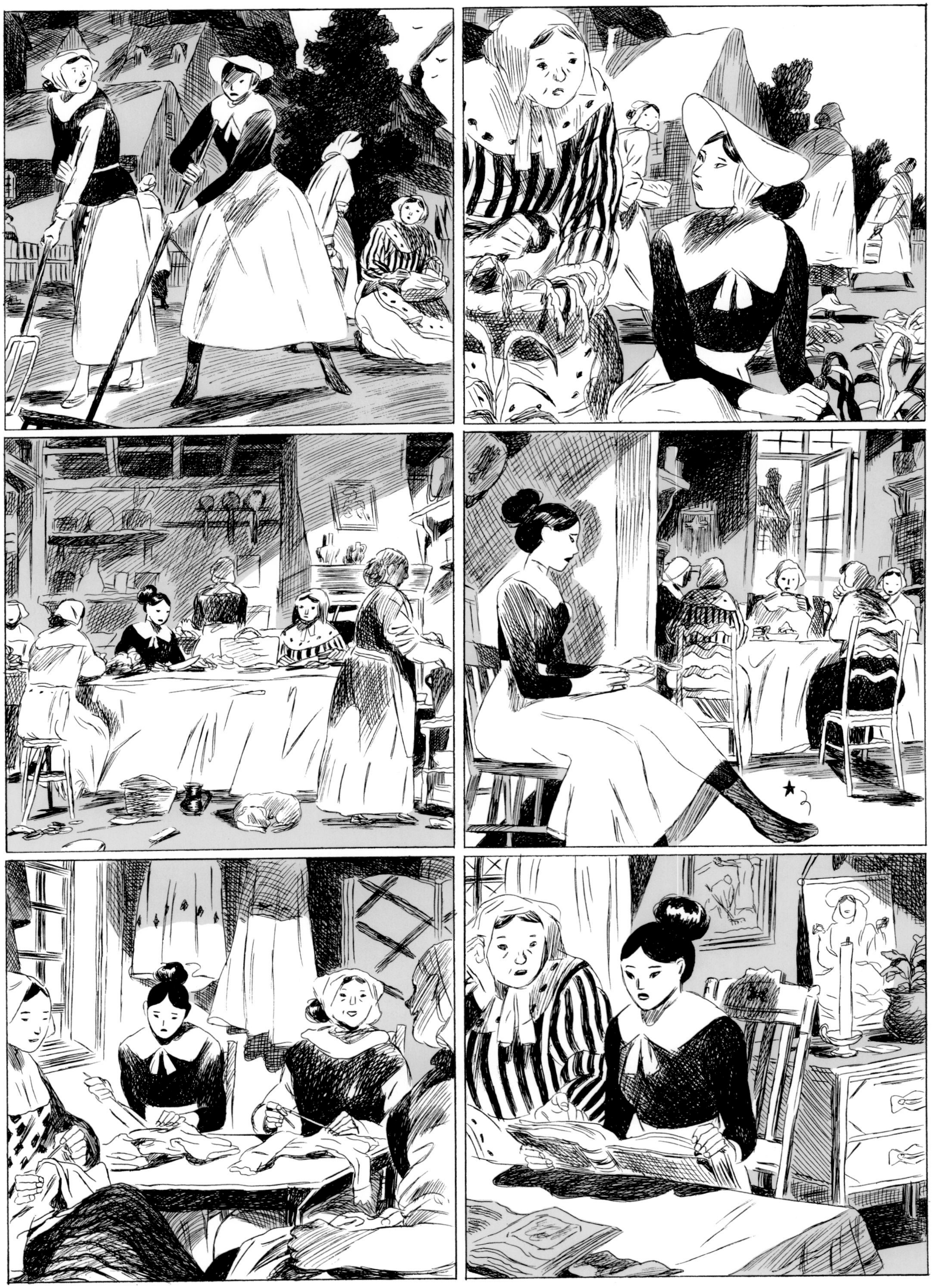

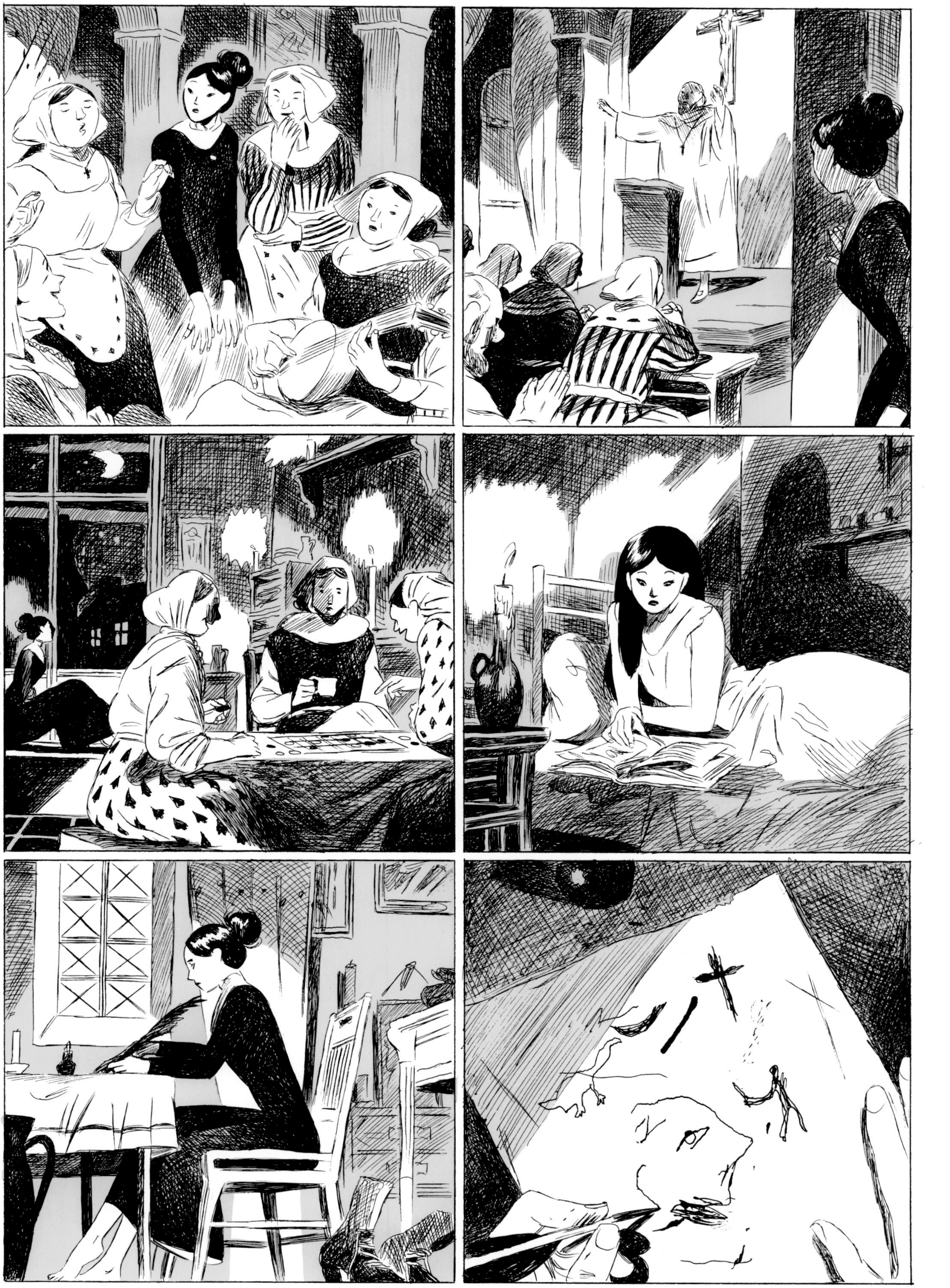

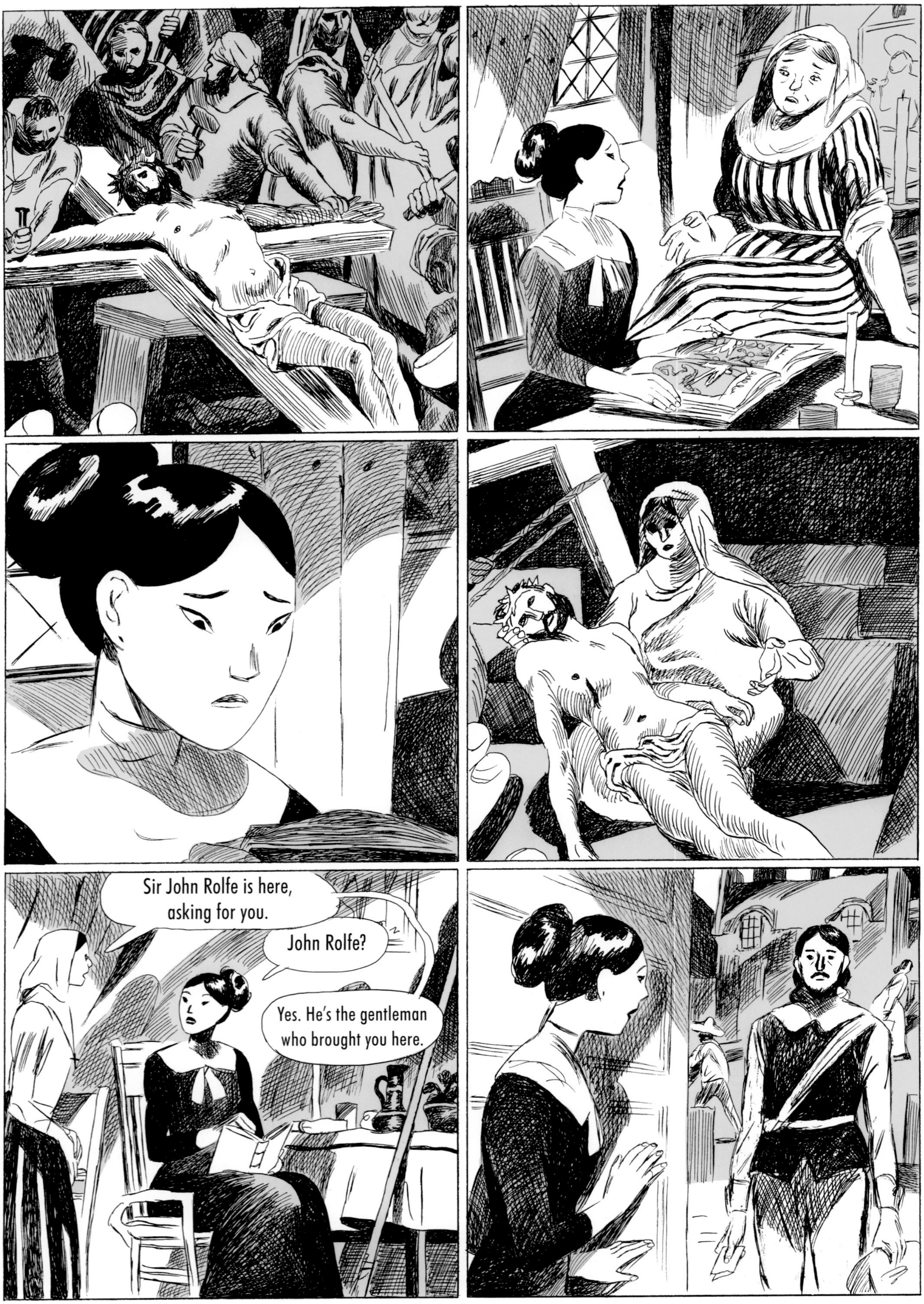
Sir John Rolfe is here, asking for you.
John Rolfe?
Yes. He's the gentleman who brought you here.

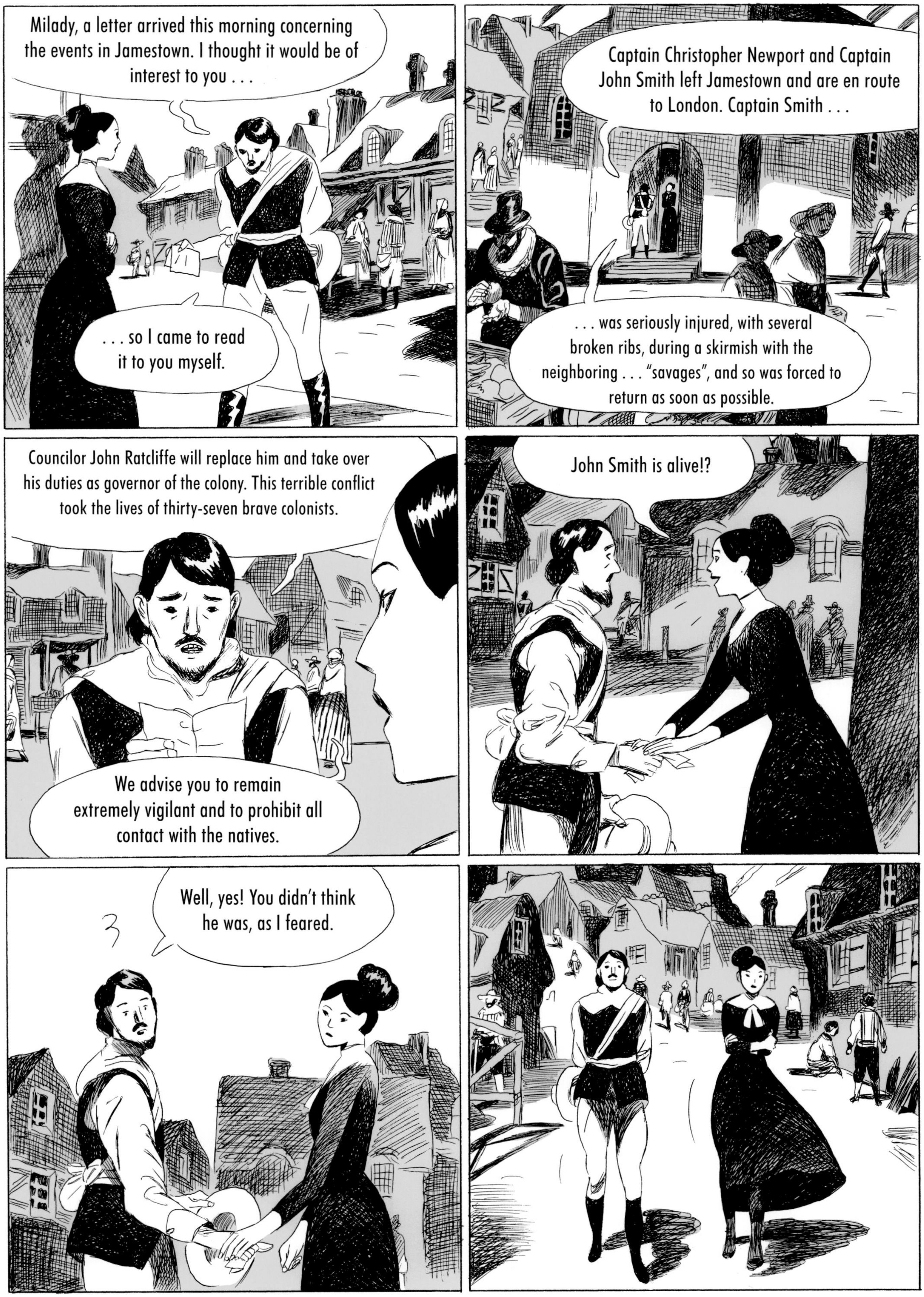
Milady, a letter arrived this morning concerning the events in Jamestown. I thought it would be of interest to you . . .
. . . so I came to read it to you myself.
Captain Christopher Newport and Captain John Smith left Jamestown and are en route to London. Captain Smith . . .
. . . was seriously injured, with several broken ribs, during a skirmish with the neighboring . . . "savages", and so was forced to return as soon as possible.
Councilor John Ratcliffe will replace him and take over his duties as governor of the colony. This terrible conflict took the lives of thirty-seven brave colonists.
We advise you to remain extremely vigilant and to prohibit all contact with the natives.
John Smith is alive!?
Well, yes! You didn't think he was, as I feared.

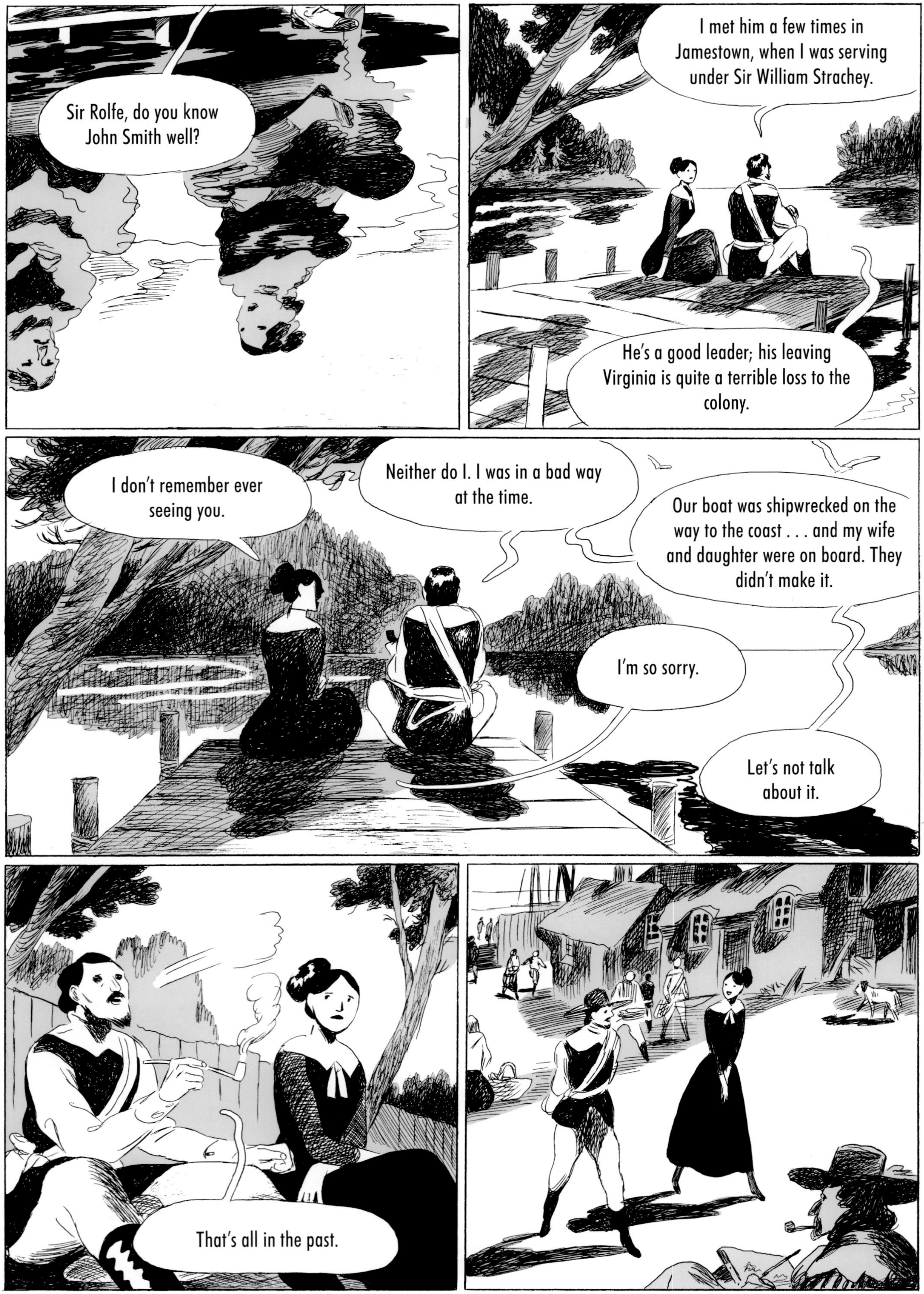
Sir Rolfe, do you know John Smith well?
I met him a few times in Jamestown, when I was serving under Sir William Strachey.
He's a good leader; his leaving Virginia is quite a terrible loss to the colony.
I don't remember ever seeing you.
Neither do I. I was in a bad way at the time.
Our boat was shipwrecked on the way to the coast . . . and my wife and daughter were on board. They didn't make it.
I'm so sorry.
Let's not talk about it.
That's all in the past.

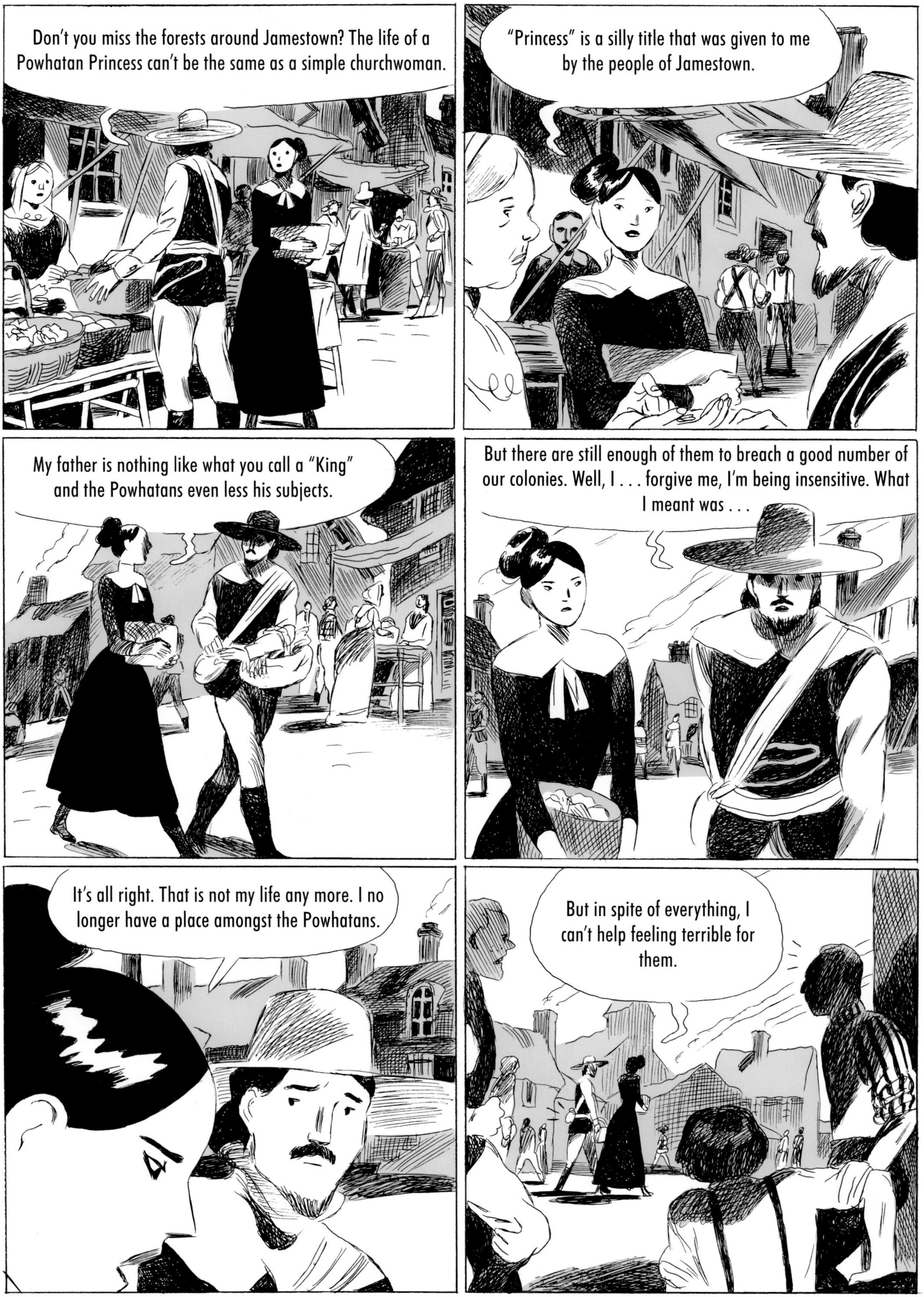
Don't you miss the forests around Jamestown? The life of a Powhatan Princess can't be the same as a simple churchwoman.
"Princess" is a silly title that was given to me by the people of Jamestown.
My father is nothing like what you call a "King" and the Powhatans even less his subjects.
But there are still enough of them to breach a good number of our colonies. Well, I . . . forgive me, I'm being insensitive. What I meant was . . .
It's all right. That is not my life any more. I no longer have a place amongst the Powhatans.
But in spite of everything, I can't help feeling terrible for them.

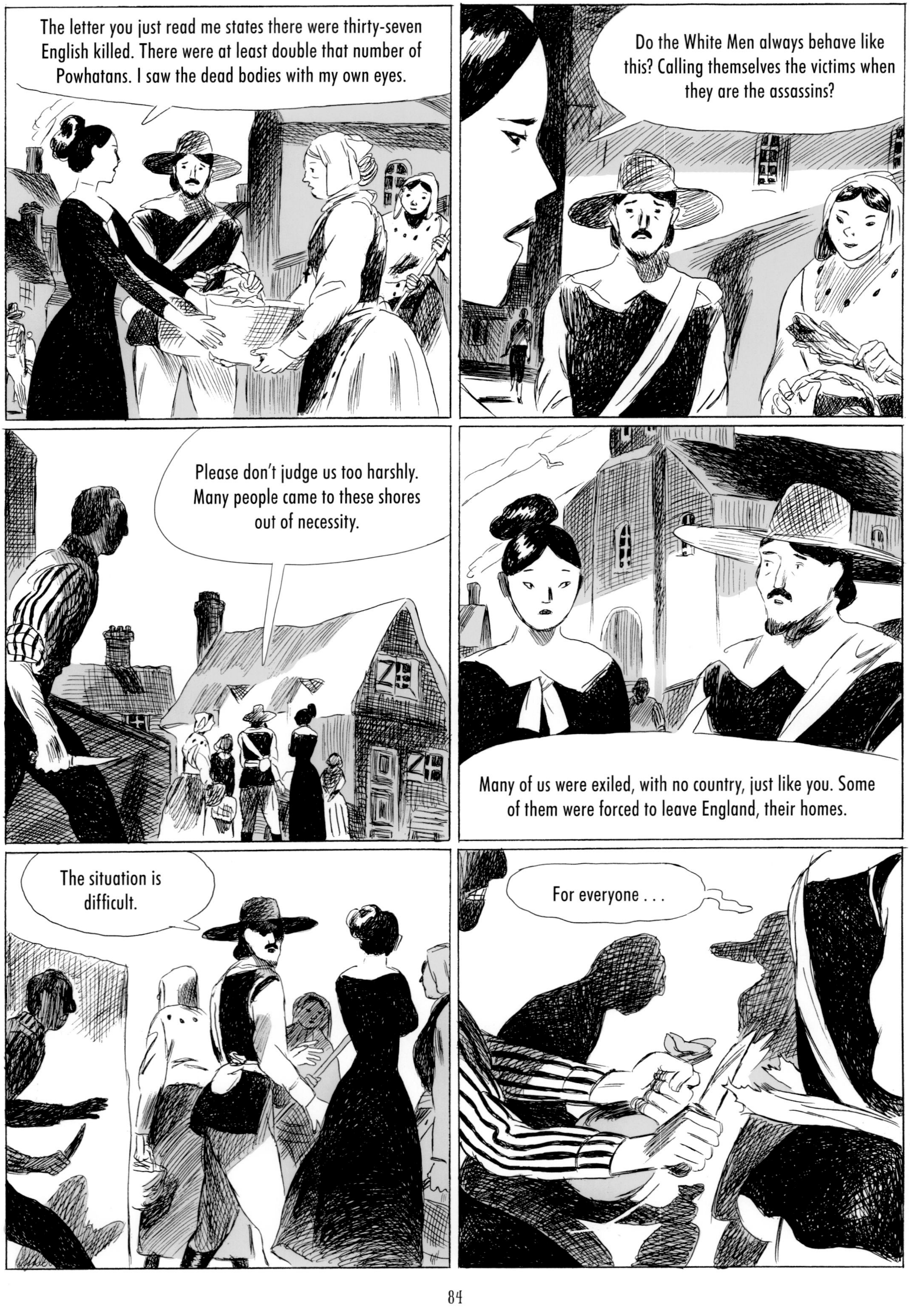
The letter you just read me states there were thirty-seven English killed. There were at least double that number of Powhatans. I saw the dead bodies with my own eyes.
Do the White Men always behave like this? Calling themselves the victims when they are the assassins?
Please don't judge us too harshly. Many people came to these shores out of necessity.
Many of us were exiled, with no country, just like you. Some of them were forced to leave England, their homes.
The situation is difficult.
For everyone . . .

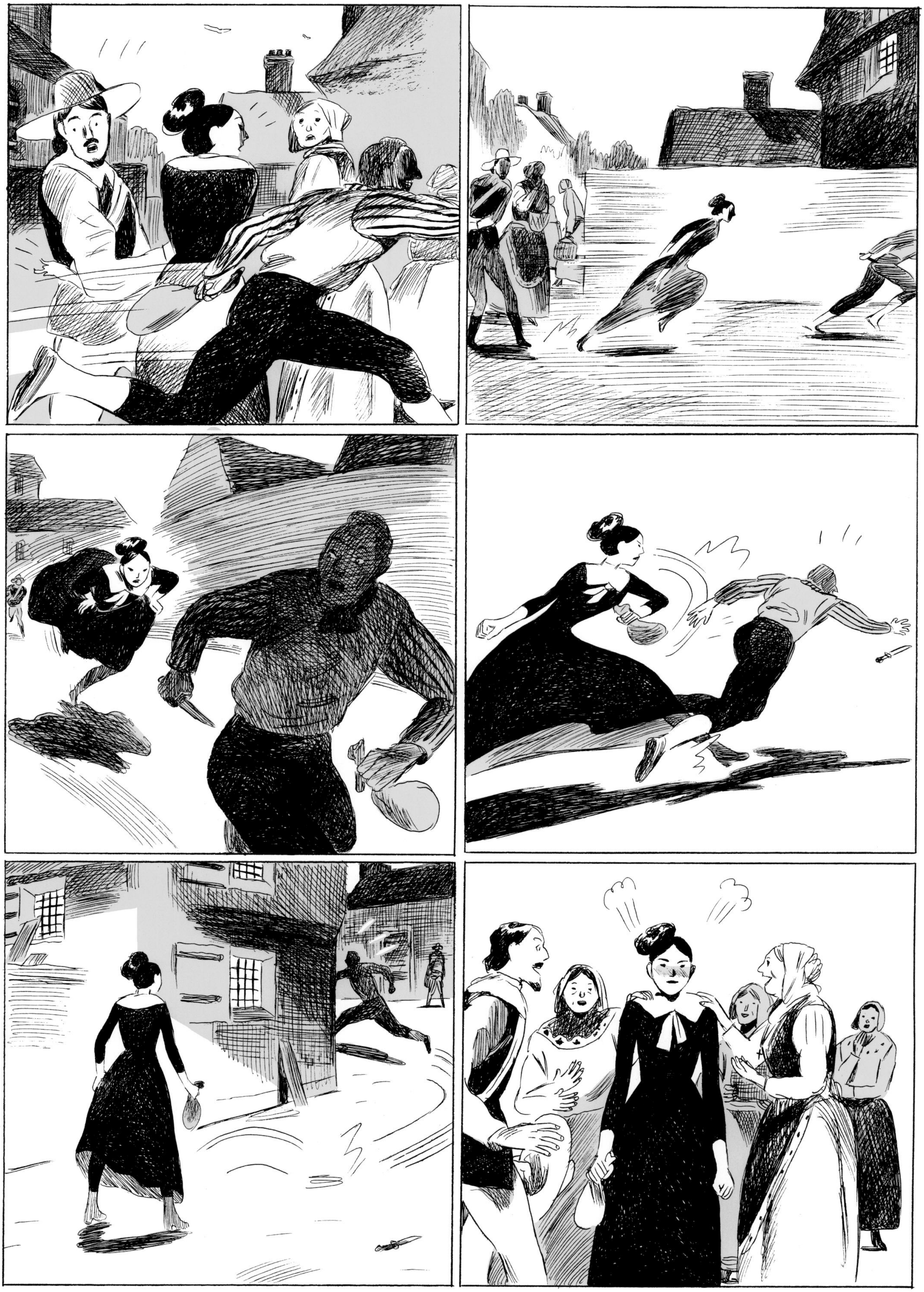

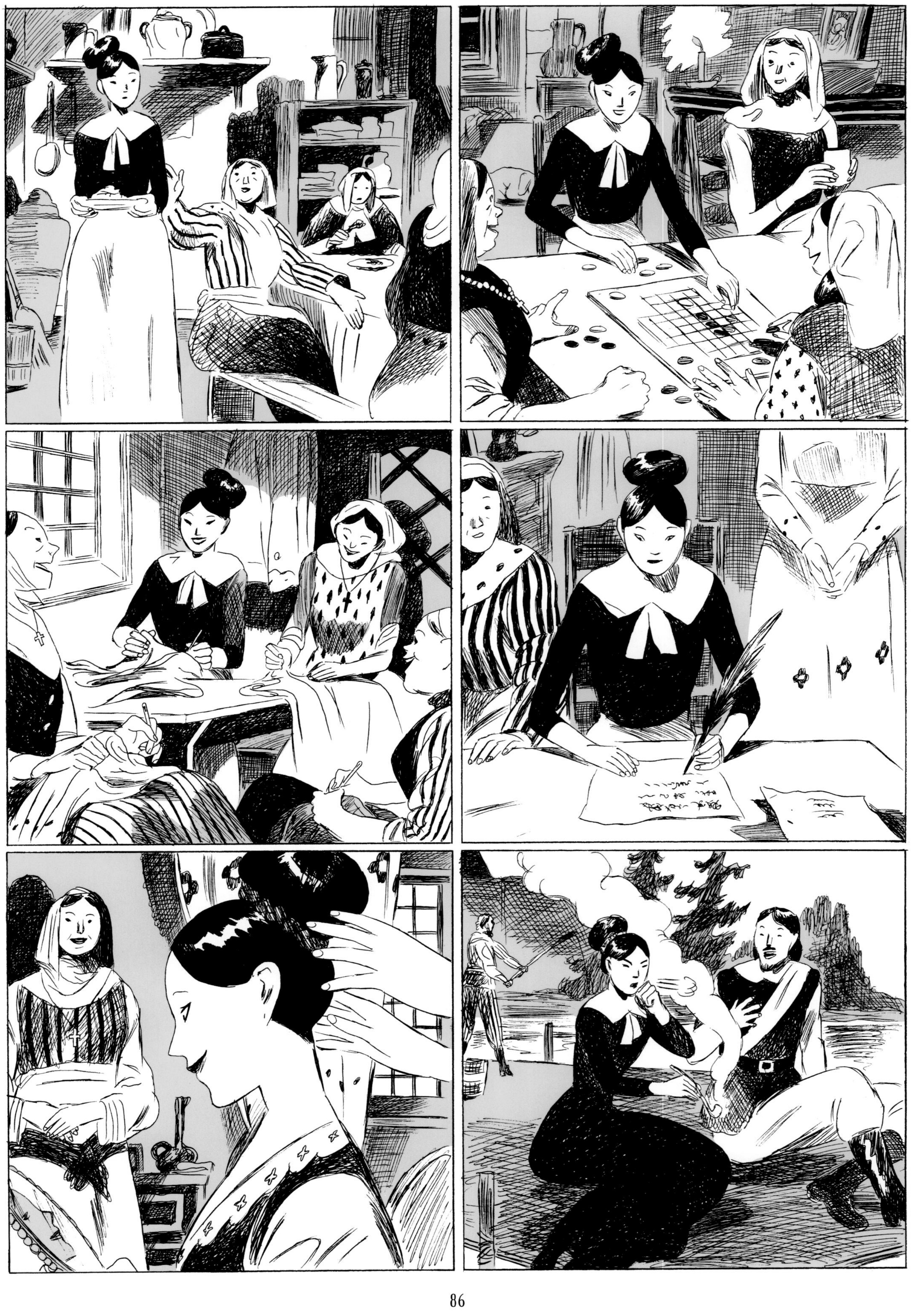

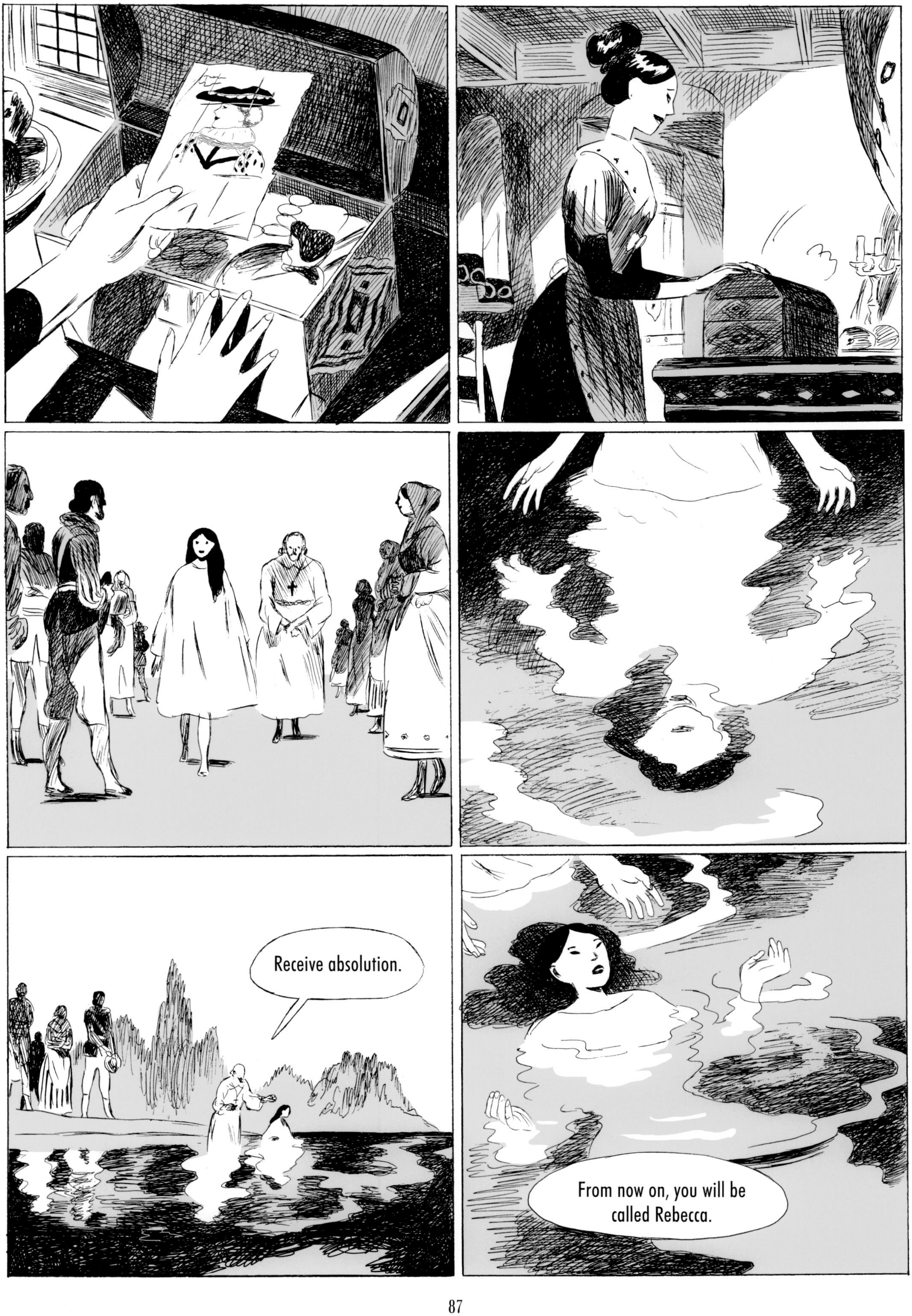
Receive absolution.
From now on, you will be called Rebecca.

Rebecca

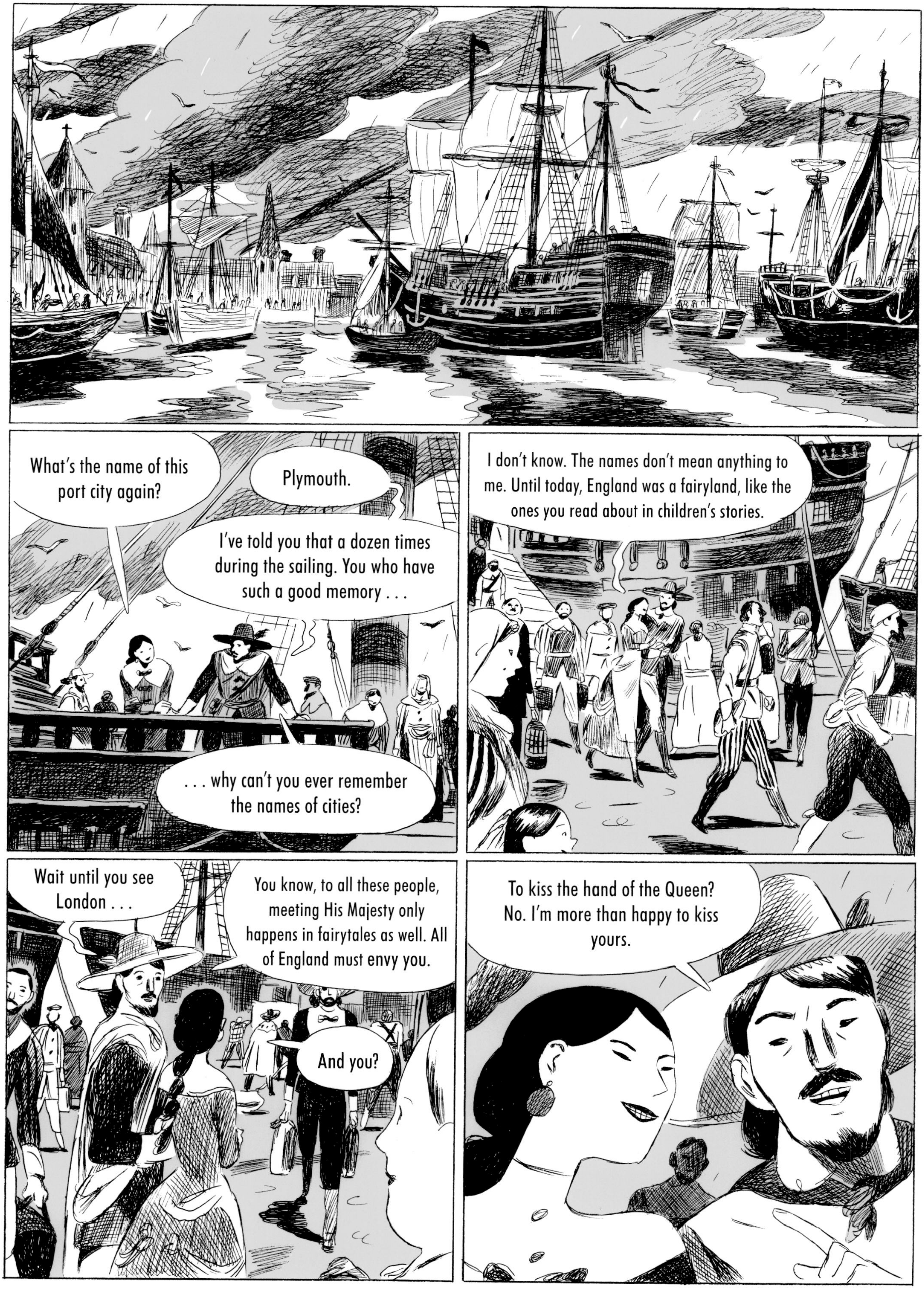
What's the name of this port city again?
Plymouth.
I've told you that a dozen times during the sailing. You who have such a good memory . . .
. . . why can't you ever remember the names of cities?
I don't know. The names don't mean anything to me. Until today, England was a fairyland, like the ones you read about in children's stories.
Wait until you see London . . .
You know, to all these people, meeting His Majesty only happens in fairytales as well. All of England must envy you.
And you?
To kiss the hand of the Queen? No. I'm more than happy to kiss yours.

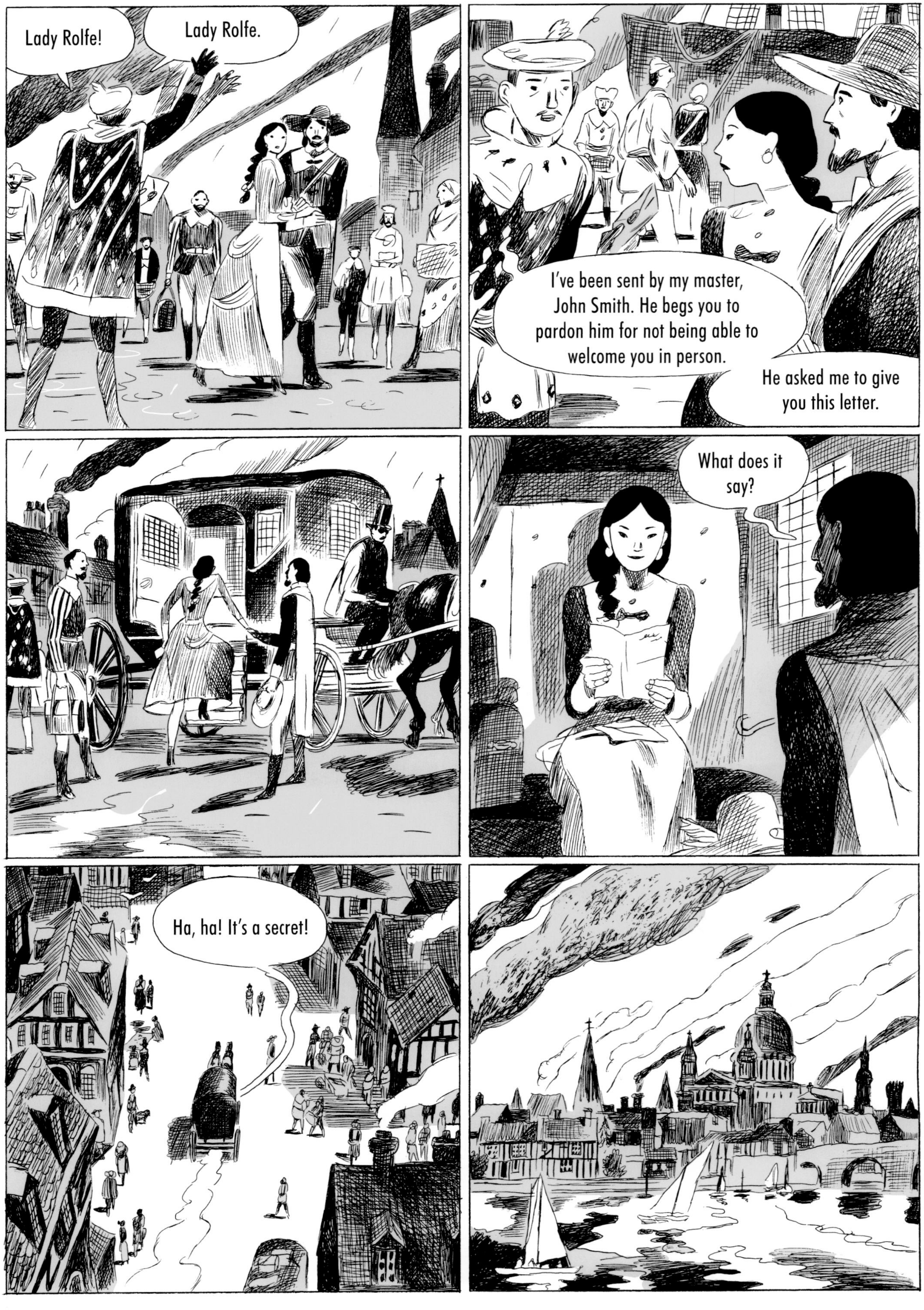
Lady Rolfe!
Lady Rolfe.
I've been sent by my master, John Smith. He begs you to pardon him for not being able to welcome you in person.
He asked me to give you this letter.
What does it say?
Ha, ha! It's a secret!

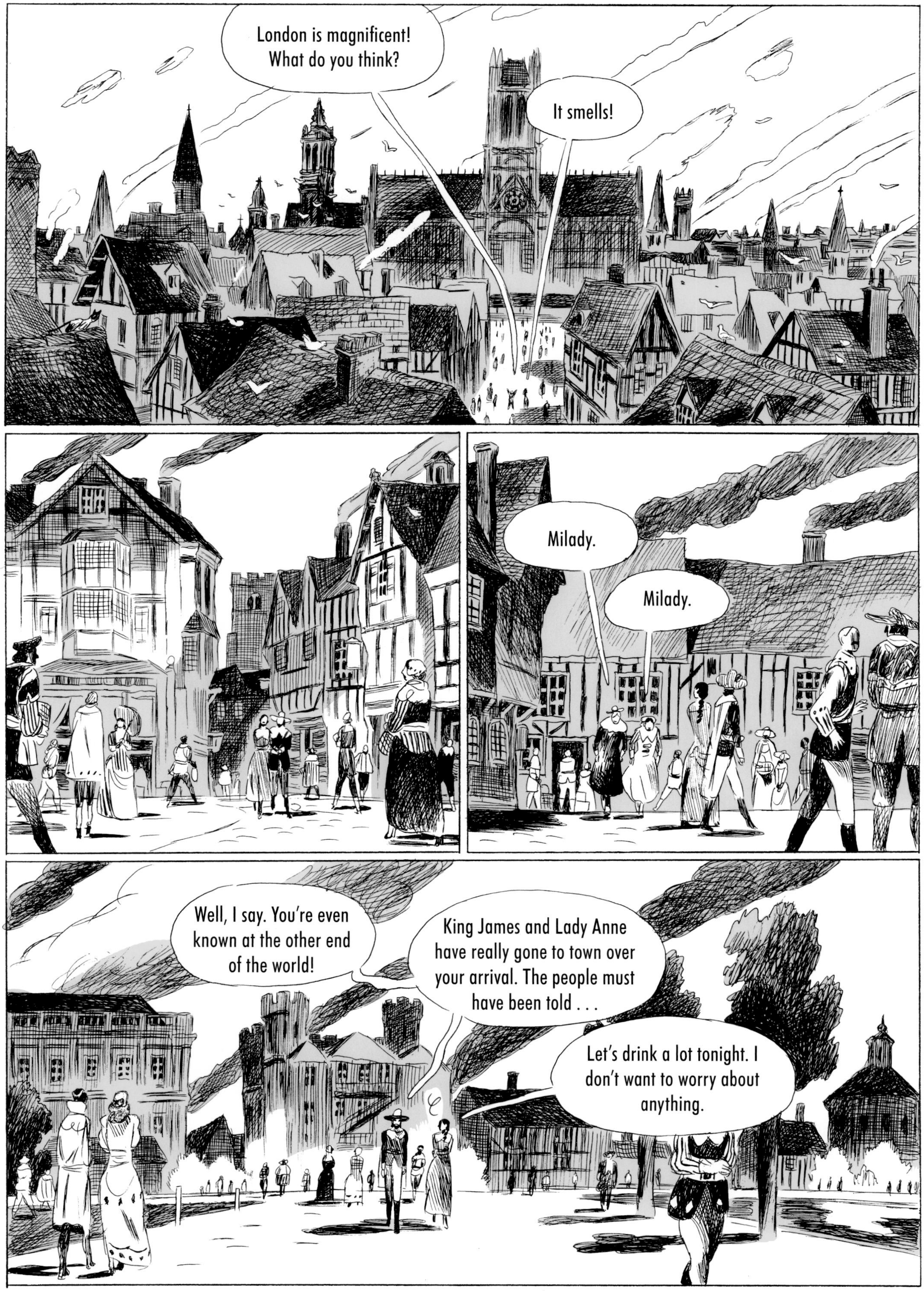
London is magnificent! What do you think?
It smells!
Milady.
Milady.
Well, I say. You're even known at the other end of the world!
King James and Lady Anne have really gone to town over your arrival. The people must have been told . . .
Let's drink a lot tonight. I don't want to worry about anything.

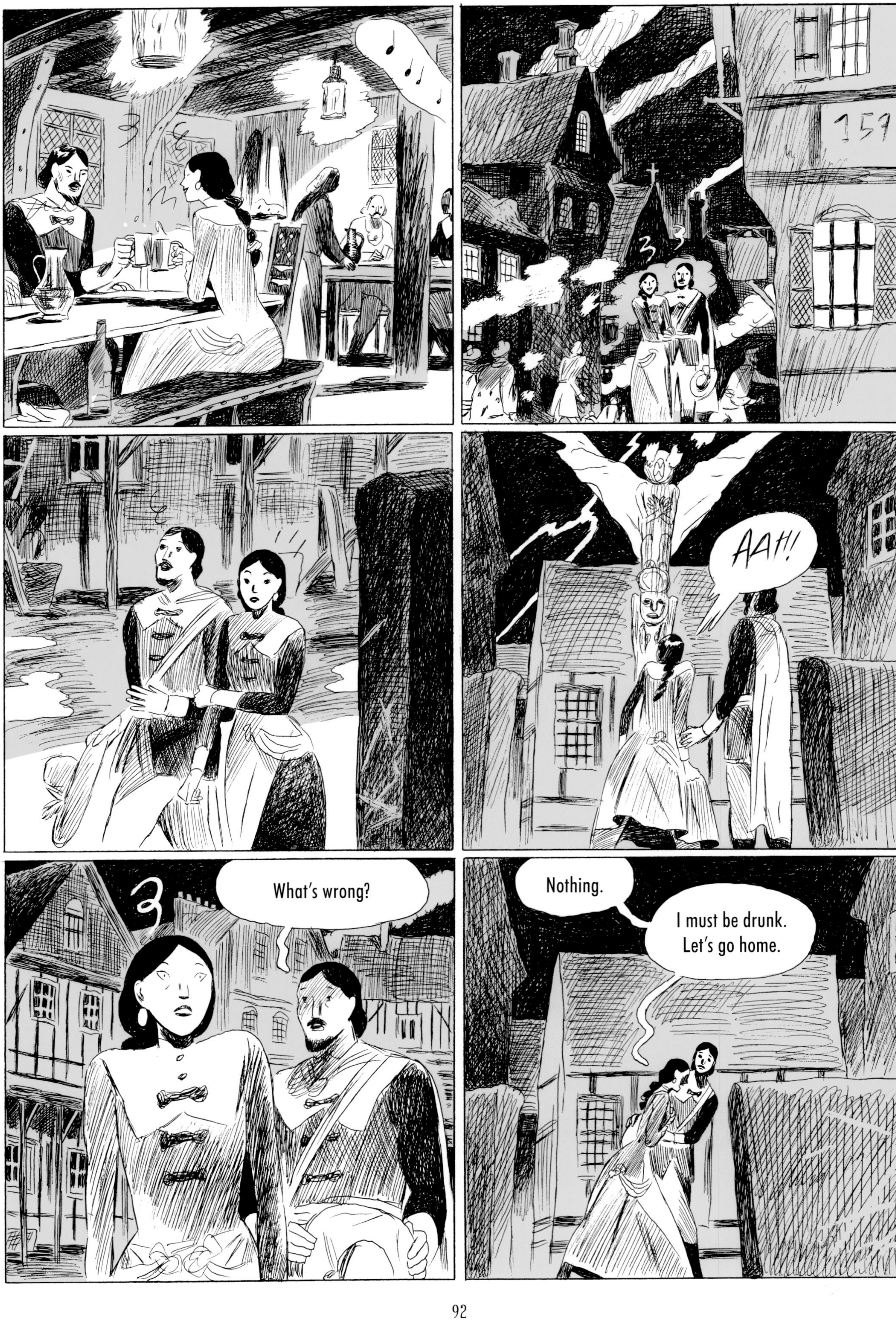
1575
AAH!
What's wrong?
Nothing.
I must be drunk.
Let's go home.

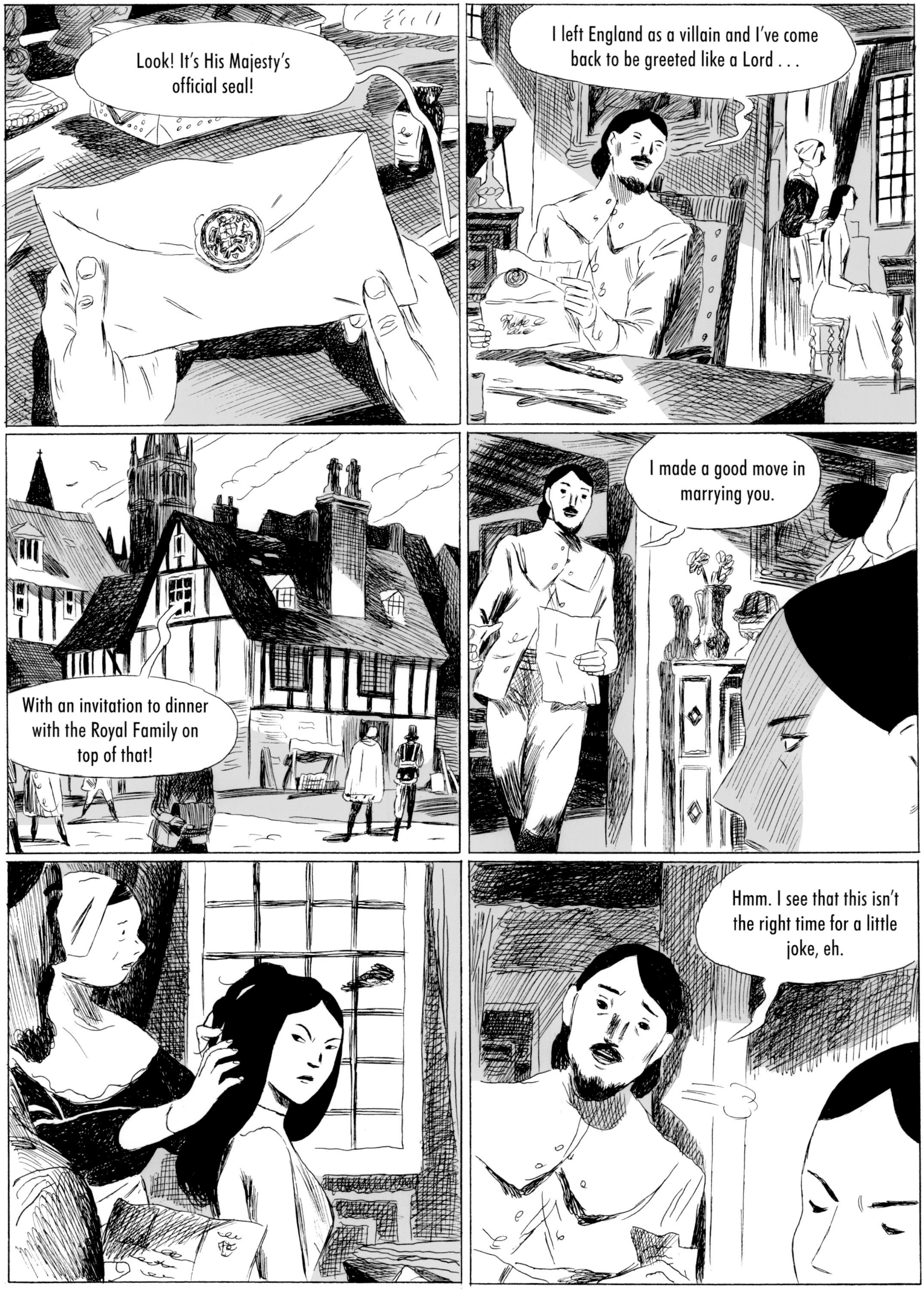
Look! It's His Majesty's official seal!
I left England as a villain and I've come back to be greeted like a Lord . . .
With an invitation to dinner with the Royal Family on top of that!
I made a good move in marrying you.
Hmm. I see that this isn't the right time for a little joke, eh.

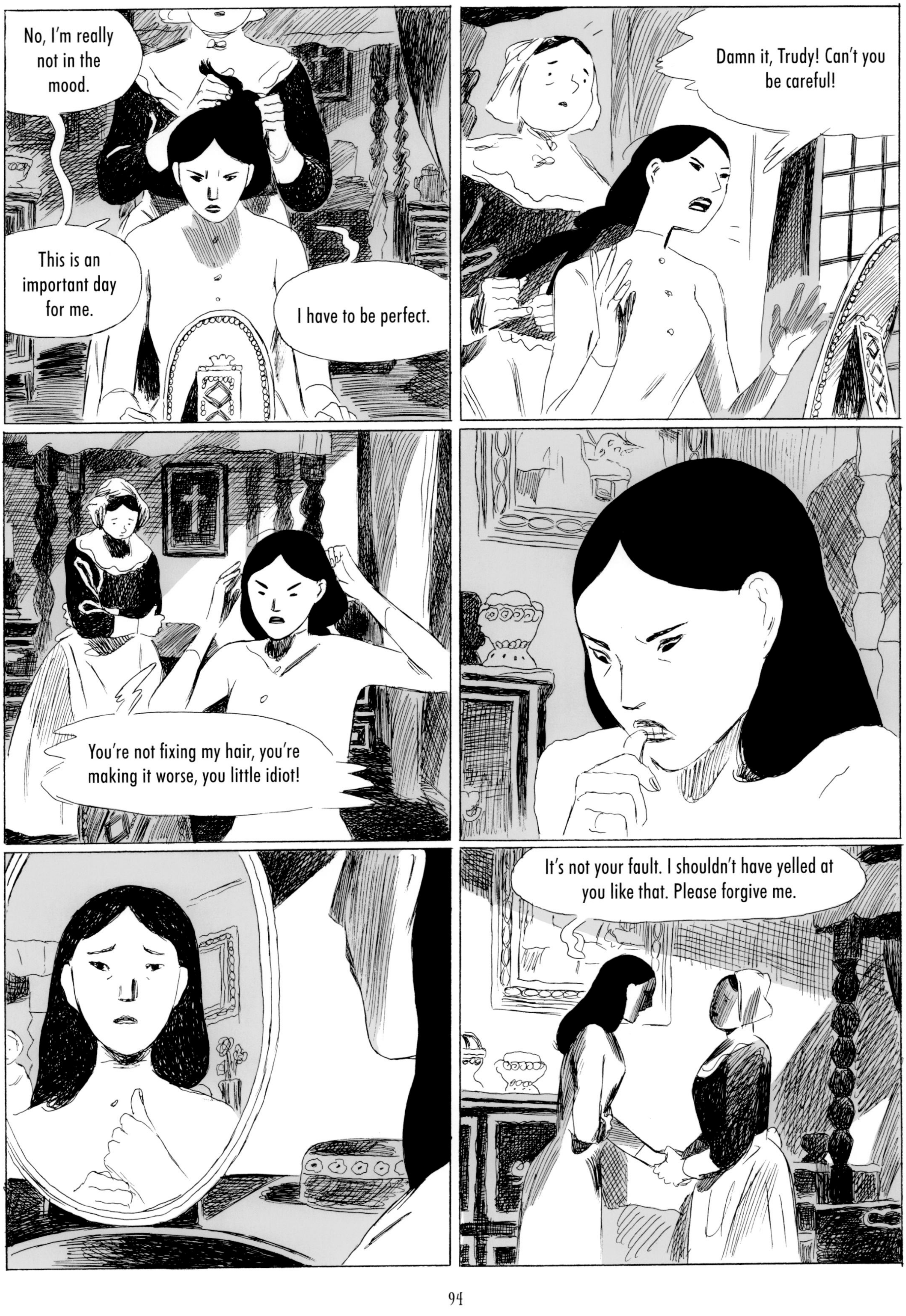
No, I'm really not in the mood.
This is an important day for me.
I have to be perfect.
Damn it, Trudy! Can't you be careful!
You're not fixing my hair, you're making it worse, you little idiot!
It's not your fault. I shouldn't have yelled at you like that. Please forgive me.

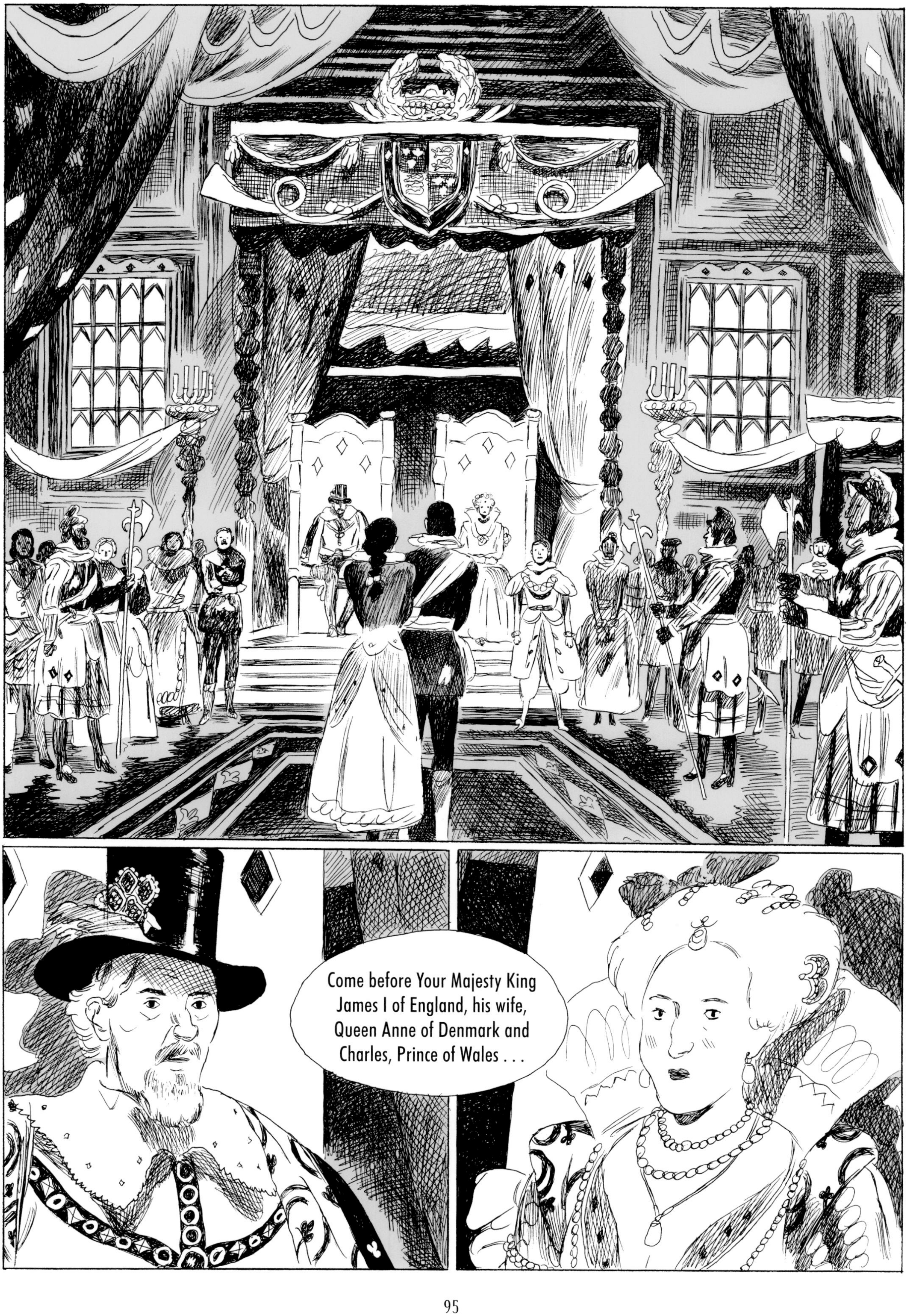
Come before Your Majesty King James I of England, his wife, Queen Anne of Denmark and Charles, Prince of Wales . . .

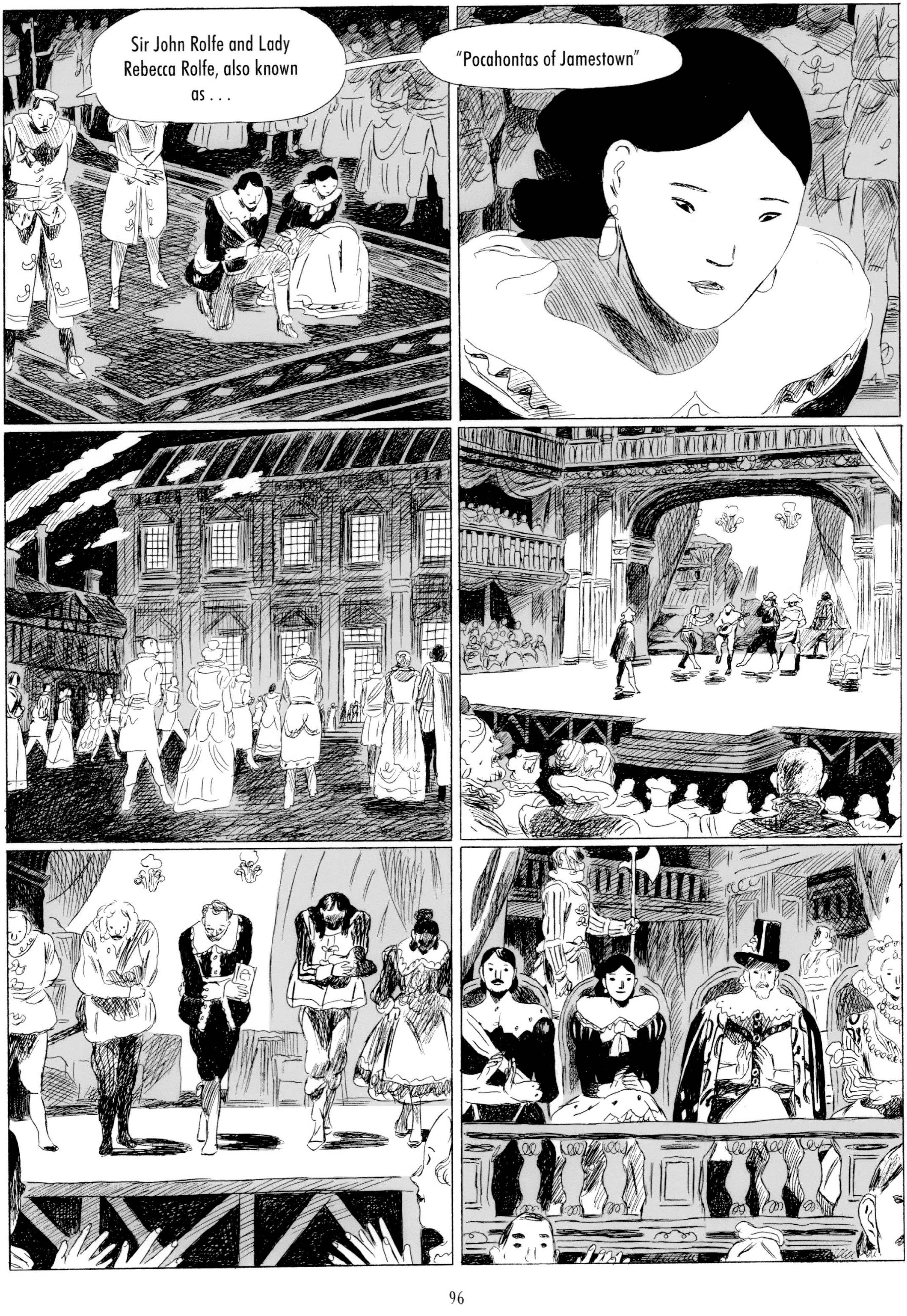
Sir John Rolfe and Lady Rebecca Rolfe, also known as . . .
"Pocahontas of Jamestown"

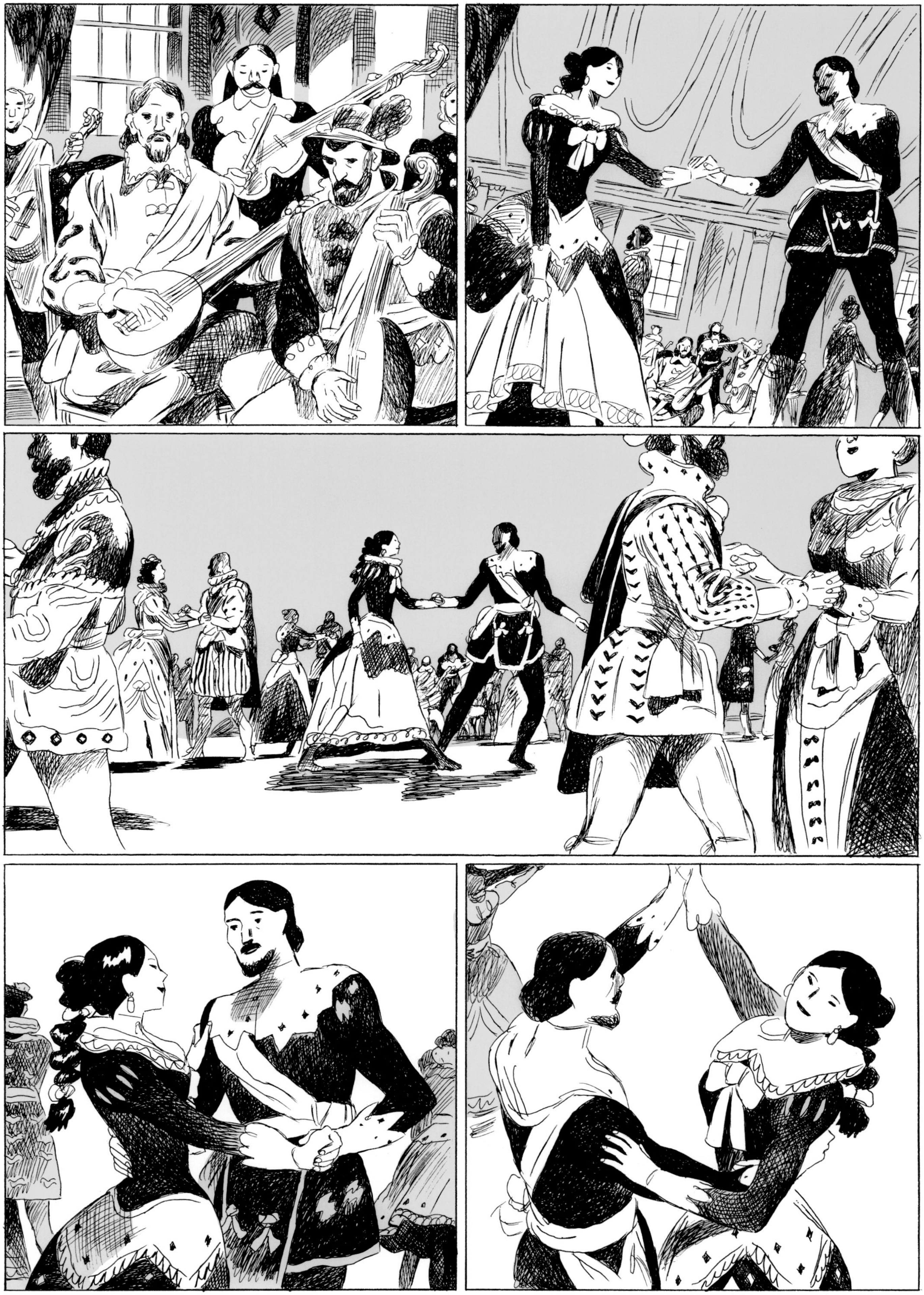

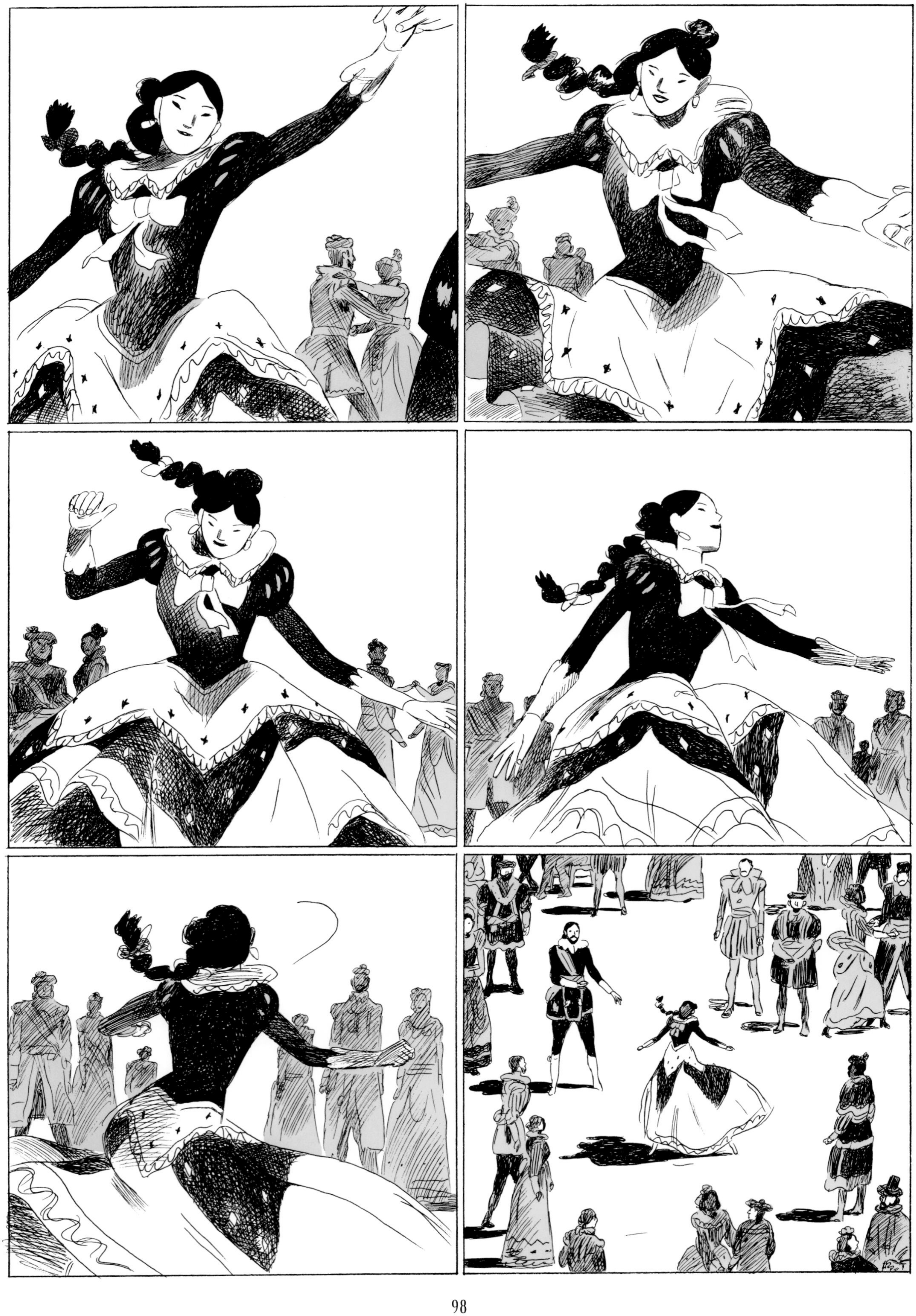

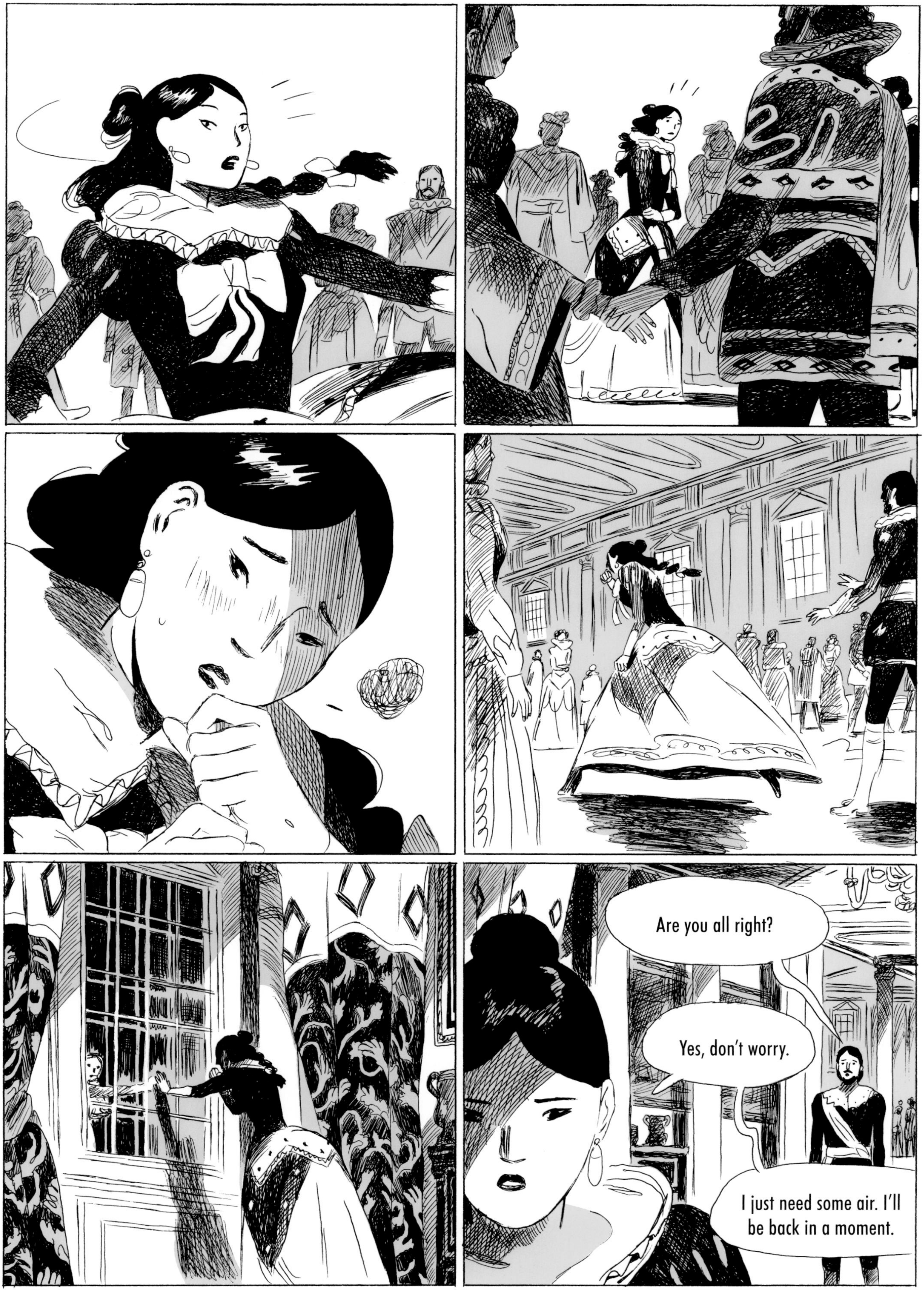
Are you all right?
Yes, don't worry.
I just need some air. I'll be back in a moment.

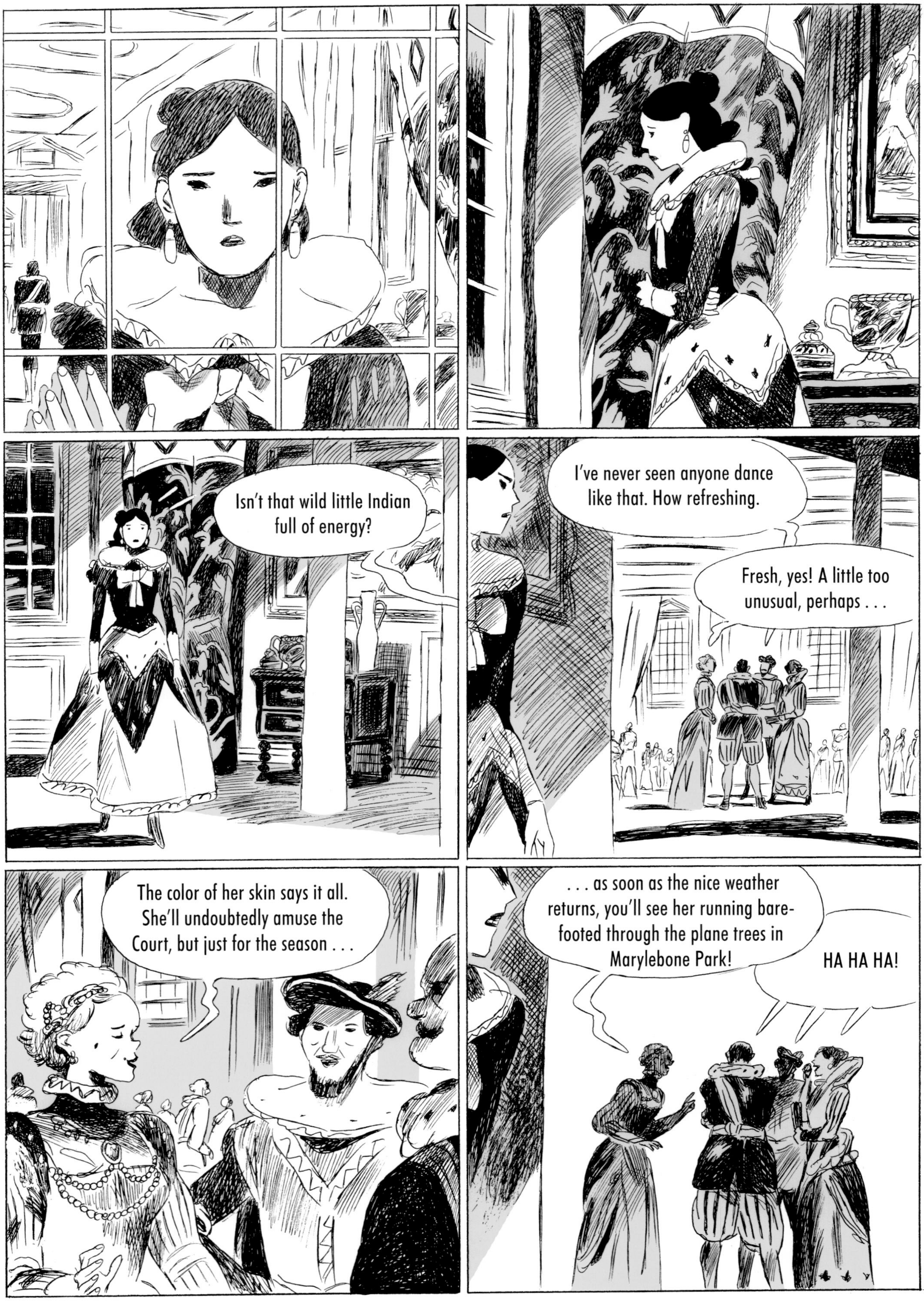
Isn't that wild little Indian full of energy?
I've never seen anyone dance like that. How refreshing.
Fresh, yes! A little too unusual, perhaps . . .
The color of her skin says it all. She'll undoubtedly amuse the Court, but just for the season . . .
. . . as soon as the nice weather returns, you'll see her running bare-footed through the plane trees in Marylebone Park!
HA HA HA!

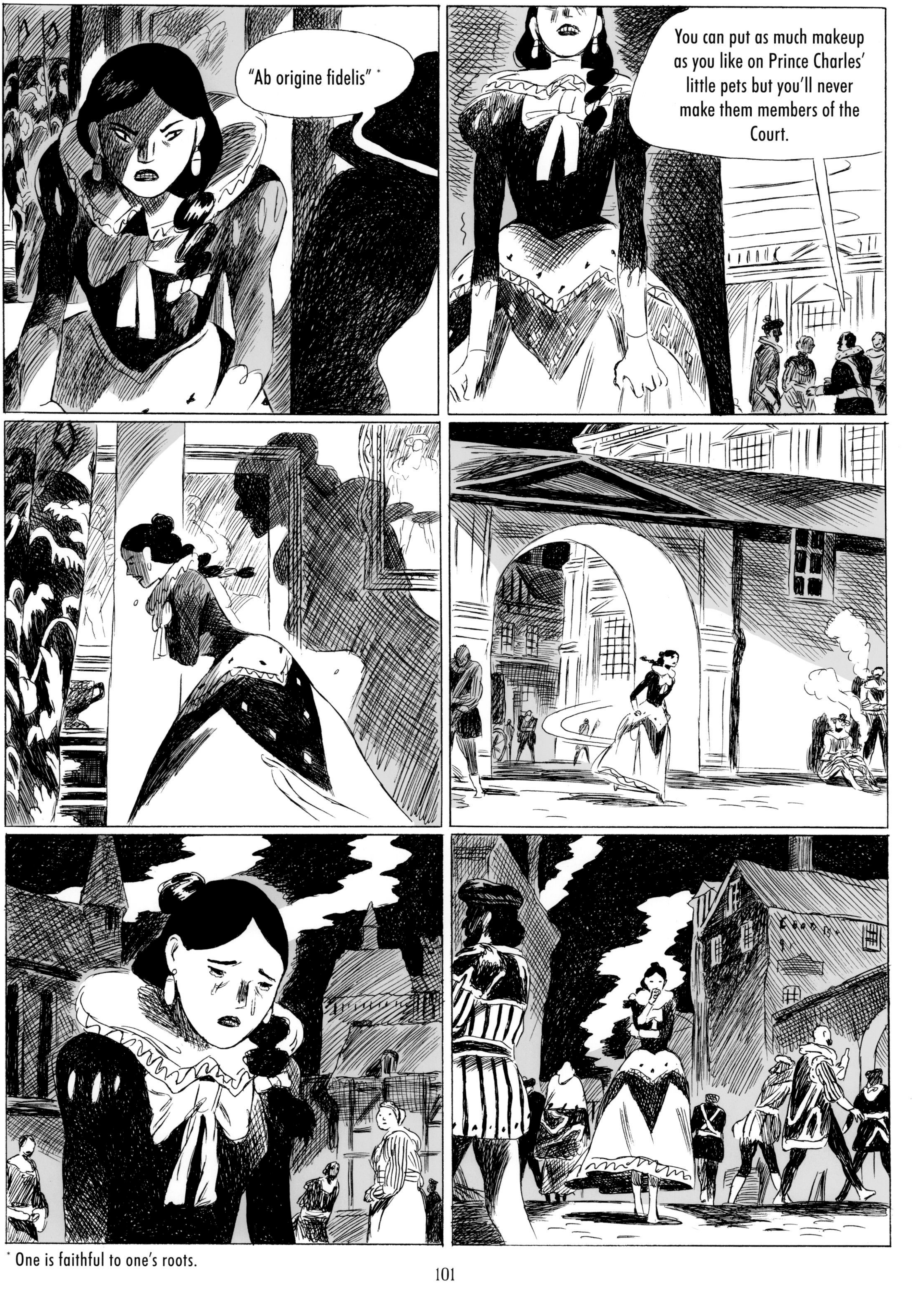
"Ab origine fidelis" *
You can put as much makeup as you like on Prince Charles' little pets but you'll never make them members of the Court.

* One is faithful to one's roots.

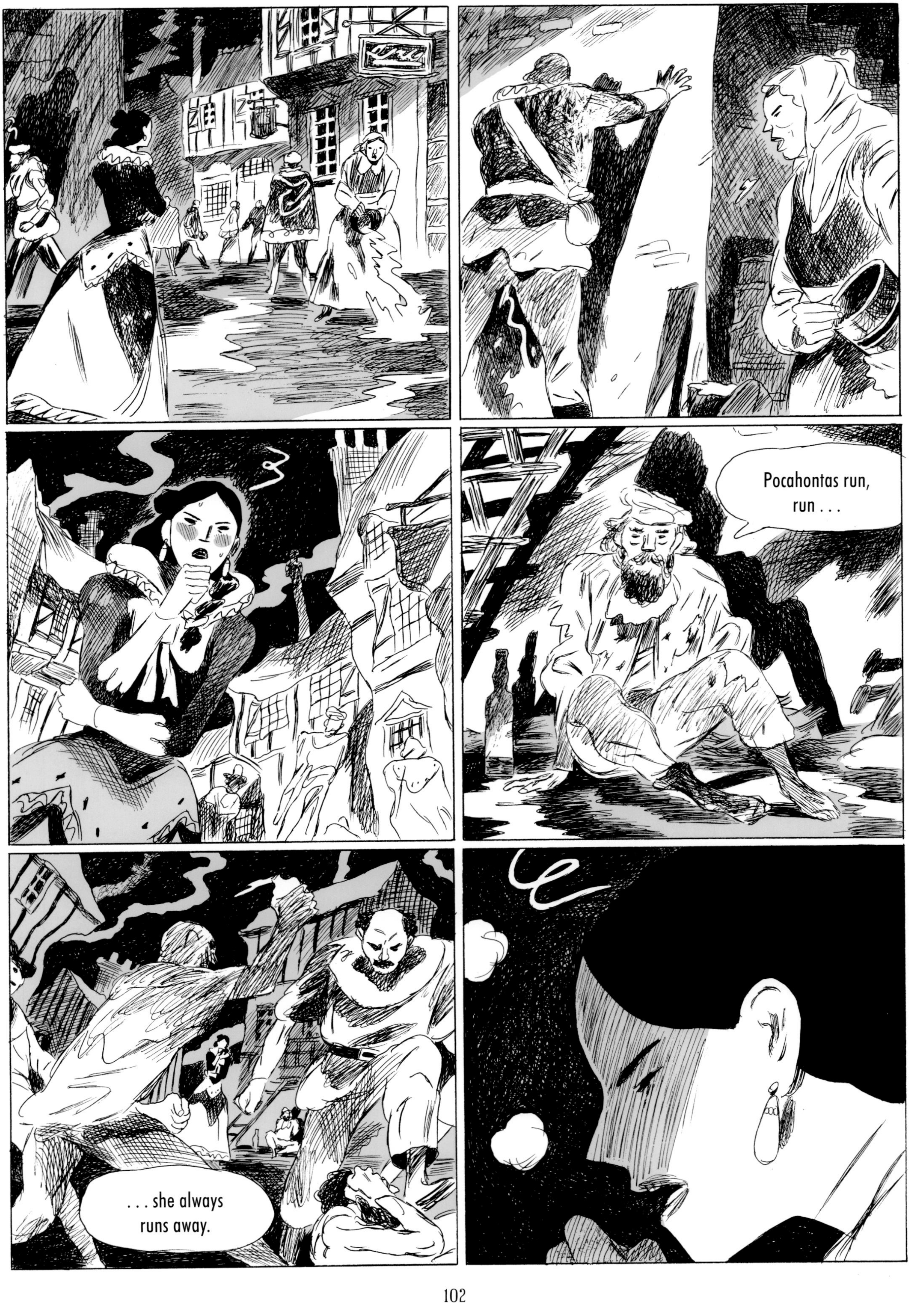
Pocahontas run, run . . .
. . . she always runs away.

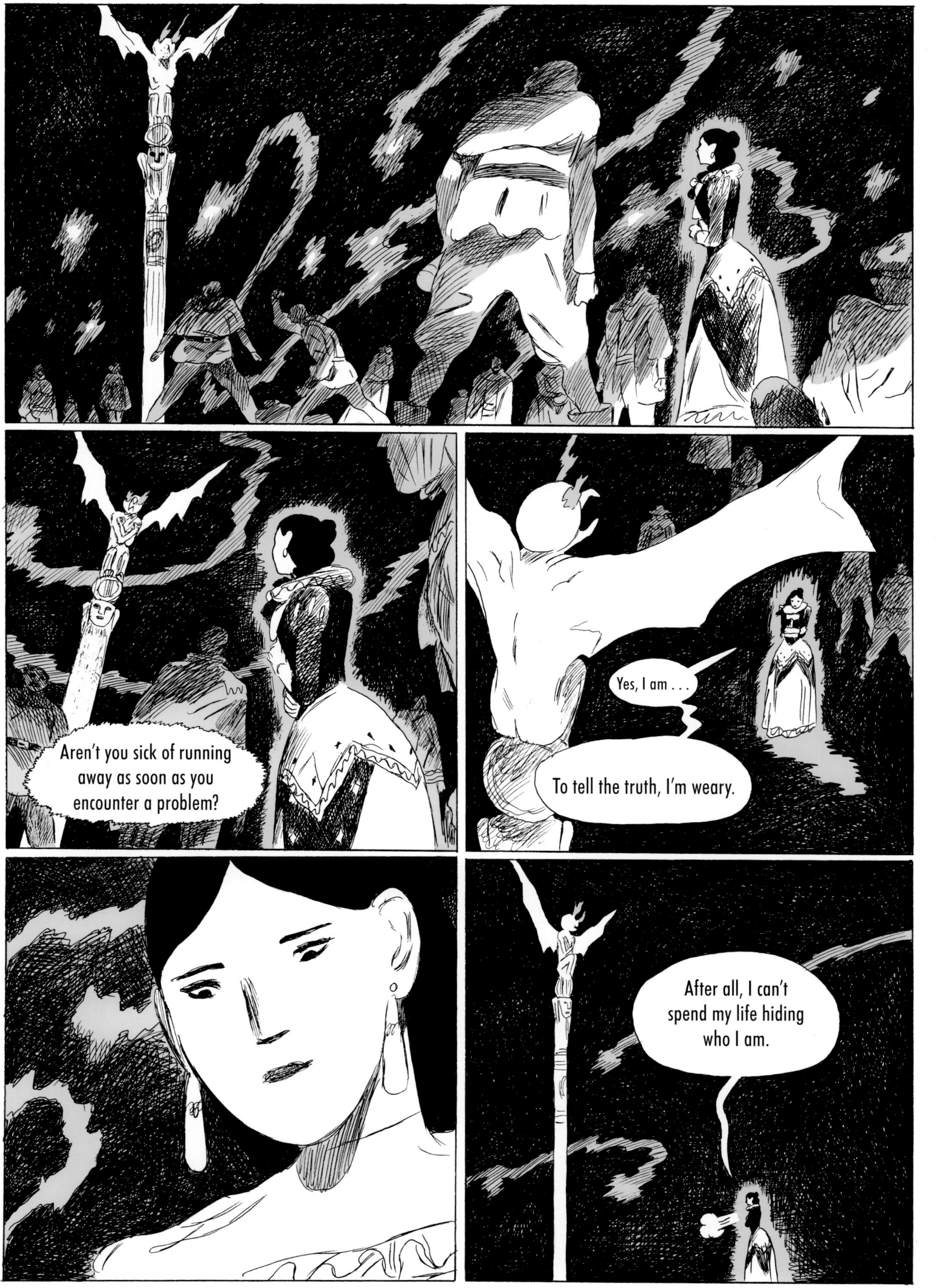

Aren't you sick of running away as soon as you encounter a problem?
Yes, I am . . .
To tell the truth, I'm weary.
After all, I can't spend my life hiding who I am.

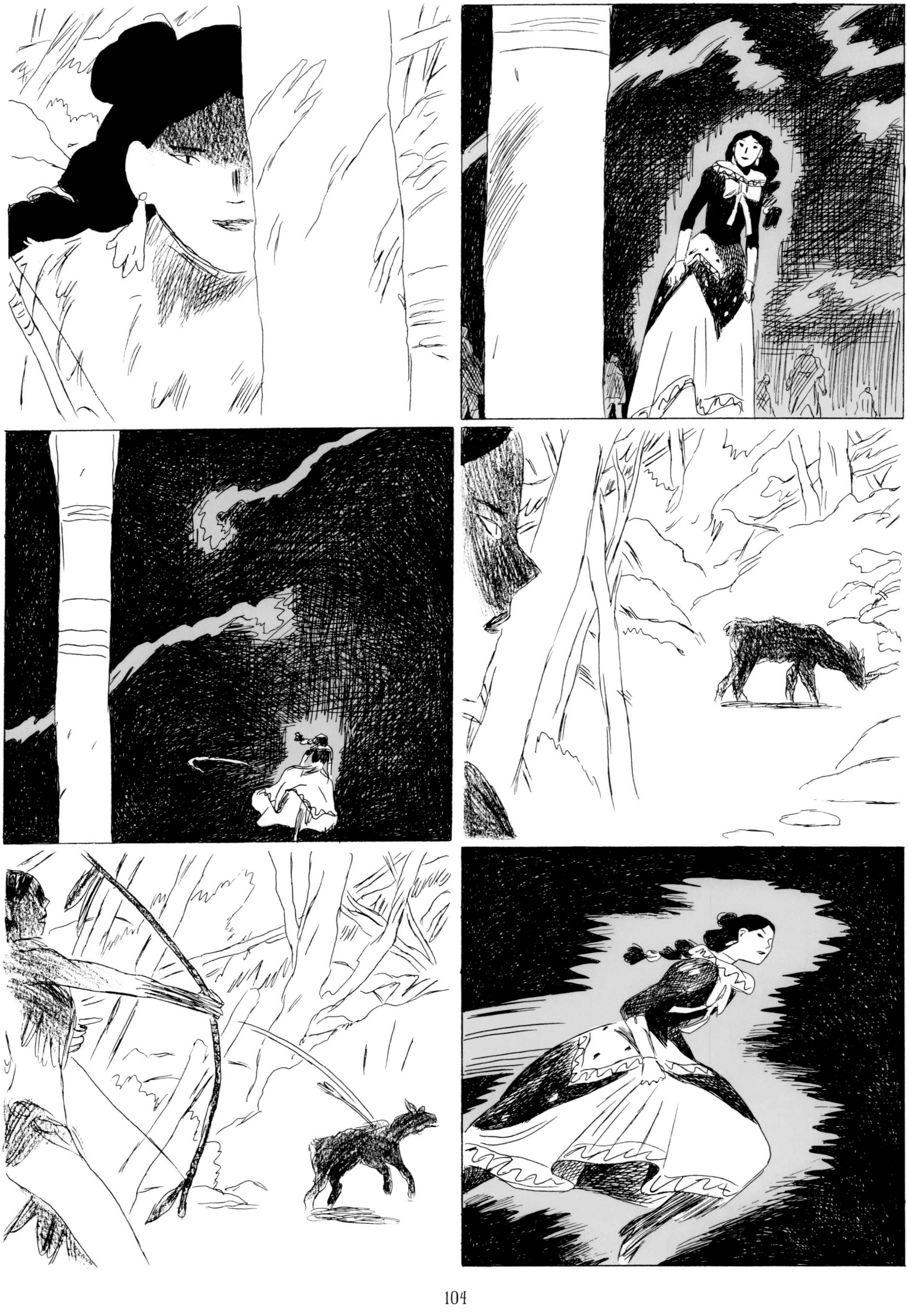

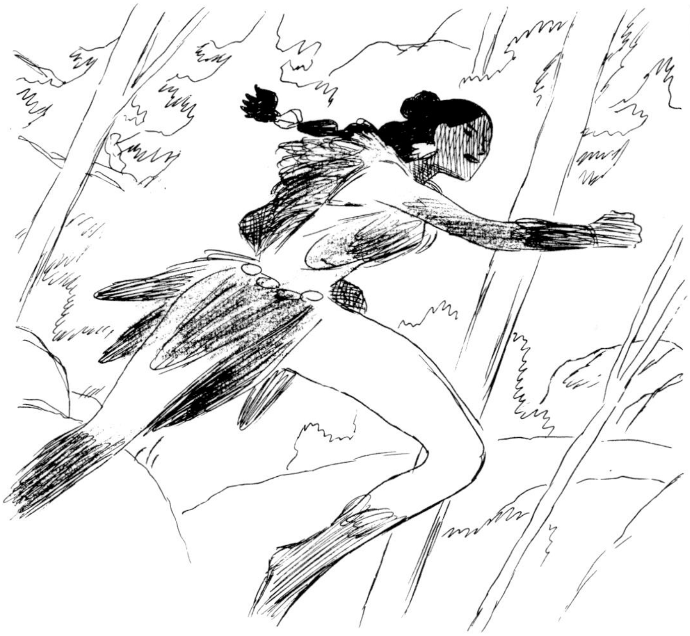

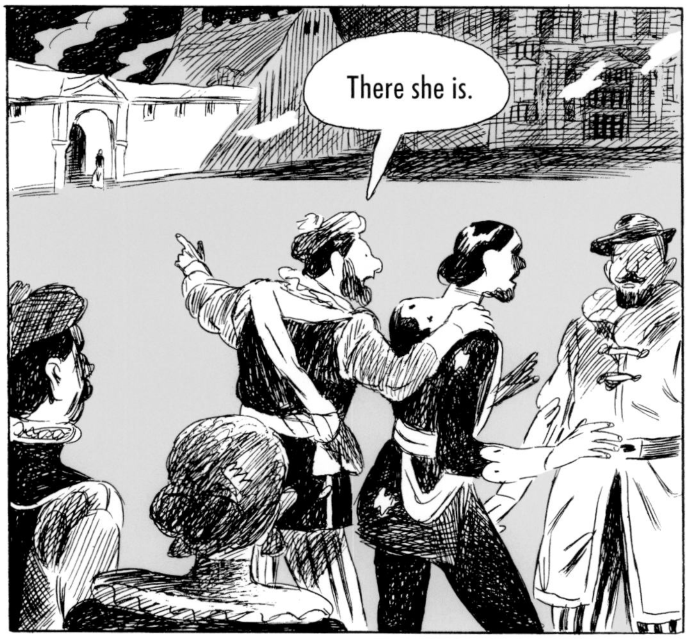
There she is.

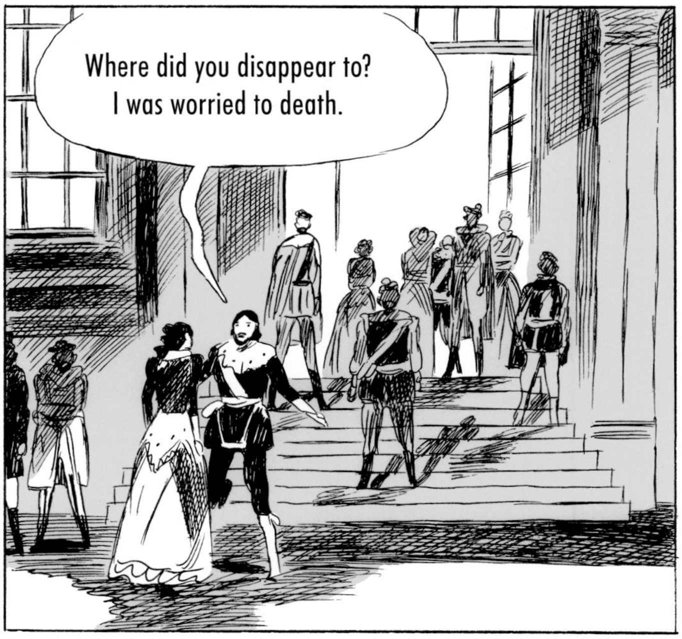
Where did you disappear to?
I was worried to death.

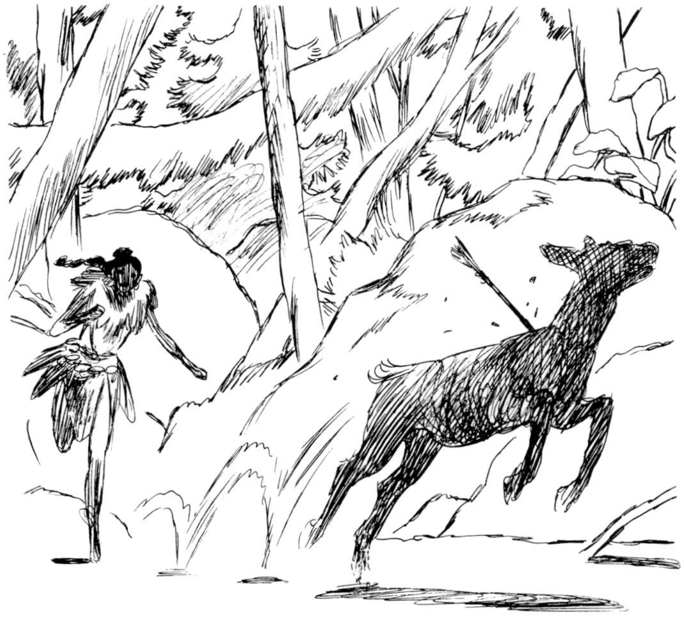

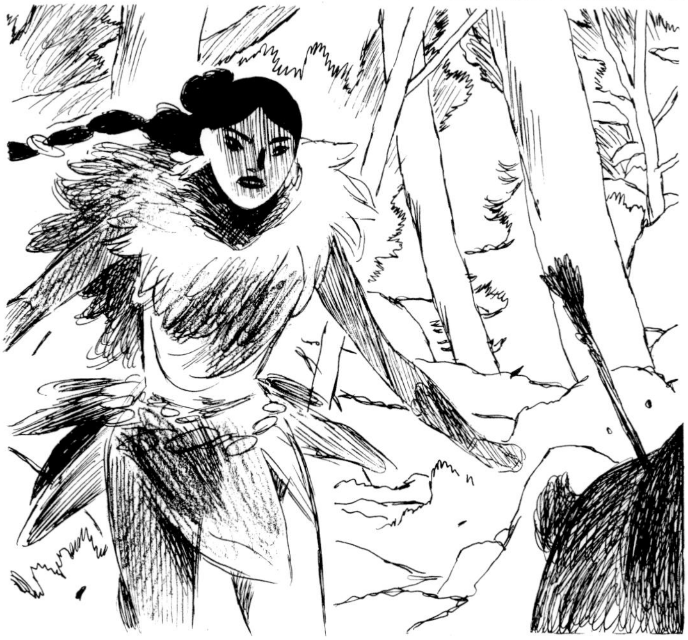

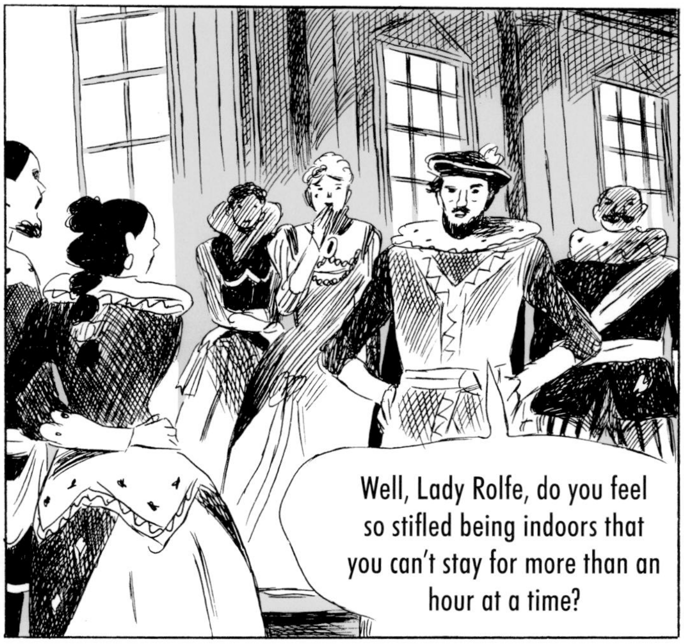
Well, Lady Rolfe, do you feel so stifled being indoors that you can't stay for more than an hour at a time?

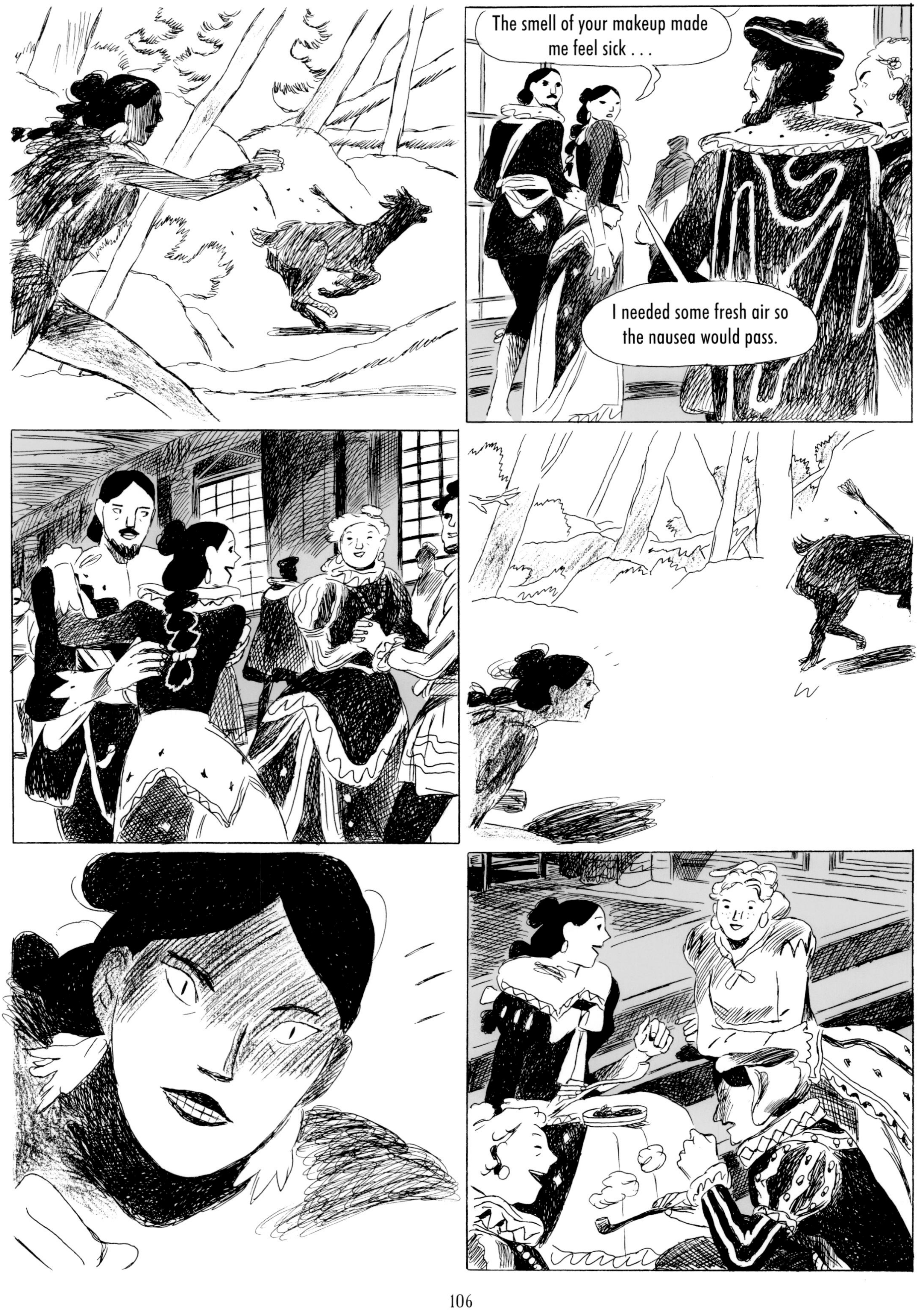
The smell of your makeup made me feel sick . . .
I needed some fresh air so the nausea would pass.

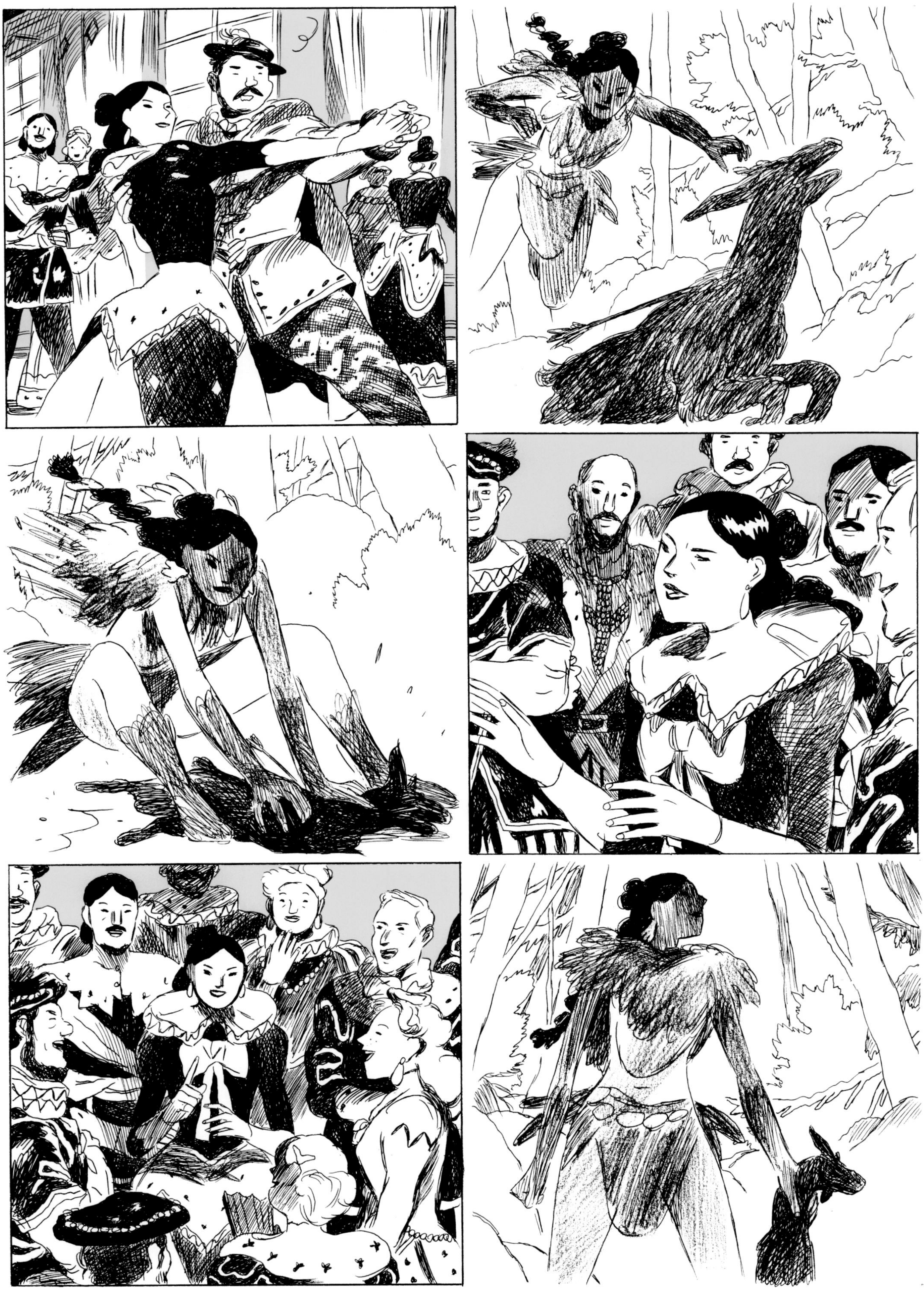

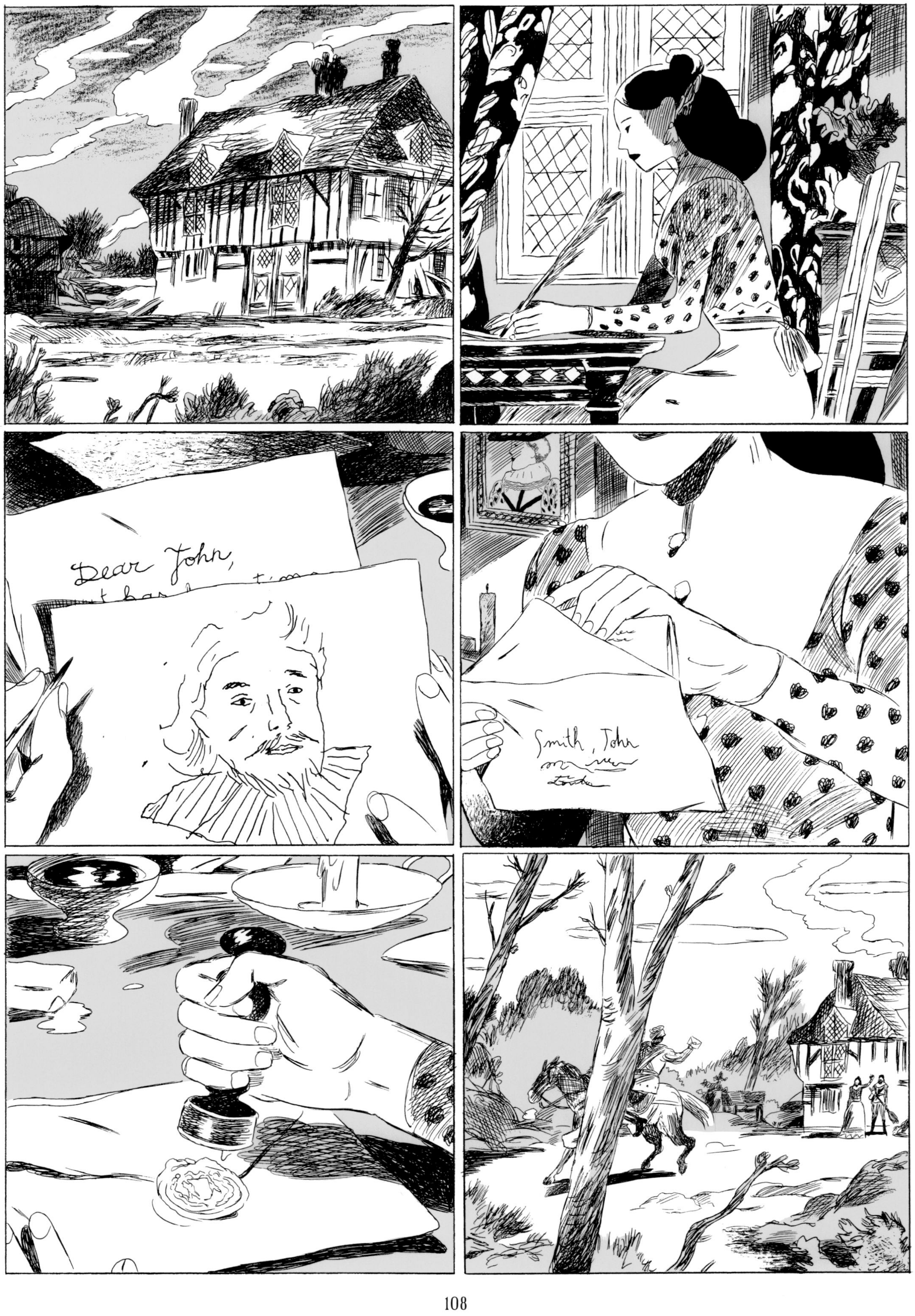
Dear John,
Smith, John

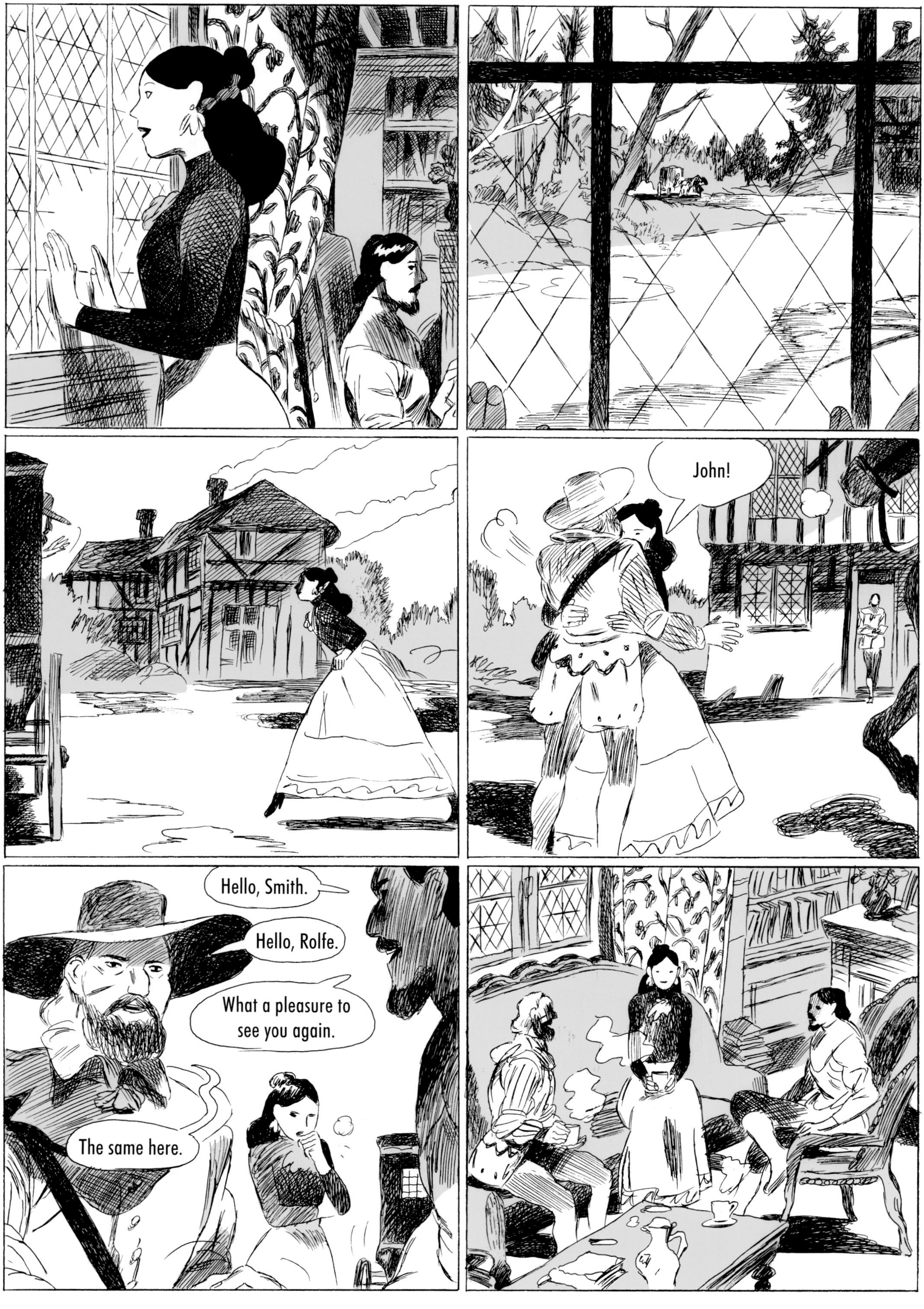
John!
Hello, Smith.
Hello, Rolfe.
What a pleasure to see you again.
The same here.

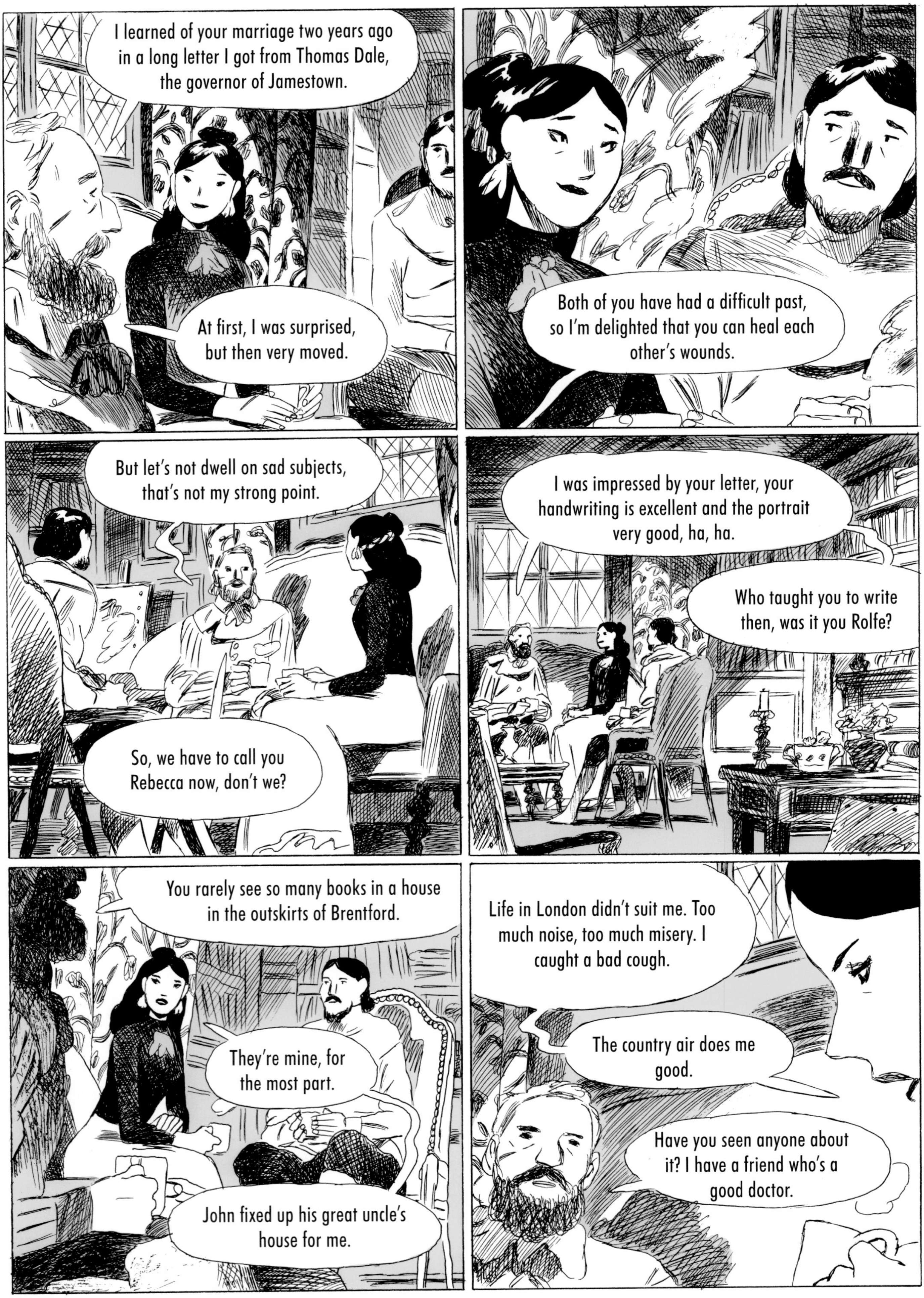
I learned of your marriage two years ago in a long letter I got from Thomas Dale, the governor of Jamestown.
At first, I was surprised, but then very moved.
Both of you have had a difficult past, so I'm delighted that you can heal each other's wounds.
But let's not dwell on sad subjects, that's not my strong point.
So, we have to call you Rebecca now, don't we?
I was impressed by your letter, your handwriting is excellent and the portrait very good, ha, ha.
Who taught you to write then, was it you Rolfe?
You rarely see so many books in a house in the outskirts of Brentford.
They're mine, for the most part.
John fixed up his great uncle's house for me.
Life in London didn't suit me. Too much noise, too much misery. I caught a bad cough.
The country air does me good.
Have you seen anyone about it? I have a friend who's a good doctor.

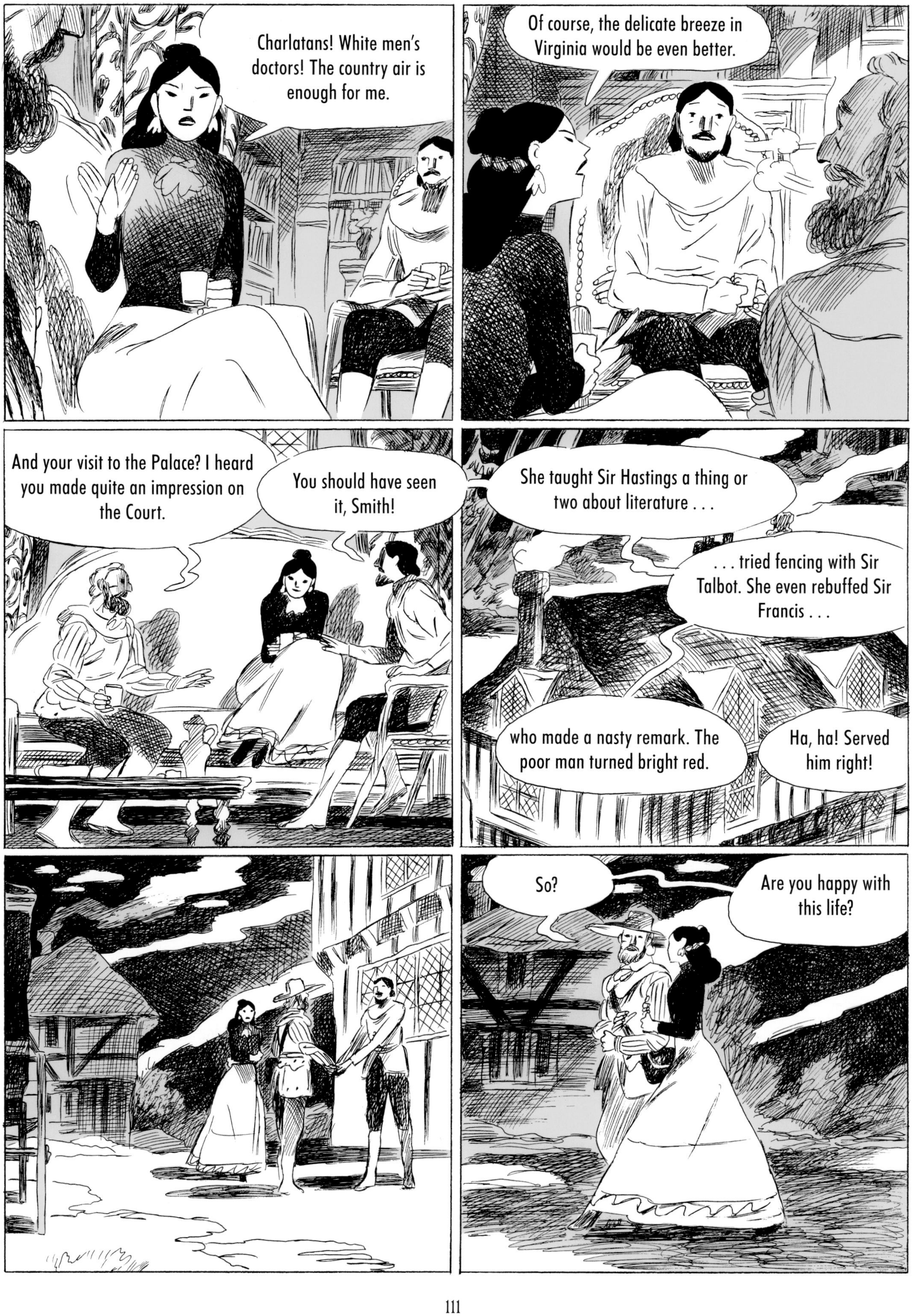

Charlatans! White men's doctors! The country air is enough for me.
Of course, the delicate breeze in Virginia would be even better.
And your visit to the Palace? I heard you made quite an impression on the Court.
You should have seen it, Smith!
She taught Sir Hastings a thing or two about literature . . .
. . . tried fencing with Sir Talbot. She even rebuffed Sir Francis . . .
who made a nasty remark. The poor man turned bright red.
Ha, ha! Served him right!
So?
Are you happy with this life?

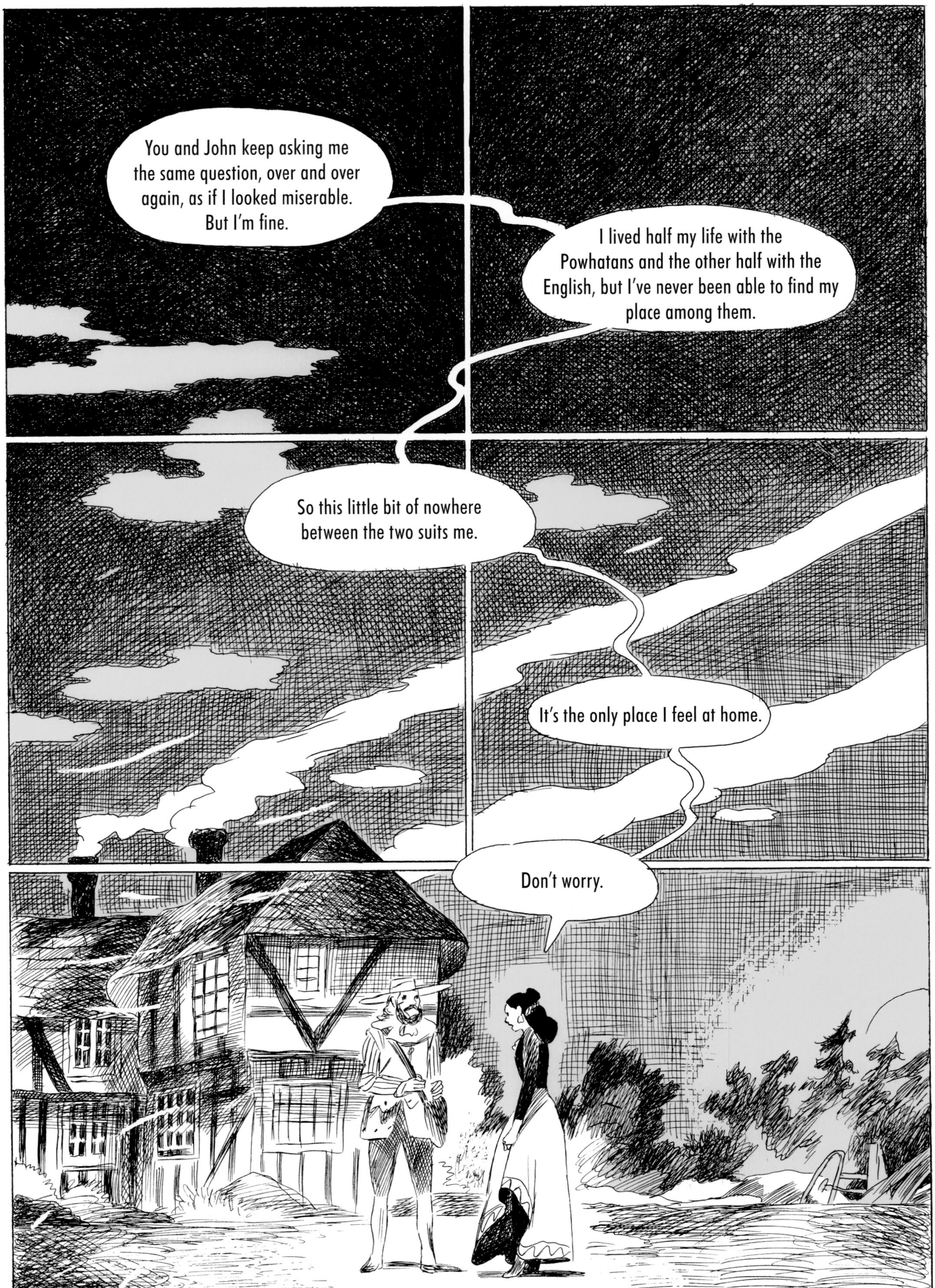

You and John keep asking me the same question, over and over again, as if I looked miserable. But I'm fine.
I lived half my life with the Powhatans and the other half with the English, but I've never been able to find my place among them.
So this little bit of nowhere between the two suits me.
It's the only place I feel at home.
Don't worry.

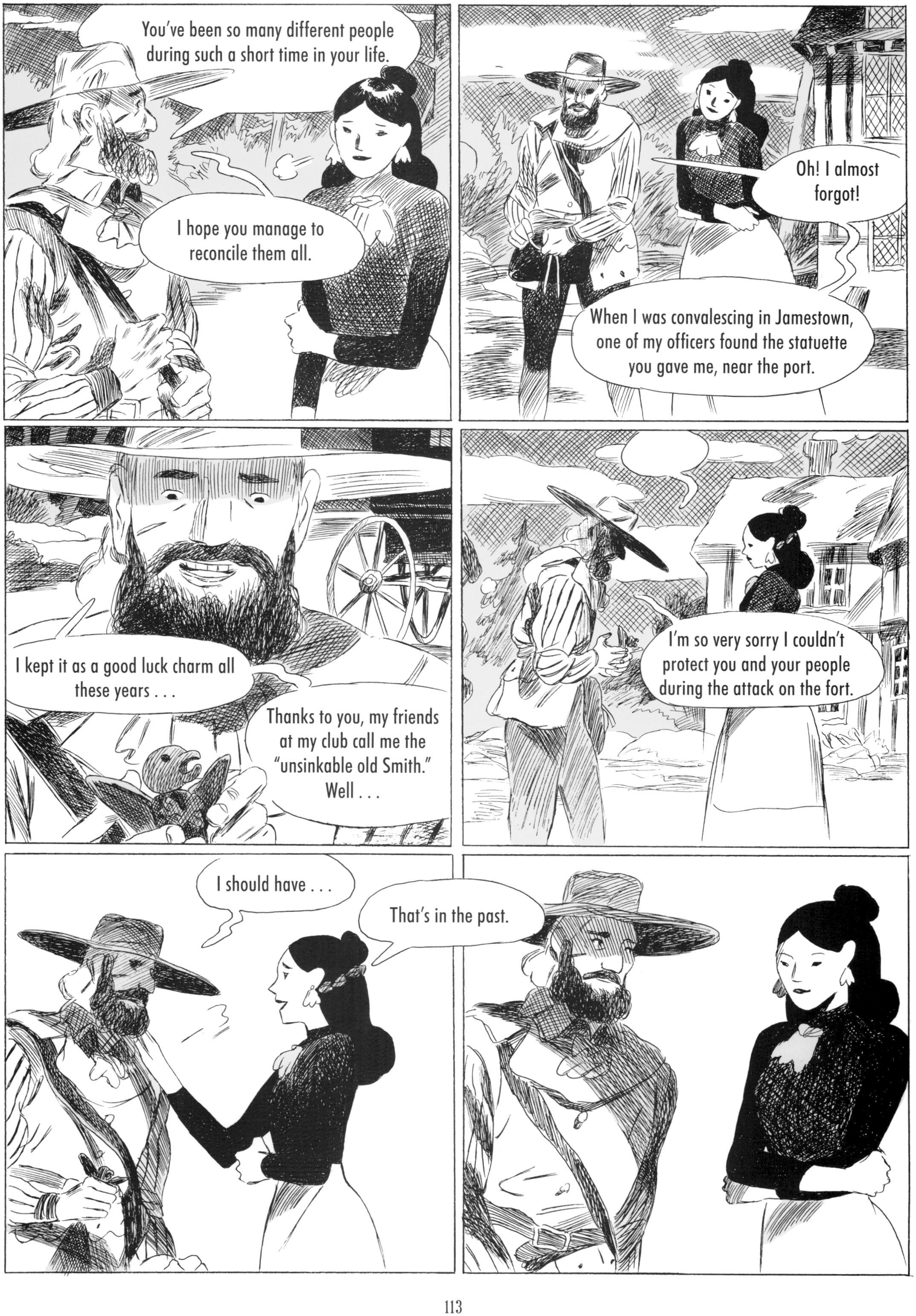
You've been so many different people during such a short time in your life.
I hope you manage to reconcile them all.
Oh! I almost forgot!
When I was convalescing in Jamestown, one of my officers found the statuette you gave me, near the port.
I kept it as a good luck charm all these years . . .
Thanks to you, my friends at my club call me the "unsinkable old Smith." Well . . .
I'm so very sorry I couldn't protect you and your people during the attack on the fort.
I should have . . .
That's in the past.

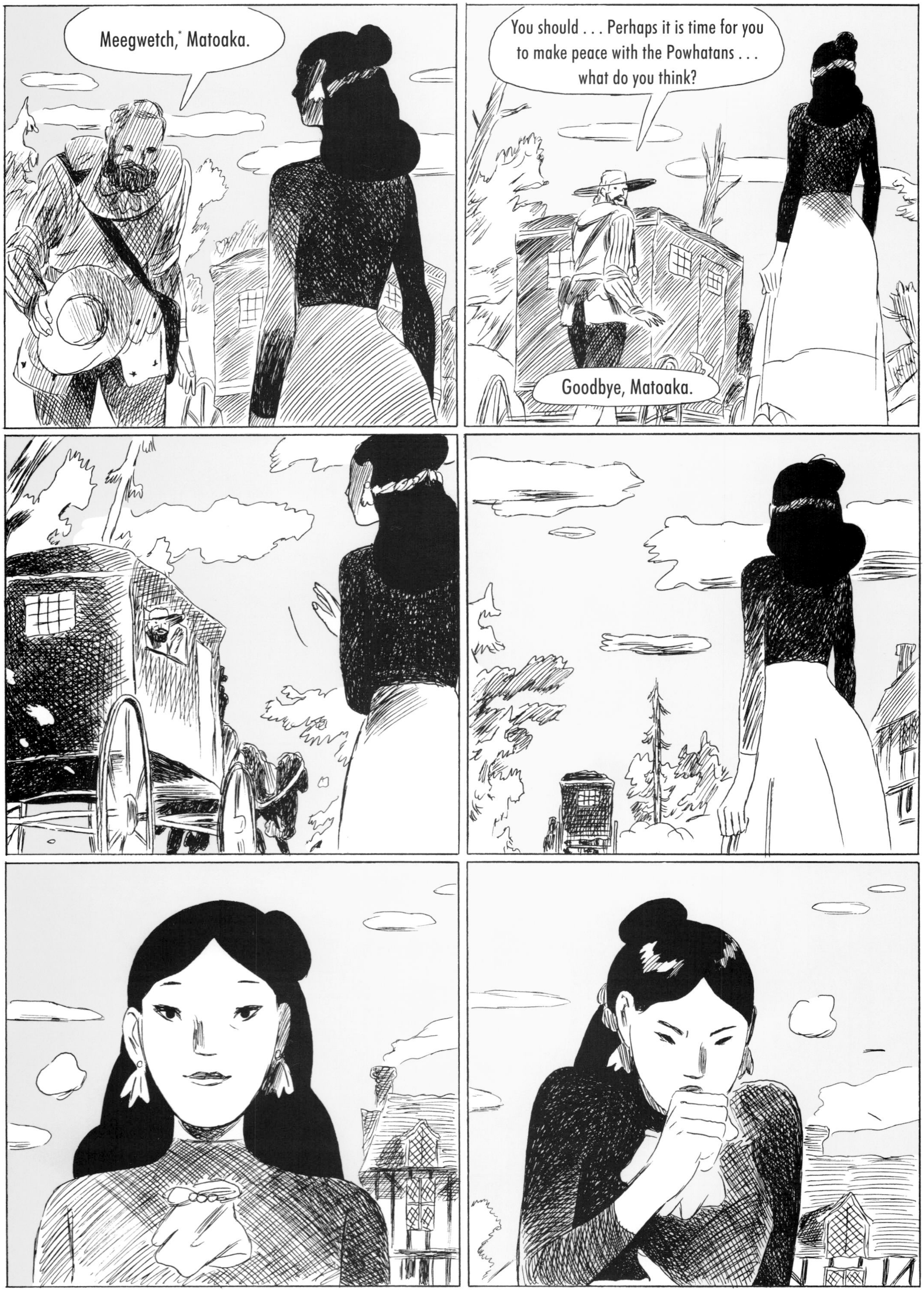
Meegwetch,* Matoaka.
You should . . . Perhaps it is time for you to make peace with the Powhatans . . . what do you think?
Goodbye, Matoaka.

* Thank you in Algonquin.

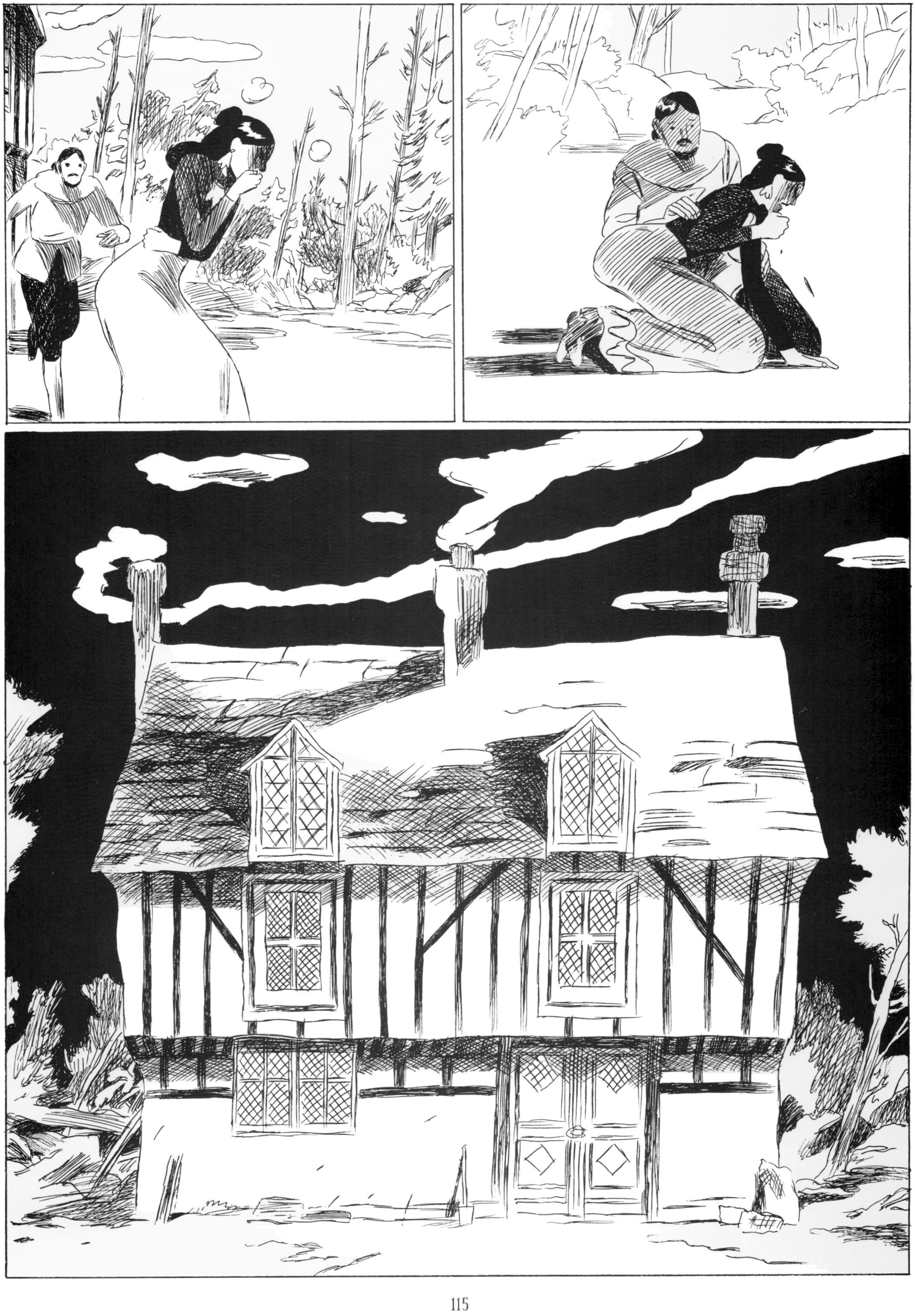

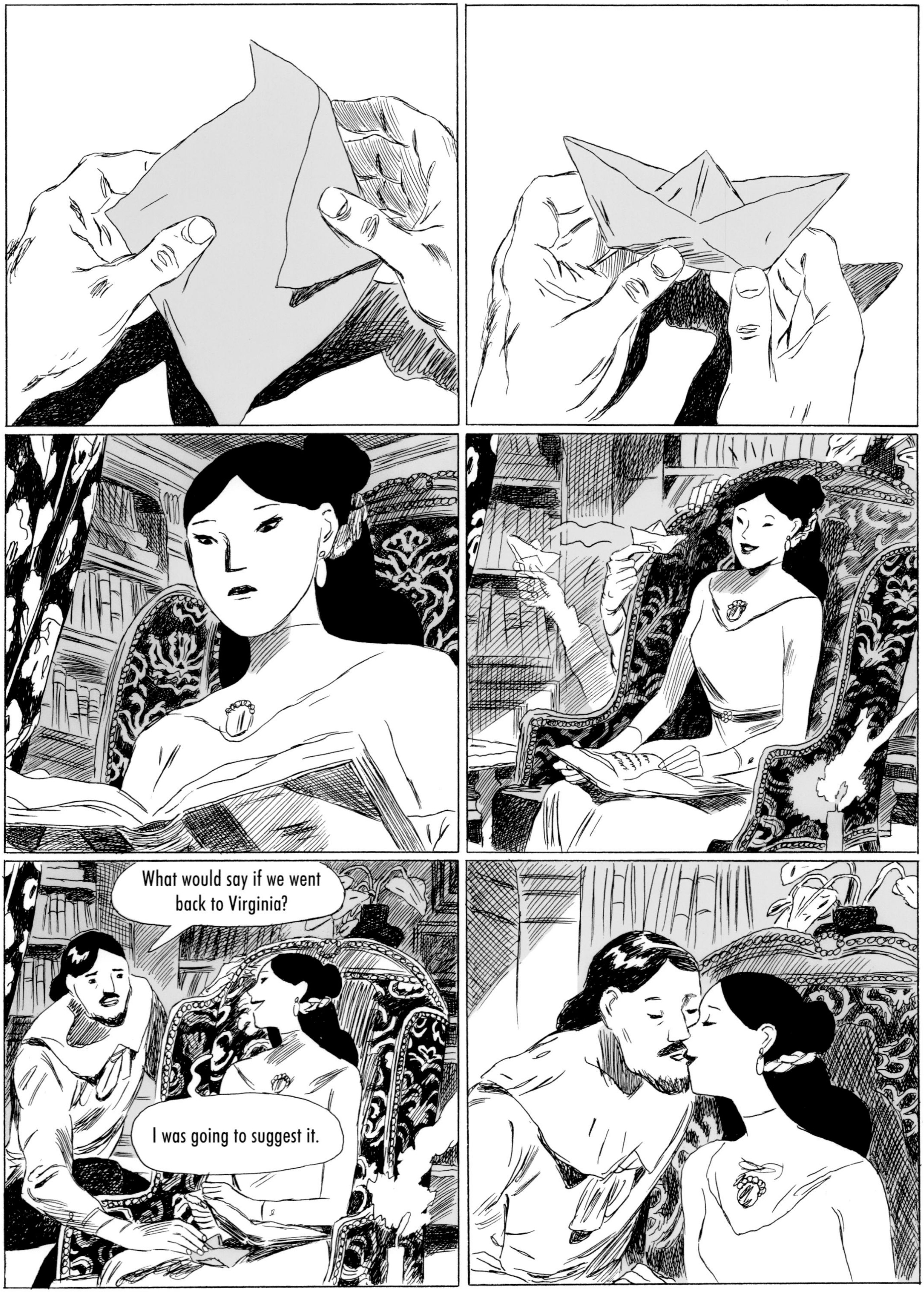
What would say if we went back to Virginia?
I was going to suggest it.

Épilogue

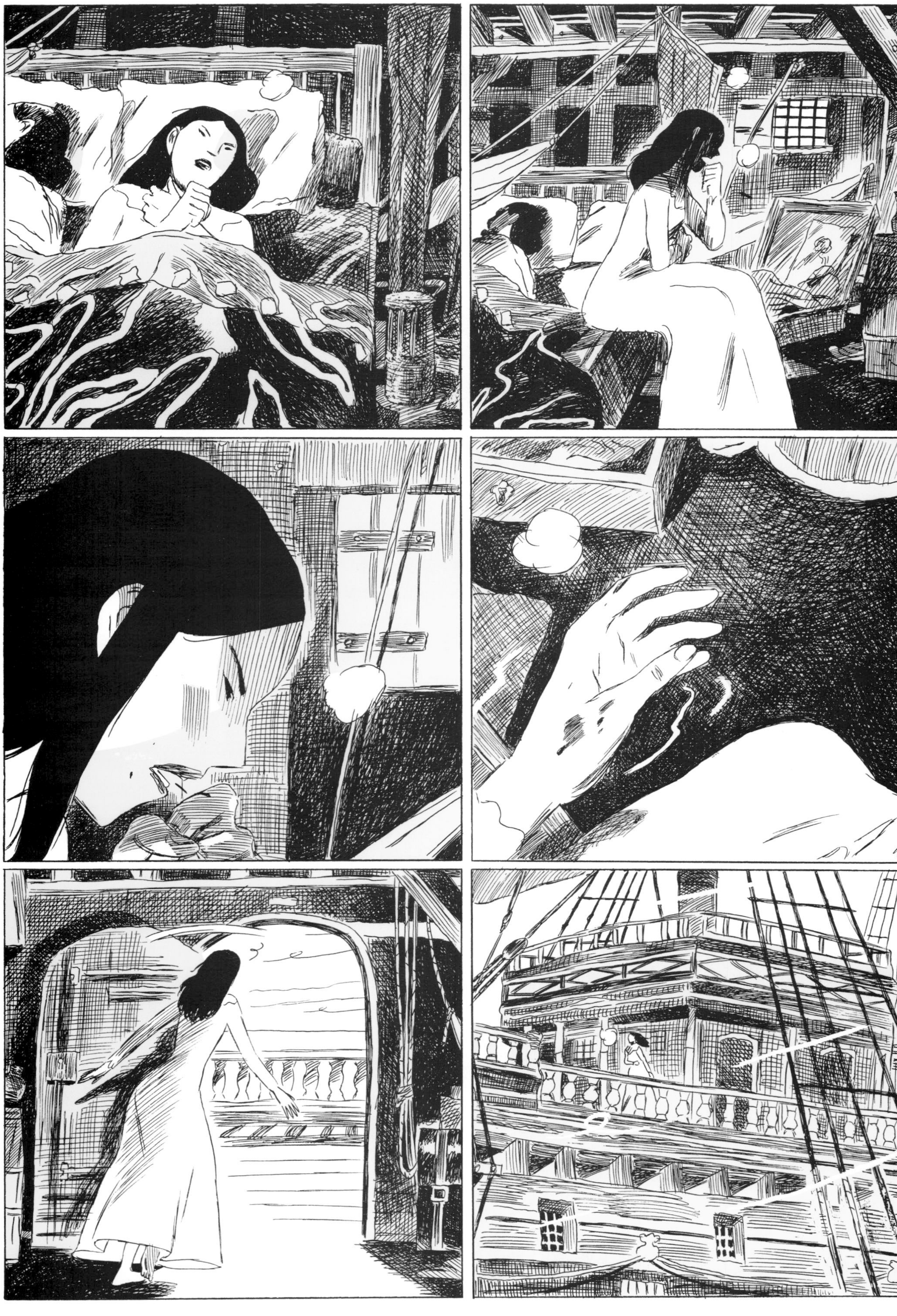

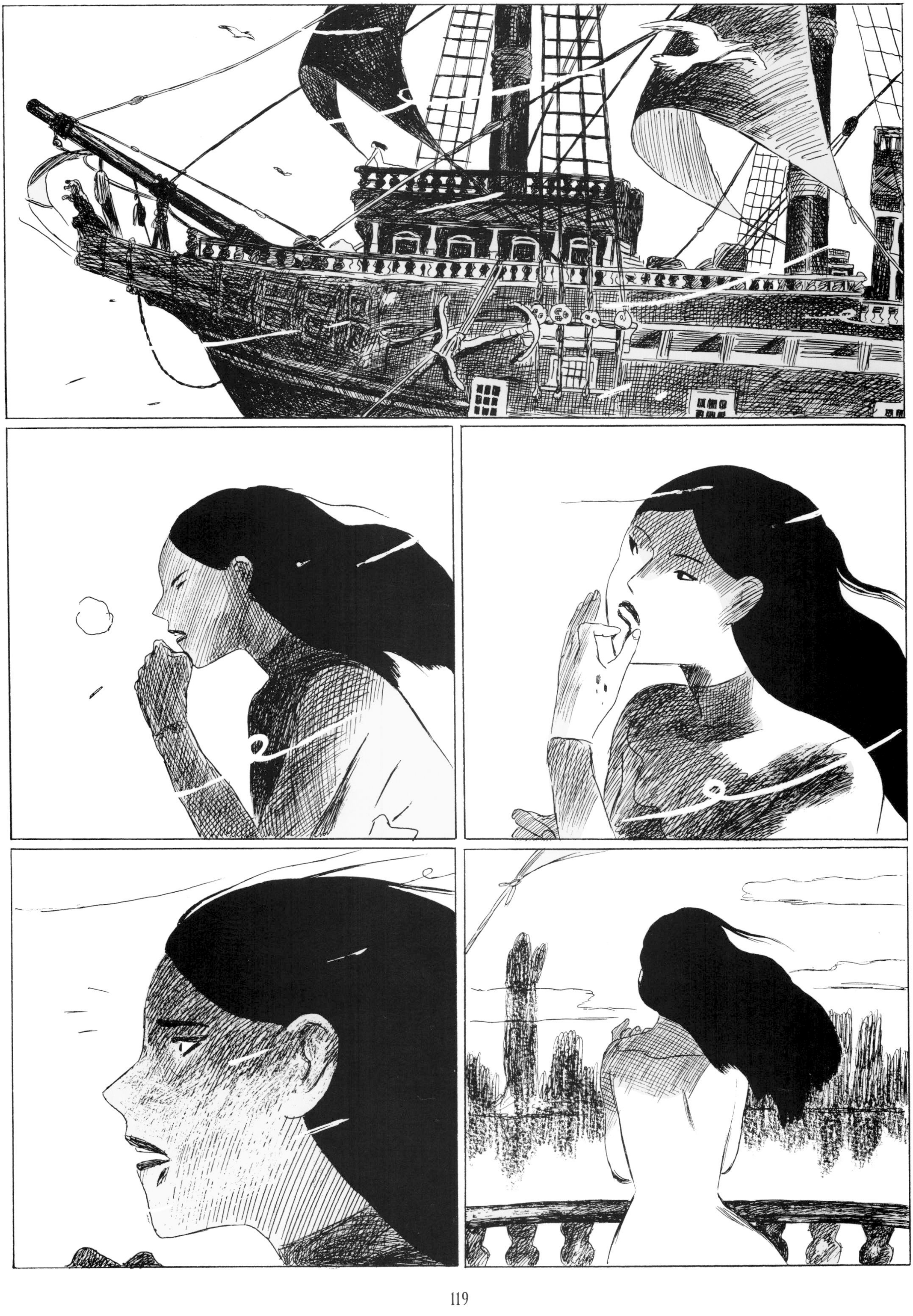

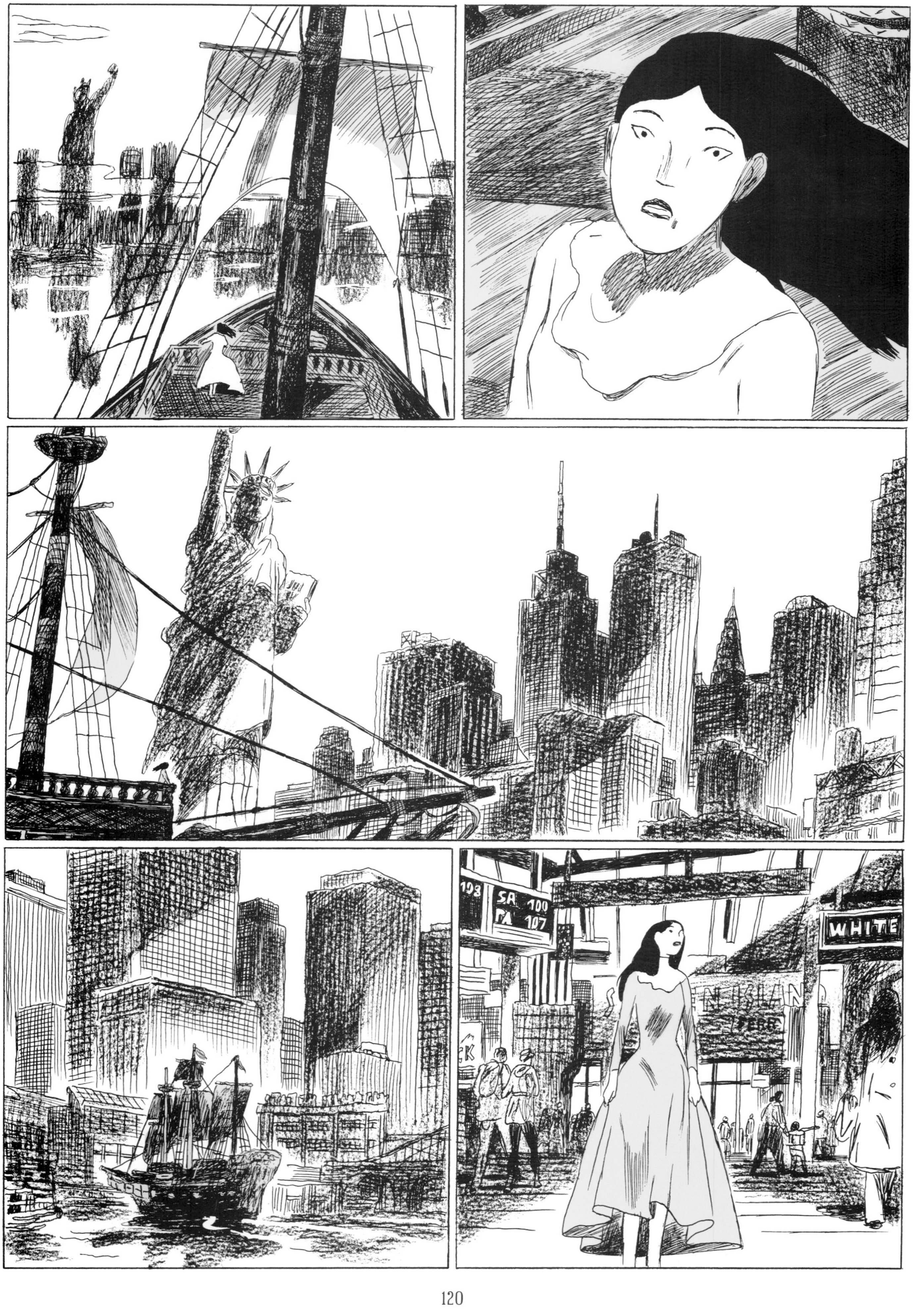
108
SA 100
107
WHITE

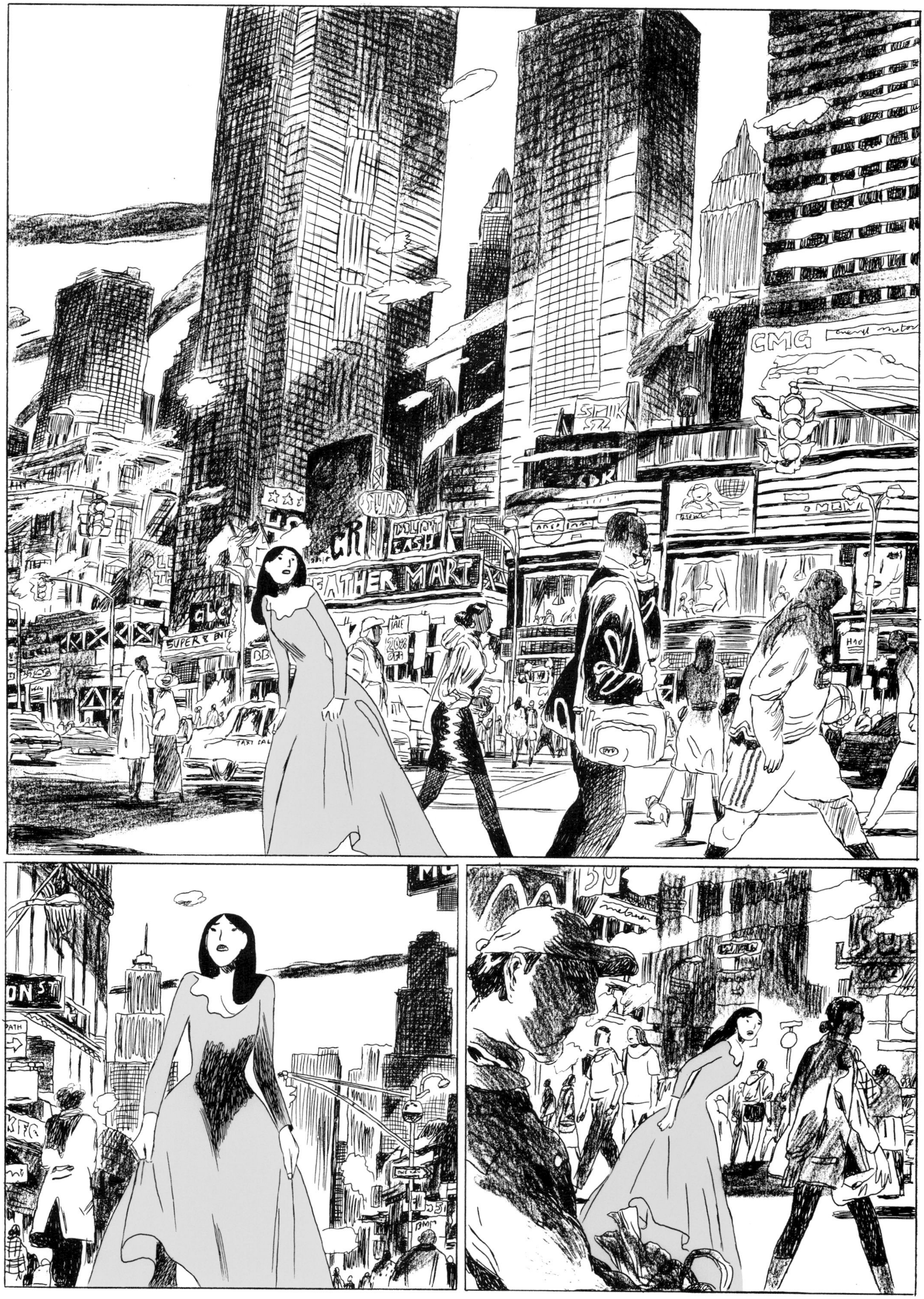
CMG
FEATHER MART
PATH

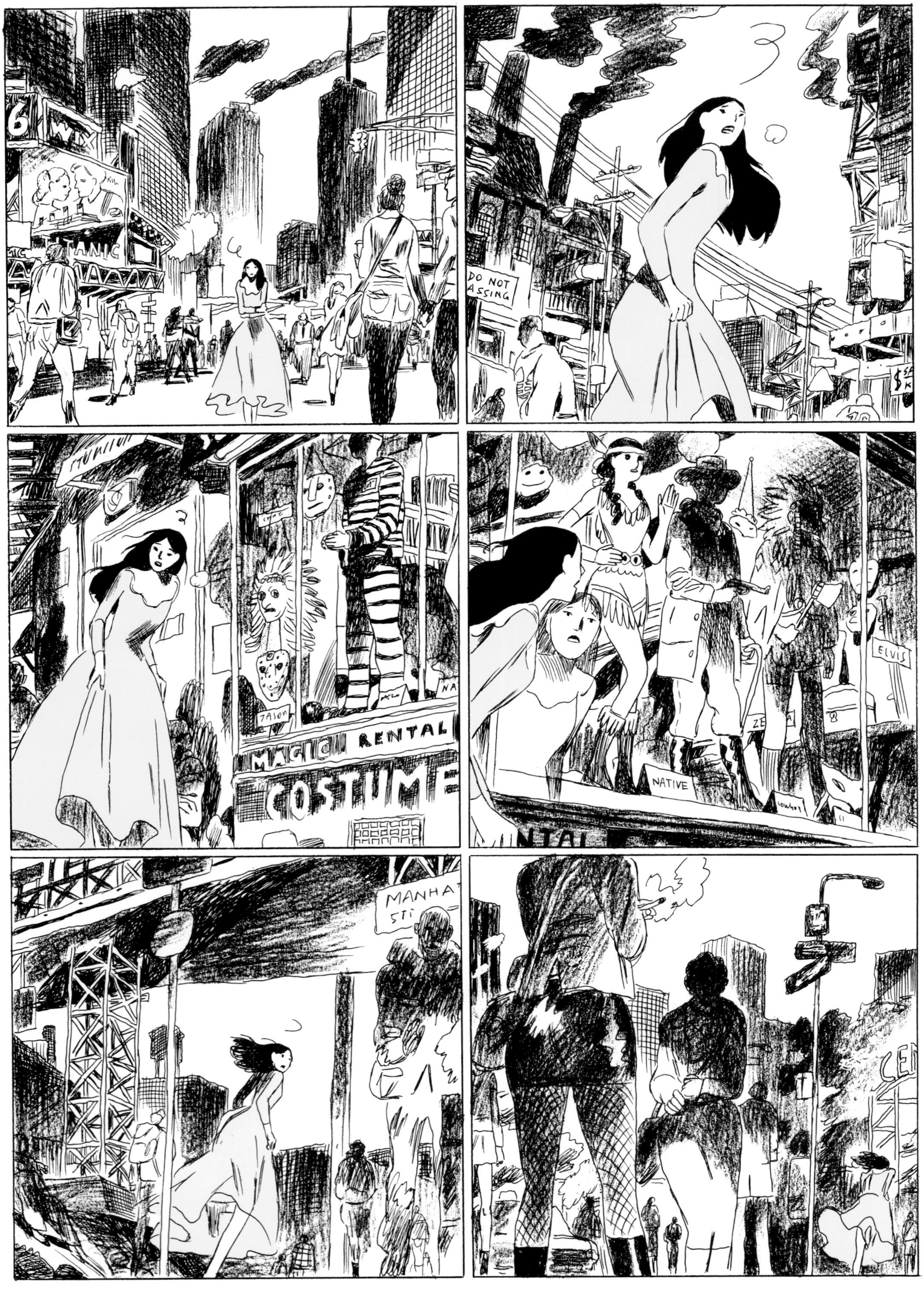
TANIC
DO NOT
ASSING
MAGIC RENTAL
COSTUME
JASON
NATIVE
ELVIS
MANHAT

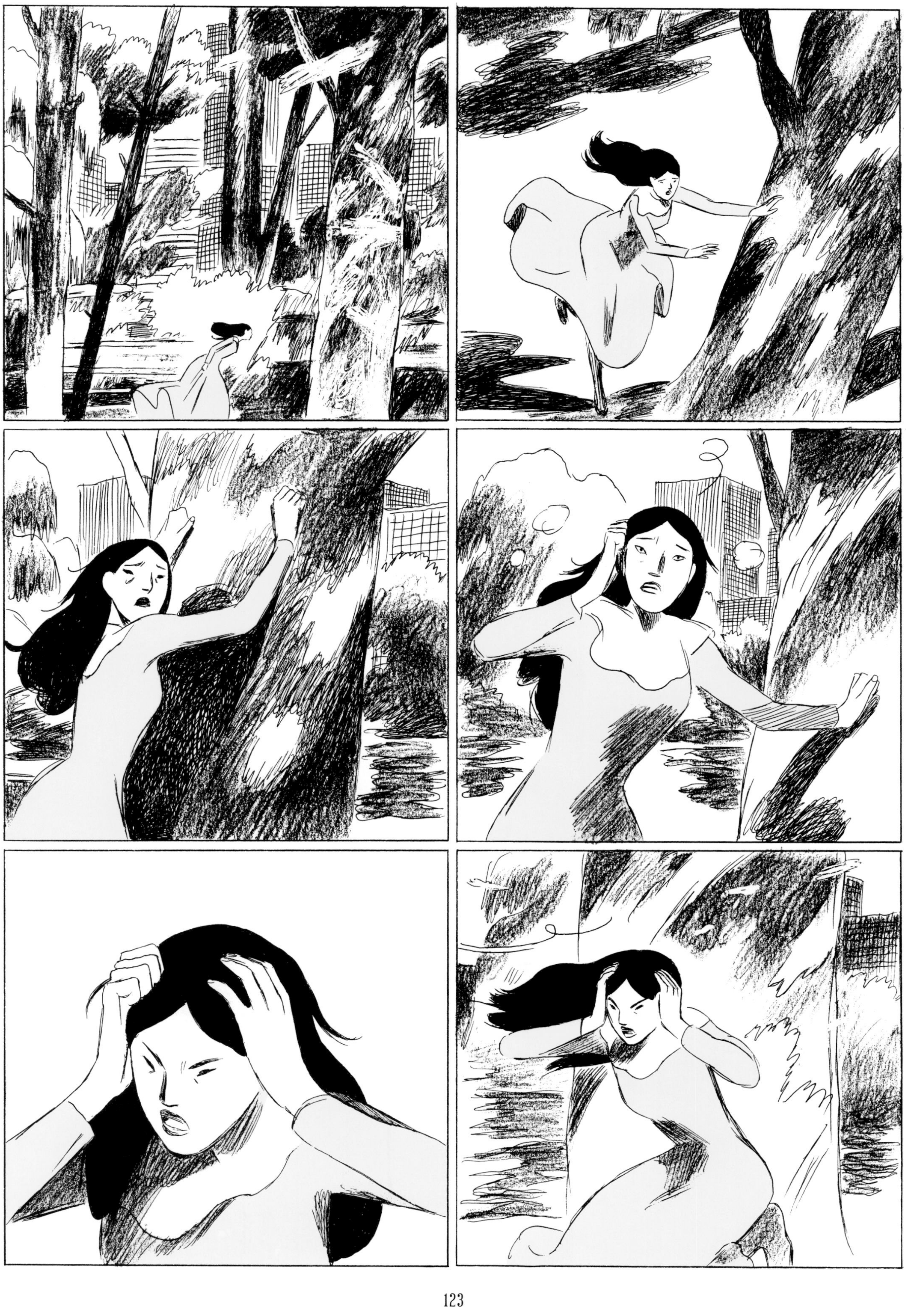

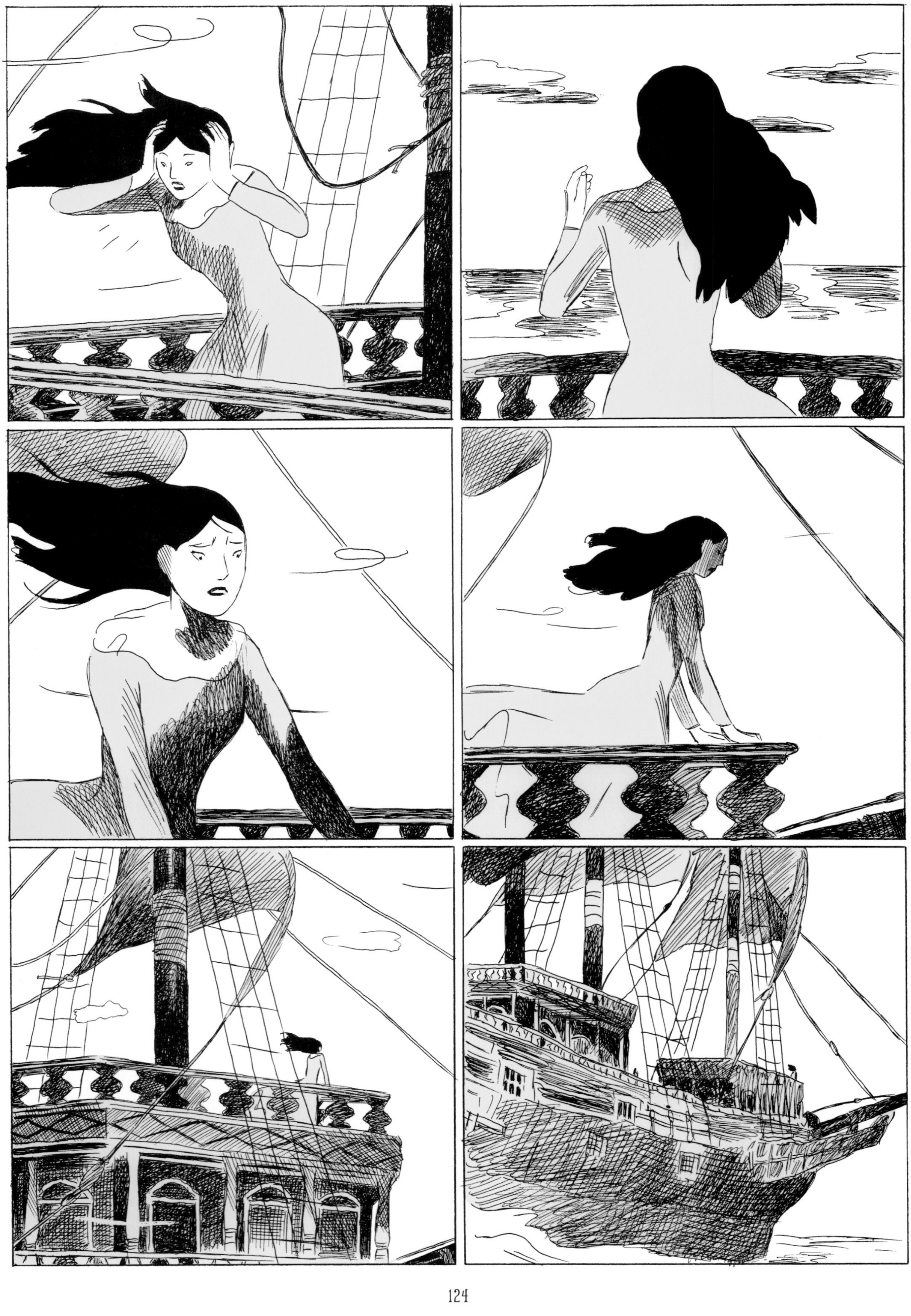

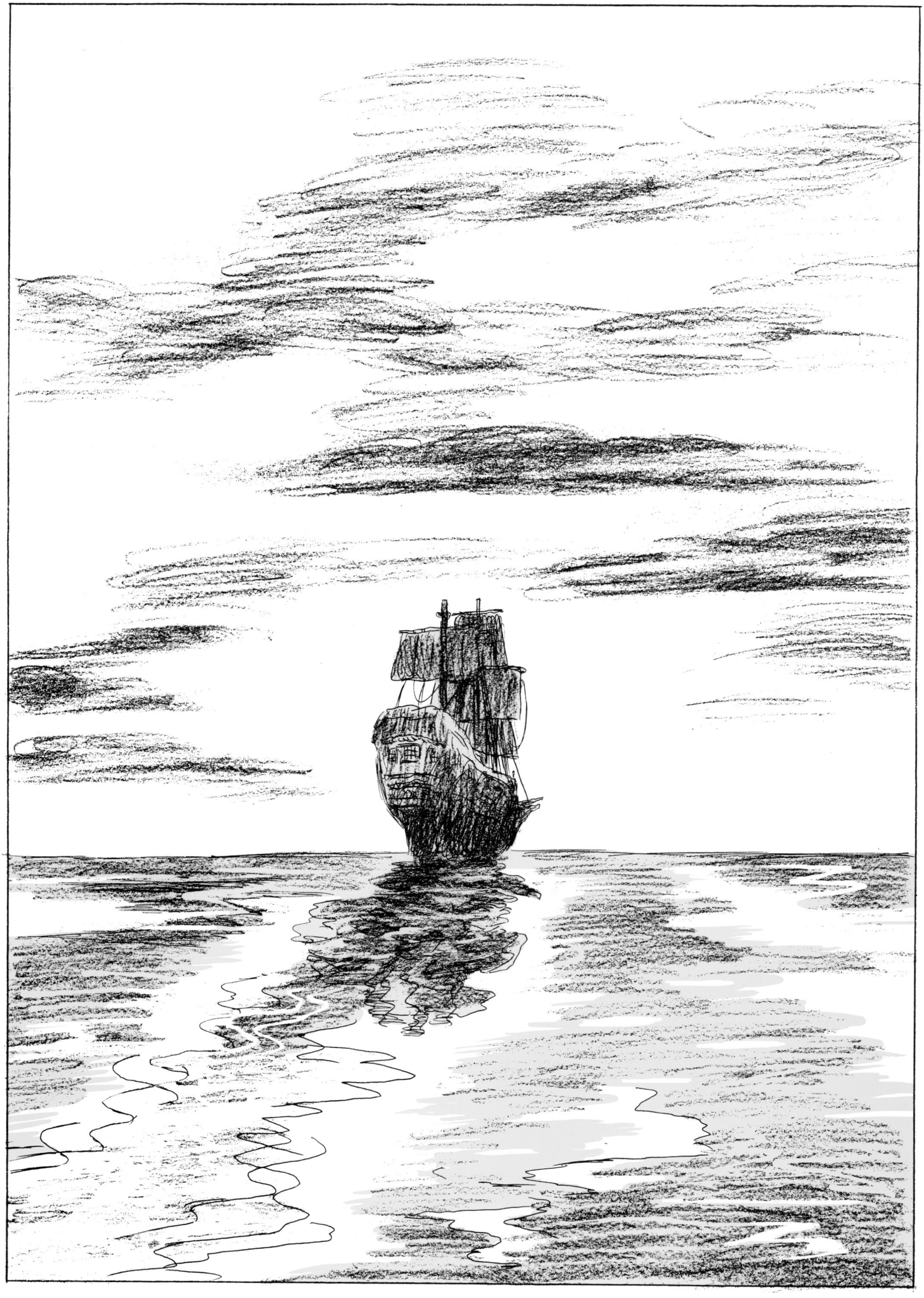

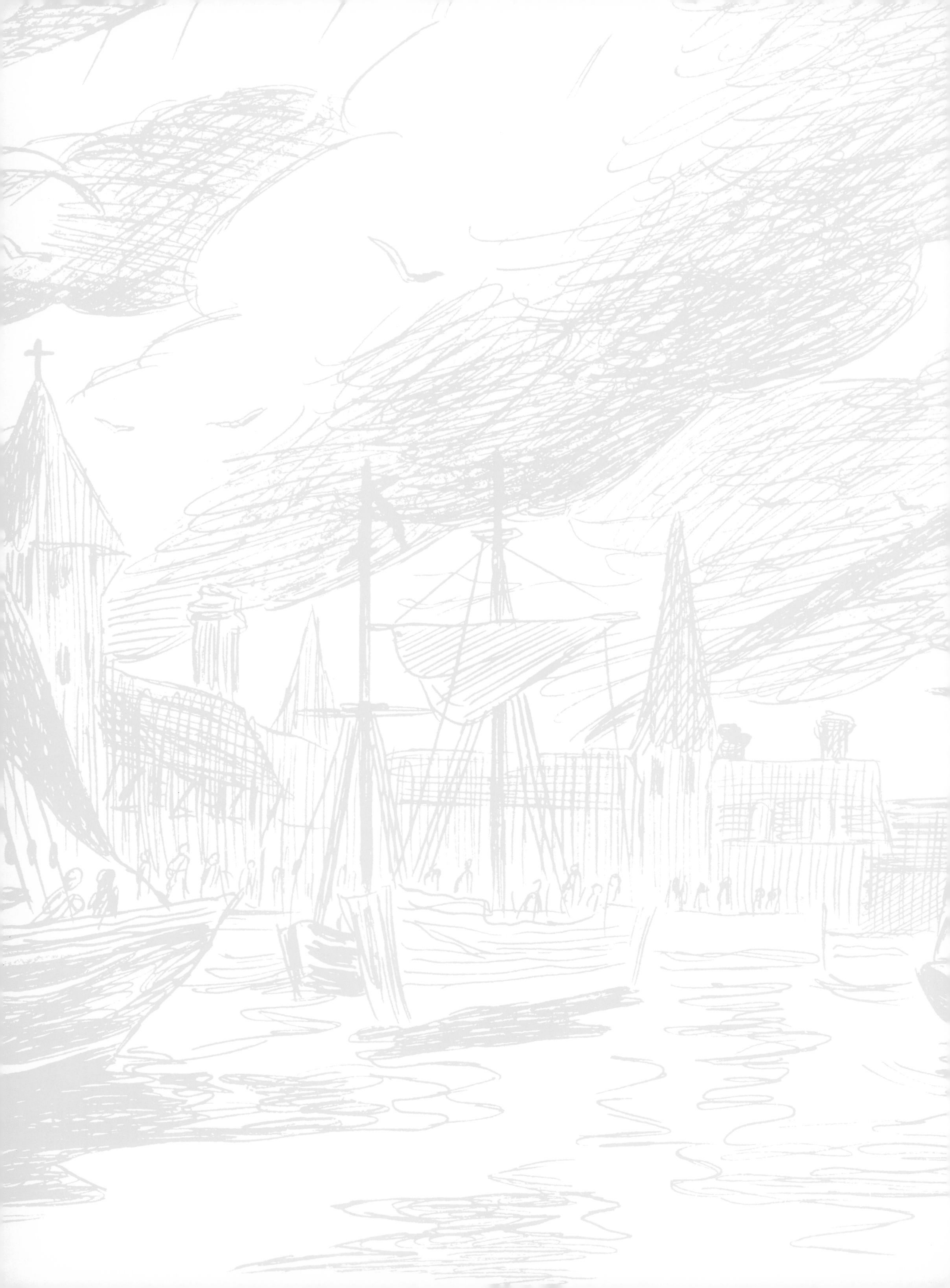

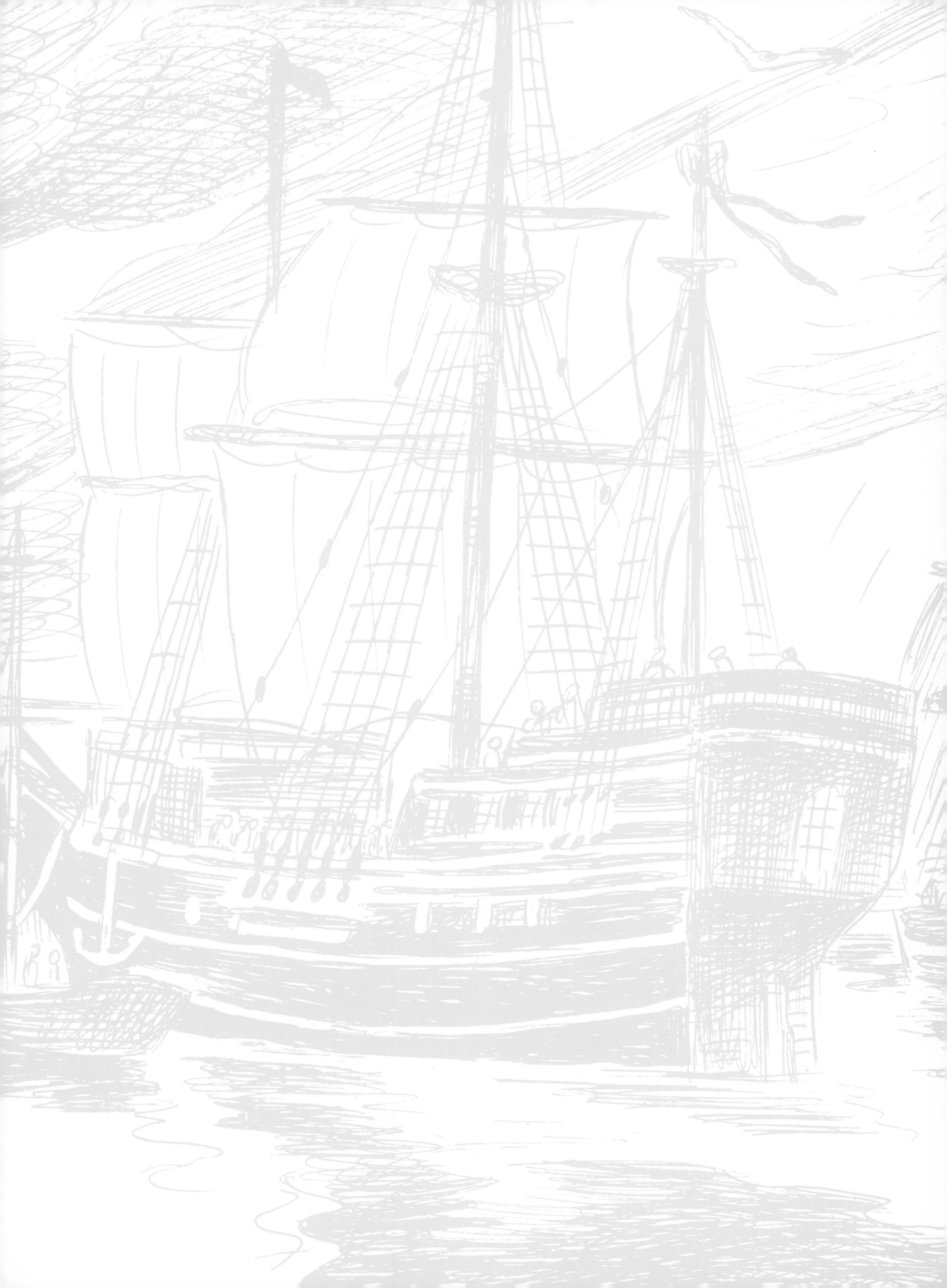

ABOUT THE AUTHOR

Loïc Locatelli-Kournwsky was born in Oyonnax in eastern France in 1987. He has published three graphic novels: *Canis Majoris,* a personal account of the trials and tribulations of suicide; *Ni Dieu Ni Maître (No God No Master)*; and the very well-received *Vaincus Mais Vivants (Conquered but Alive)*, published by Lombard Editions. This is his first graphic novel to be translated into English. He lives in Lyon.

ABOUT THE TRANSLATOR

Sandra Smith is the translator of all twelve novels by Irène Némirovsky; a new translation of Camus's *L'Etranger (The Outsider,* Penguin UK); and *The Necklace and Other Stories: Maupassant for Modern Times* (Liveright). Her translation of Némirovsky's *Suite Française* won the French American Foundation and Florence Gould Foundation Translation Prize for Fiction, as well as the PEN Book-of-the-Month Club Translation Prize. After ten years as a Fellow of Robinson College, Cambridge, Smith now lives in New York.